ESTABLISHING
ZION

FOUNDATIONS FOR A
MILLENNIAL SOCIETY

ESTABLISHING
ZION

FOUNDATIONS FOR A MILLENNIAL SOCIETY

LAWRENCE C. WALTERS

CFI

An imprint of Cedar Fort, Inc.

Springville, Utah

Paperback ISBN 13: 978–1–4621–4801–1
eBook ISBN 13: 978–1–4621–4802–8

Published by CFI, an imprint of Cedar Fort, Inc.
2373 W. 700 S., Suite 100, Springville, UT 84663
Distributed by Cedar Fort, Inc., www.cedarfort.com

LIBRARY OF CONGRESS CATALOGING NUMBER: 2024931632

Cover design by Shawnda Craig and Mario Padilla
Cover design © 2024 Cedar Fort, Inc.

Printed in the United States of America
10 9 8 7 6 5 4 3 2 1
Printed on acid-free paper

*To my wife, Carol, who has been my inspiration
and my chief promoter, my counselor and my motivator,
and my unfailing companion through all the journeys
for over fifty years.*

Contents

Acknowledgments

For years, I have thought about topics of governance and government. I developed many of the ideas and some of the principles about governance through discussions with my colleagues while I was on the faculty of the Romney Institute of Public Management at Brigham Young University. Much of the research and writing contained here was done while I served as a missionary in the Church History Department of The Church of Jesus Christ of Latter-day Saints. I benefited from access to the historians and resources the library afforded, though the references included here are all from publicly available sources.

I have also benefited greatly from comments and suggestions from my wife, Carol; my children; my good friend Gary C. Cornia; and other friends and colleagues who reviewed early drafts of the manuscript. I express my gratitude to all. I take full responsibility for any errors or odd ideas.

A great and marvelous work is about to come forth unto the children of men. . . . Now, as you have asked, behold, I say unto you, keep my commandments, and seek to bring forth and establish the cause of Zion. . . . Send forth the elders of my church unto the nations which are afar off; unto the islands of the sea; send forth unto foreign lands; call upon all nations, first upon the Gentiles, and then upon the Jews. And behold, and lo, this shall be their cry, and the voice of the Lord unto all people: Go ye forth unto the land of Zion, that the borders of my people may be enlarged, and that her stakes may be strengthened, and that Zion may go forth unto the regions round about . . . that the covenants of the Eternal Father which he hath made unto thee, O house of Israel, may be fulfilled.[1]

T he choice to come unto Christ is not a matter of physical location; it is a matter of individual commitment. People can be "brought to the knowledge of the Lord" without leaving their homelands. True, in the early days of the Church, conversion often meant emigration as well. But now the gathering takes place in each nation. The Lord has decreed the establishment of Zion in each realm where He has given His Saints their birth and nationality.[2]

---

1. Doctrine and Covenants 6:1,6; 133:8–9; Moroni 10:31.
2. Russell M. Nelson, "The gathering of scattered Israel," *Ensign*, November 2006, 81.

Introduction

*E*stablishing Zion has been a focus of The Church of Jesus Christ of Latter-day Saints since the Restoration began in the 1820s. Prophets throughout the ages have looked forward to our day when Zion would be established again on the earth. Given the number of revelations and prophetic pronouncements on the subject of Zion, what more can we say, other than "follow the prophets"?

I believe there is more to be said, and my purpose in writing this book is simple on the surface. I have devoted most of my professional career to the study, practice, and improvement of local governments. As I read the scriptures and the admonitions of the prophets, I find volumes of vitally important guidance on how to focus on the Savior to live a more Christlike life and thereby personally qualify to live in Zion. I find relatively little that describes how a Zion society will function. This book is an attempt to explore the question, What will Zion be like?

For all the references to Zion in the Bible, especially the Old Testament, Latter-day Saints have a relatively unique view of Zion. Beyond the heavenly city founded by Enoch, for most Christians and Jews, Zion is either a specific hill in Jerusalem where David established his kingdom, a reference to all of Jerusalem,[1] or a reference to the land of Israel.[2] The focus of this book is very different and should

---

1. Wikipedia, "Zion," 2022, https://en.wikipedia.org/wiki/Zion.
2. One source suggested that Zion can be translated as "indication" or "marking," suggesting that Jews are marked so as not to be lost and will return to their owner ("What is Zion?," Ask the Rabbi, Chabad.org, 2022, accessed

not be misinterpreted as a commentary on these other views of Zion. In this book, and for Latter-day Saints generally, Zion is a spiritual condition among God's people in a given place.

How will things be arranged when we step outside the chapel door? Will there be markets and, if so, how will they function? Will the role of the Church be the same as today? And what about civil governments? What lessons can we draw from past efforts? We know that "Zion cannot be built up unless it is by the principles of the law of the celestial kingdom" (Doctrine and Covenants 105:5). But how do those laws apply to all aspects of a Zion society? That is my first reason for writing this book. What can we glean about the nature of a Zion society?

By reviewing past efforts to establish Zion in scripture and prophetic teachings (particularly Doctrine and Covenants 124), can we begin to sketch a framework for a Zion society that describes residents in their roles as family members, Church members, community members, and market participants? Some of that description may seem easy (Zion is the "pure in heart" [Doctrine and Covenants 97:21]), but how do people who are pure in heart behave in the community, as workers, employers, or citizens? More broadly, how do the *institutions* in a Zion society function?

All my life, I have loved playing in the small, seasonal rivers and creeks in the western United States; rivers you can walk across in the summer; moving water strewn with bowling-ball rocks, just as rounded but not nearly so regular. Within minutes of arriving, I inevitably look for the best place to create a temporary hand-built dam, knowing full well that it won't survive the next heavy runoff. Part of the joy is knowing that no one has built a dam quite like this one in exactly this place. I also love creatively meeting the practical engineering challenges with only hands, a smorgasbord of rocks, and a bit of mud. I rarely finish in the time available, but that is not the point. The attempt never fails to produce pleasure in the effort.

In this book, I find myself building again, not with rocks but with ideas and words. There is no fantasy that I am the first. There

---

7 Jan 2023, https://www.chabad.org/library/article_cdo/aid/1543702/jewish/What-Is-Zion.htm).

is no expectation that I can do it alone. All my ideas and words may amount to no more than a small stone in the magnificent structure of Zion. In time, even the connection I have to that stone will be forgotten. And that is fine. There is joy in productively striving with others to meet the challenges of creating Zion.

My second reason for writing this book is that little has been written about non-Church institutions and organizations in Zion. There is every reason to believe there will be people living in Zion who are not members of the Church.[3] Consequently, the organization of Zion will need to accommodate and meet the needs of those citizens as well. I believe that a richer understanding and vision of a Zion society may contribute in some small way to its realization. My hope is that this book may help readers understand and more fully keep the covenants they have made to build the kingdom and establish Zion. As President Russell M. Nelson taught, "Anytime we do anything that helps anyone—on either side of the veil—to make and keep their covenants with God, we are helping to gather Israel."[4]

Some may argue that our sole obligation is to live a life that qualifies for Zion, and we can either ignore or withdraw from other, more worldly considerations. But to qualify to live in Zion is to qualify to live in a community. God did not call Enoch Zion, "the Lord called *his people* Zion" (Moses 7:18; emphasis added). The fruit of Enoch's ministry was a city full of united, righteous people: God's covenant people. God called the whole assemblage of Saints Zion. Achieving Zion is a group effort, and it requires more than personal righteousness.

Establishing Zion requires that we live and serve together in peace, harmony, and fairness; that we change (or leave) the organizations we belong to; that we engage with our neighbors to create Zion communities; that we strengthen and organize our families to shoulder the responsibilities of Zion; that we actively engage in community governance. Zion in this sense applies to groups, not individuals.

---

3. Joseph Fielding Smith, *Doctrines of Salvation: Sermons and Writings of Joseph Fielding Smith*, ed. Bruce R. McConkie, vol. 1 (Salt Lake City, UT: Bookcraft, 1954), 86–87.
4. Russell M. Nelson, "Let God Prevail," *Ensign*, November, 2020, 92–93.

Groups, even righteous and unified groups, living together create both formal and informal social relationships and social institutions. Giving thought to what those relationships and institutions should look like and how they should function can promote their realization.

The social nature of Zion was emphasized in an 1834 revelation to Joseph Smith in which the Lord explained that the Saints' failure to "redeem Zion" was caused by the collective shortcomings of the Church in Missouri and elsewhere.

> Behold, I say unto you, were it not for the transgressions of my people, *speaking concerning the church and not individuals*, they might have been redeemed even now. . . . I speak *concerning my churches abroad*—there are many who will say: Where is their God? Behold, he will deliver them in time of trouble, otherwise we will not go up unto Zion, and will keep our moneys. Therefore, in consequence of the *transgressions of my people*, it is expedient in me that mine elders should wait for a little season for the redemption of Zion. (Doctrine and Covenants 105:2, 8–9, emphasis added)

"Redeeming" Zion is a joint and collective effort by God's covenant people. It is not sufficient for individuals to be righteous. They must live together and be "united according to the union required by the law of the celestial kingdom" (Doctrine and Covenants 105:4). Hence the need to consider what that unity will look like in practice.

So, what is this book? It has a healthy measure of history, both ancient and modern. There is a good bit of reasoning and system-building from first principles. There is a large dollop of faith and willingness to take prophetic teachings at face value. And inevitably, there is aspiration—lots of aspiration, as history, a bit of social science, system building, and faith come together to provide a vision of the tumbled streamed before us, with a structure far more permanent and glorious than piled river rock.

The vision I hope to provide is not a distant view of a future Zion. Rather, I seek to articulate the principles and goals that should motivate and guide the efforts of those who actively seek to establish Zion today. Personal righteousness is required of all, but that alone will not establish Zion. Those who seek to live in Zion will recognize that building the kingdom and establishing Zion requires that we create, adjust, support, and actively lead the institutions and organizations in this current world to a higher and holier plane. This book is an effort to identify some of those guiding principles and offer suggestions on their implications.

I have no special claim to authority, and I certainly do not speak for The Church of Jesus Christ of Latter-day Saints. While I quote extensively from scripture and from the prophets, ultimately each reader must decide where truth lies. If you, as my reader, disagree with my interpretations and theories, I will not be offended. I will feel like George A. Smith when, in 1844, he commented regarding the incomplete efforts of the Council of Fifty to draft a new constitution: "Our researches have done us good. By taking this course we gain wisdom & prudence much better than we would if we had set down like chickens to wait for the Lord to give it."[5]

The ideas developed in this book are grouped into four parts: historical perspectives, principles, practices, and governance. Each part treats related concepts, organized into chapters divided into short sections.

Part 1 begins by reviewing past efforts to establish Zion or Zion-like societies in order to establish a context for what follows. My review is not exhaustive, and a number of other writers have treated the subject in much greater depth. I draw on several of these studies in an effort to glean important insights for our day.

I observed several recurring themes and lessons as I reviewed these accounts. From the days of Enoch, Zion has been associated with the elimination of poverty. From society's perspective, how is this to be accomplished? We know that it must follow eternal celestial principles, and we know that the "poor shall be exalted in that the rich are made low" (Doctrine and Covenants 104:16). Beyond that general description, how will poverty be eliminated?

---

5. Grow, Matthew J., Ronald K. Esplin, Mark Ashurst-McGee, Gerrit J. Dirkmaat, and Jeffrey D. Mahas, eds. *Council of Fifty, Minutes, March 1844–January 1846.* First volume of the Administrative Records series of *The Joseph Smith Papers*, edited by Ronald K. Esplin, Matthew J. Grow, and Matthew C. Godfrey. Salt Lake City: Church Historian's Press, 2016.

During the Restoration, we have come to associate the elimination of poverty in Zion with the law of consecration and stewardship as understood by the Saints in Missouri. Under the law of the Church (see Doctrine and Covenants 42), the Saints were to consecrate their donations for the poor to the bishop. In both Missouri and in Utah, this consecration was interpreted to include all that the donor possessed. After this initial consecration, the bishop would assign stewardships to all, make distributions to those in need, and retain a certain portion for future needs and public purposes. In the discussion here I raise the question, Was formal deeding of all assets to the Church the pattern followed prior to the nineteenth century, and is this pattern needed in creating Zion today?

A second recurring theme I've observed relates to urban management. Every scriptural account of Zion or Zion-like societies involved building a city. In the latter days, Joseph envisioned building a city of Zion. But cities bring with them both opportunities and challenges in managing urban services. What were the opportunities that made building cities desirable, and how were the challenges overcome?

A third theme that I see in past efforts is land for a perpetual inheritance. God's covenants with His people nearly always involve promises regarding land. While this feature has not received much emphasis in recent decades, the covenants are still in place and must be fulfilled. What does fulfilling these covenants mean, and how will it be accomplished?

Finally, there is the recurring theme of unity among the Saints. In Enoch's city, the people were of one heart and one mind. Similar wording is used to describe the early Christians in Judea and the Nephites following the Savior's appearance. What did unity look like in these earlier periods, and how did they combat divisions such as we see today?

After a review of past efforts, I turn in part 2 to a more careful consideration of the principles that should guide organizations in a Zion society. Individuals will, of course, be guided by the doctrine of Christ and the teachings of the prophets. But how might the Savior structure the institutions and organizations that affect everyday life in a Zion society?

Part 2 is about principles. I begin with a chapter on five foundation stones for Zion: devotion to the Father and the Son, Christlike charity or love for all God's children, individual agency, personal accountability, and unity. Love of God and love for our neighbors are both commandments. Agency and accountability are divine gifts and part of our nature. Unity is different.

The need for unity among the Saints is a recurring theme in past efforts to establish Zion. Although the Saints are commanded to be unified, we cannot keep this commandment on our own. In an era of extremism and polarization, many despair of achieving unity in our society. What will unity among the Saints look like?

The next principles chapter considers Doctrine and Covenants 124. In that revelation, the Lord states four times that Nauvoo is the cornerstone of Zion. With that kind of emphasis, it is worth carefully considering the structure and message of section 124 as it relates to the organization of temples, the Church, and non-church organizations in Zion.

The role of the Church appears to have changed over the years, and the trajectory of this change places increased emphasis on the family. This trend is likely to continue, and a Zion society will also place a greater emphasis on the family than we see in the world around us. The role of the Church and the importance of families as the fundamental unit in Zion are discussed in the final two principles chapters.

Part 3 turns to the practical implications of the five foundation stones for society's institutions and organizations. The chapter on poverty elimination uses scripture and development economics to lay out an approach for lifting nearly all people out of poverty. The chapter on land both articulates why land is important in Zion and discusses how our concepts of ownership and property rights may need to change, though the technical discussion of property rights appears in an appendix.

The implications of the five foundation stones for institutions and organizations are discussed in the concluding practices chapter which poses and attempts to answer the question, What kind of people should organizations in Zion foster?

Some believe that in Zion there will be no need for a separate and distinct civil government. I do not share that view and neither did

Joseph Smith. I discuss governance in part 4. Based on my reading of history, and on the foundation stones and principles identified in part 2, I explore how civil government will function in Zion.

The chapter on the need for good government draws together what we know about the inspired principles for structuring and operating government. The chapter on governance in Zion focuses on the implementation of these principles and how we might bring our communities closer to Zion. Some of the practical but more technical implications of the discussion are relegated to an appendix on deliberative processes.

I conclude with a summary chapter that provides a description of what I see as a possible framework for establishing Zion in the latter days, including various institutions and types of organizations. My hope is that this multidimensional view of Zion may guide future individual and collective action, as together we strive to establish Zion in preparation for the return of the Savior.

Again, I stress that the conclusions and observations offered here are mine alone, and I suffer from the limited views and experiences of a single individual. The Lord will return when we as a people are prepared and have become a Zion people. I do not believe the Savior will deliver a neatly bound handbook on how to accomplish this goal beyond what we have in the Doctrine and Covenants and other prophetic teachings.

We must work out, with the Lord's help, how to change our society to conform to the celestial principles underlying Zion. Eventually, Zion will fill the earth, although initially Zion may exist within an indifferent and even incredulous world as it did in the days of Enoch and Melchizedek. But, as in the days of Enoch and as foretold in scripture, we will create a Zion society that will be a place of peace and safety.

In contemplating the workings of a Zion society, we should never forget why we are striving to build Zion: to prepare for the coming of Jesus Christ; to prepare ourselves, our homes and families, and our communities to receive the Savior. Our goal is to create in our hearts and in our day-to-day living a place and environment where the Lord will walk and conclude, "Here I will make my abode."

A complex society has many moving parts. In 1829, the Lord chided Oliver Cowdery, saying, "Behold, you have not understood; you have supposed that I would give it unto you, when you took no thought save it was to ask me" (Doctrine and Covenants 9:7). It is in the spirit of "studying it out in [my] mind" that I offer the following. As with my rock dams in summer streams, others who come after me will approach the subjects raised here with greater insight than I bring to the effort. But who knows? I may stumble on a small stone that fits in the larger structure.

PART 1
Historical Perspective

There are several ways to approach history. One approach is to become immersed in a single event, document, or relic, delving deeply into its connections to people, other documents, and even other relics. That is not feasible for approaching a subject as vast as the history of Zion over the centuries. Rather, I want to look for principles and patterns: principles of action that must be followed to establish Zion in our day and social patterns that can provide clues on how we should organize life in Zion.

In these three chapters, I identify important gospel insights and principles of action. Some of those principles may take us in somewhat unexpected directions. Helpful social patterns to be emulated, on the other hand, are more difficult to ferret out. Some of the patterns that are discernible are negative and should likely be avoided. But the lessons learned are important and provide the beginning of a foundation for Zion.

CHAPTER 1

Ancient Efforts to Create Zion

Enoch and Melchizedek

*I*t may be helpful at the onset to ask what we hope to learn by revisiting what we know about Enoch and Melchizedek. First, we are looking for guiding principles, the commandments and principles that formed the foundations of their societies. Second, we are looking for clues about how those guiding principles influenced their social organization. How did they organize themselves to accomplish their common purposes, including unity and the elimination of poverty? We will see that it is easier to answer the first question than the second, but there are clues and suggestions of a pattern.

Enoch left the land of Cainan, which he described as a "land of righteousness unto this day" (Moses 6:41) to preach to the rest of God's children, many of whom denied the existence of God. As prophets often do, he began by teaching the plan of salvation, including the doctrine of Christ and the importance of individual agency (see Moses 6:41–56).

When God called Enoch to "go forth" and preach, He also provided direction on what to teach: "Say unto this people: Choose ye this day, to serve the Lord God who made you" (Moses 6:33). Later, He told Enoch, "And unto thy brethren have I said, and also given commandment, that they should love one another, and that they should choose me, their Father" (Moses 7:33). From Enoch's experience we learn the vital principle that achieving Zion is a choice to accept God the Father and His Son Jesus Christ, and to live the second great commandment.

Enoch was successful in helping many to choose God and embrace the doctrine of Christ. As they did so, the people became righteous, unified, and poverty-free. Only then did Enoch build a city called "the City of Holiness, even Zion" (Moses 7:16–19). It is significant that "the Lord came and dwelt with his people, and they dwelt in righteousness" (Moses 7:16) and "the Lord said unto Enoch: Behold mine abode forever" (Moses 7:21). Ultimately, "Enoch and all his people walked with God, and he dwelt in the midst of Zion; and it came to pass that Zion was not, for God received it up into his own bosom; and from thence went forth the saying, Zion is Fled" (Moses 7:69).

We know a bit more about one group during the life of Abraham that approached the level of righteousness achieved in the city of Enoch because of a brief description in the Joseph Smith translation of Genesis 14. We learn that under Melchizedek's leadership, the people of Salem "wrought righteousness, and obtained heaven, and sought for the city of Enoch which God had before taken" (JST, Genesis 14:34).

We know that Melchizedek was "ordained an high priest after the order of the covenant which God made with Enoch, It being after the order of the Son of God" (JST, Genesis 14:27–28).

> And this Melchizedek, having thus established righteousness, was called the king of heaven by his people, or, in other words, the King of peace. And he lifted up his voice, and he blessed Abram, being the high priest, and the keeper of the storehouse of God; Him whom God had appointed to receive tithes for the poor. Wherefore, Abram paid unto him tithes of all that he had. (JST, Genesis 14:36–39)

Elder Bruce R. McConkie believed that the record in the Joseph Smith Translation is sufficiently clear to conclude that Melchizedek and his people were eventually translated and joined the city of

Enoch.[1] BYU Professor Frank F. Judd Jr. has pointed out the similarities between Enoch and Melchizedek. Just as scriptural passages such as "the Lord came and dwelt with his people" and "people walked with God" (Moses 7) suggest a temple-like experience, Judd sees other similarities between the two leaders:

> Melchizedek was privileged to lead a life remarkably similar to Enoch's. Both of these great men held the same priesthood authority, performed similar miracles, received temple blessings, established Zion communities, and were, along with their people, eventually translated and taken up to heaven.[2]

To support his claim that both Enoch and Melchizedek had access to temple blessings, Professor Judd cites several latter-day prophets, including President Ezra Taft Benson:

> Adam and his descendants entered into the priesthood order of God. Today we would say they went to the House of the Lord and received their blessings. . . . But this order is otherwise described in modern revelation as an order of family government where a man and woman enter into a covenant with God—just as did Adam and Eve—to be sealed for eternity. . . . Adam followed this order and brought his posterity into the presence of God. He is the greatest example for us to follow. Enoch followed this pattern and brought the Saints of his day into the presence of God.[3]

Regarding the temple blessings enjoyed by the people of Melchizedek, Judd states:

---

1. Bruce R. McConkie, *Doctrinal New Testament Commentary,* 3 vols., vol. 3 (Salt Lake City, UT: Deseret Book, 1965), 202–3.
2. Frank F. Judd, Jr., "Melchizedek: Seeking After the Zion of Enoch," ed. Paul Y. Hoskisson, *Sperry Symposium Classics: The Old Testament* (Provo and Salt Lake City, UT: Religious Studies Center, Brigham Young University and Deseret Book, 2005), https://rsc.byu.edu/sperry-symposium-classics-old-testament/melchizedek.
3. Ezra Taft Benson, "What I Hope You Will Teach Your Children about the Temple," *Ensign,* August, 1985, 9.

This order of the priesthood authorized Melchizedek "to stand in the presence of God" (JST, Genesis 14:31). According to the Doctrine and Covenants, that is the reason temples are built; namely, "that the Son of Man might have a place to manifest himself to his people" (Doctrine and Covenants 109:5). Therefore, it seems that the society of Melchizedek, like the society of Enoch, enjoyed priesthood blessings associated with the temple of the Lord.[4]

Eliminating Poverty

Three key features characterized the residents of Enoch's city and qualified them as a Zion people: they dwelt in righteousness, they were of one heart and one mind, and there were no poor among them. I briefly discussed how the people of Enoch and Melchizedek sought to live righteously, but how were there no poor among them? How is poverty to be eliminated in Zion? The record is clear that Abram paid tithes of all that he had into the storehouse maintained by Melchizedek for the care of the poor. It also seems clear that while Abram made a significant contribution to the storehouse, it was not all that he possessed. While Melchizedek maintained a storehouse for his poor, it is not clear whether Enoch had a storehouse for his poor. Whatever institutional mechanism was employed, Enoch's people were able to eliminate poverty.

As discussed below, the Nephites, following the appearances of the Savior, also achieved a condition in which "there were not rich and poor" because "they had all things common" (4 Nephi 1:3). Likewise among the early Christians at the time of Peter, "neither was there any among them that lacked" because those Saints "had all things common" and "distribution was made unto every man according as he had need" (Acts 4:32–34). But did having "all things common among them" mean that these people formally transferred all of their possessions to the Church?

There is another possible interpretation for the word "common." Enoch recognized and taught that God created the heavens and the earth (see Moses 6:44). As the Creator, everything belongs to God.

---

4. Judd, "Melchizedek: Seeking After the Zion of Enoch."

However, from the story of Cain and Abel we see that there were private personal possessions, suggesting that stewardships differed. When Cain rose in his pride and committed the first murder, he gloried that his personal possessions would increase (see Moses 5:33). But until Cain's pride got the best of him, he tilled the ground, Abel raised livestock, and all the fruits of their labors were most likely shared by the whole family.

It is important that we not impose our contemporary western ideas of ownership, especially of land, on the ancients. The example from Cain and Abel makes it clear that the ancients had personal private possessions. But I see no reason to think that in the run-up to Enoch's city, the locals recognized private land ownership as we understand the term. Any concepts of deeds or formal transfer of titles would be unnecessary and likely not understood.

What I am suggesting is that in a nomadic society that includes personal possessions but has no concept of private land ownership, it may well be that the notion of "all things common" is not relevant. Consecration in such a society would amount to freely making available all that one has to share with those in need.

What we learn definitively from Enoch's people is that creating Zion is a choice—a choice to follow the Savior, to love one another, and to assure that all have similar access and opportunity to obtain life's necessities.

Establishing a City

For purposes of this discussion, it is also worth considering why Enoch built a city. Hugh Nibley wrote extensively on Enoch and Zion. In his book *Enoch the Prophet*, Nibley discusses how various sources describe conditions in Enoch's day. In Nibley's view, "Joseph Smith places the action amidst pastoral nomads ranging the mountains and valleys—and so do other sources."[5]

The challenges of moving a nomadic people into an urban environment are enormous, especially if that urban environment must be

---

5. Hugh Nibley, *Enoch the Prophet*, ed. Stephen D. Ricks (Salt Lake City, UT: Deseret Book, 1986), 194.

newly created in a mountainous environment. Scholars of the history of cities have argued that cities came about because the advantages of urban life outweighed the disadvantages.[6] While this may be true, it is not very helpful unless we consider more deeply what Enoch and his people gained through urban dwelling. Here are a few possibilities.

1. Central to any concept of Zion is the temple. God always commands His servants to build temples (see Doctrine and Covenants 124:39–41). Moses was instructed to make a portable "temple" while Israel sojourned in the wilderness. Similarly, many ancient cities were built up around a central sacred space, often characterized as the center of the world. Enoch's city would have been built around a temple, a sacred connection between heaven and earth. I suspect that the city of Enoch's layout, with the temple in the center, became a pattern that other ancient people would later follow in their own cities, including the people of Melchizedek.

2. As people were converted by Enoch's preaching, they would undoubtedly want to gather with other converts and to be close to Enoch and the temple. With greater success, there would be higher densities around Enoch's camp, with all the challenges of providing food, clean water, sanitation, and so on associated with large crowds. Creating a city would create a location for gathering and a potentially orderly organization for meeting the needs of a denser population.

Emphasizing that there were no poor in Enoch's Zion also acknowledges that there could be poverty, and likely would be, but for the righteous actions of the people that led to its elimination. Poverty is a relative and comparative concept. To say that someone is poor is to say that there is someone else who has more—whether food, clothing, shelter, or other possessions—and there are social distinctions made based on those differences. If everyone in a community has roughly

---

6. See for example Marc Van De Mieroop, *A History of the Ancient Near East: ca. 3000–323 BC*, 3rd ed. (West Sussex, United Kingdom: John Wiley & Sons, Ltd., 2016).

the same living standard, whatever that standard may be, there are no poor in that community.

3. In many ancient cities, the religious center also served as a redistribution center. As agriculture became more productive, surplus production from the area surrounding the city was transported to the temple and then redistributed to the broader population.[7] Again, I suspect this pattern emulated Zion. A city with a temple (or temple complex) at its heart could also have the capacity to receive, store, and redistribute food and other necessities to assure that all were adequately provided for.

4. Similarly, higher population density reduces the logistical challenges and makes providing short-term assistance to the needy easier for both the donors and the recipients.

5. Urban living also results in labor specialization. Urban dwellers can specialize in particular tasks and obtain other necessities through trade and barter. This would also likely mean that the poor would have more opportunity to find gainful employment. At least, this seems to be the pattern in much of the developing world today.

6. Protection from their enemies. While Enoch was effective in defending Zion (moving mountains, changing rivers, and so on), the residents in Zion would probably feel a greater sense of safety within the city than pursuing their more traditional dispersed lifestyle.

If this list has merit, there are both spiritual (temple, gathering) and temporal (caring for the poor, providing economic opportunity, protection) reasons for Enoch to build a city. But urban life comes with several significant challenges:

1. Providing communal services such as clean water, sewage disposal, and solid waste disposal. For thousands of years, cities have confronted the challenge of providing clean water by using central water systems, often building aqueducts, pipes, and water retention systems to deliver and store fresh

---

7. Van De Mieroop, *A History of the Ancient Near East: ca. 3000–323 BC*, 3rd ed.

water. Sewage disposal has also often been confronted on a communal basis with centralized systems removing sewage from the city to the nearest river or large body of water. Solid waste disposal in ancient cities has provided archeologists in our day with a major data resource, but when the city was active, there had to be provision for waste disposal and agreement on a location. Other services such as land regulation (who gets to build what, where)[8], communication, and fuel seem to have been handled in ancient cities less systematically, varying by location and environment.

2. In addition to the design, production, and maintenance of these basic public utilities, there would also be the need for labor to build the temple, to construct and maintain roads, and to build and maintain public buildings. These needs could be met through a combination of hired labor (paid for through taxes) or assigned work obligations.

3. Food production and pastures. In many ancient cities, food was produced in the areas surrounding the city, but not so much in the city. This was the approach envisioned by Joseph Smith and the First Presidency as they laid out the plat maps for Kirtland, Far West, and the city of Zion in Jackson County, Missouri. People would live in the city, but most of the agriculture would be in surrounding areas. Was this the approach Enoch used in his city? It seems likely, although to what extent it could be implemented in a mountainous region is unknown. Did Enoch's city require communal irrigation the way many Middle Eastern and U.S. Western cities did? That is also unknown. It also seems likely that the former nomads would wish to retain their herds to the extent possible, again requiring negotiation and agreement on the allocation of pasture lands and animal enclosures.

4. Most ancient cities developed systems of writing and record keeping. Whether to keep track of market transactions, taxes paid, contracts entered into, or simply communication

---

8. G. Kendall and G. Wickham, "Lessons from an old millennium: Law and regulation in the ancient city" (The Australian Sociological Association [TASA] 1999 Conference, Melbourne, Australia, December 1999).

between parties, written communication systems emerged fairly early on. We know that Enoch had a written language and a book of remembrance. Prophecies and revelations were recorded. The need for knowledge of the written language to be transmitted to subsequent generations would suggest some sort of educational system.

Realizing the potential and confronting the challenges of urban life in Enoch's new city suggests the need for a fairly sophisticated city organization, one sufficiently robust to support an urban population for at least 365 years (see Moses 7:68). Those who have written on Enoch's Zion have focused largely on the spiritual, on the environmental upheaval in his day, and on Enoch's defense of the city. As previously noted, Hugh Nibley has written extensively on Enoch and Zion, but his book on Enoch seems focused on the importance of Enoch as a prophet and on validating passages about Enoch in the book of Moses.

While we know next to nothing about how Enoch and his nomadic converts worked in unison to found the city of Zion or how they overcame the challenges of this new urban living, we know a good deal about the principles that guided them. They lived in righteousness and were unified in their efforts to eliminate poverty and meet the challenges they confronted. We know they were taught to choose Jesus Christ and to love one another, two principles that continue to form part of the foundations of Zion. We must draw on those same principles as we look to the future.

CHAPTER 2

Early Christians

While the early Christians believed the Second Coming was near, neither the Christians under the Apostles nor the remnant of Israel in the Americas saw themselves as creators of a Zion society. But both groups had the benefit of being instructed by the Savior Himself. After they received the gift of the Holy Ghost, as they lived the principles of the gospel, they approached in their communities conditions that will prevail in Zion. As such, there is much to be learned from them.

Context and Conditions among the First Christians in Judea

There are two aspects of early Christian societies that we need to try and understand as they relate to efforts to establish Zion in our day. The first is the phrase "all things common." Both the Saints in Judea and in the Americas are described as having all things common: "they had all things common" (Acts 4:32) and "they had all things common among them" (4 Nephi 1:3). What did the writers mean by the phrase, and is that concept relevant for building Zion today?

The second social aspect we need to understand is unity as it existed both in Judea and in the Americas. Luke declares that "the multitude of them that believed were of one heart and of one soul" (Acts 4:32). Mormon states multiple times that "there was no contention in the land" (4 Nephi 1:2, 13, 15) and "they were in one, the children of Christ" (4 Nephi 1:17). What type of unity was achieved in these societies and how? Both questions are explored in this chapter.

Following the ascension of the Savior, the Saints in Jerusalem had to establish a community of believers within the Jewish region of Judea and the encompassing Roman Empire. They sought to implement the teachings of Jesus, but it is not clear that they consciously set about to create a Zion society. The word "Zion" appears only seven times in the entire New Testament, generally with quotations from the Old Testament (see Matthew 21:5; John 12:15; Rom 9:33, Romans 11:26) or references to a future Zion (see Hebrews 12:22–25; Revelation 14:1). Thus, explicit teachings on how Zion should be organized are sparse to nonexistent in the New Testament.

It is also helpful to bear in mind the context experienced by the first Christians. The authors of the *Expositor's Bible Commentary*[1] and Alexander Wedderburn[2] point out many of the disciples at the time were fishermen and farmers from Galilee and were not able to pursue their trades and professions in Jerusalem.

Wedderburn also points out that the early followers of Jesus were Jews, and believing in Jesus did not make them less Jewish. They believed Jesus to be the fulfillment of the promises made to Israel. Jews in this period connected resurrection with the end times. Early Christians shared this view and expected the Second Coming to happen soon. Those who thought the end was near would not feel a great need to manage their resources to make them last. According to Alexander Wedderburn, "This lack of long-term planning and stewardship of their resources may well also have contributed to the financial vulnerability of the Jerusalem community, making it more heavily dependent on the gifts and subventions of others."[3]

---

1. Frank E. Gaebelein, ed., *Volume 9: John–Acts*, 12 vols., vol. 9, (Grand Rapids, MI: Zondervan Publishing House, 1981), 310.
2. Alexander J. M. Wedderburn, *A History of the First Christians (Understanding the Bible and Its World)* (London, UK: Bloomsbury Publishing, 2004), 33.
3. Wedderburn, *A History of the First Christians*, 33–34.

The *Expositor's Bible Commentary* agrees that the early Christians considered themselves "the righteous remnant within Israel."[4] It further explains, "Other Jewish groups that thought of themselves in terms of a remnant theology expressed their spiritual oneness by sharing goods, and the Jerusalem church seems to have done likewise."[5]

Paul was committed to "remember[ing] the poor" (Galatians 2:10), a phrase that appears only twice in scripture, in this passage in Galatians and in Doctrine and Covenants 42:30.[6] Dieter Georgi suggests that the phrase means both more and less than we might suppose as it relates to the early Christians.[7] We need to consider what Paul meant by the phrase in context and what we know about "the poor" that he referred to.

> Being "the poor" appears to be the essential dignity held by the congregation in Jerusalem, to be granted and respected by all other Jesus congregations. . . . In [the Jewish Bible], and especially in the Psalms, the name "the poor" is used in very specific contexts and is further elaborated in later periods of early Judaism, until eventually it is used synonymously with such designations as "pious" and "just." Since the Maccabean wars [167 BC] the denomination "the poor" had been used as self-designation by a variety of Jewish groups, all of whom meant to express that they alone were the true devotees, the true Israel, the "Holy Remnant."[8]

Georgi also considers the verb "remember" as used in Galatians 2:10. He suggests that the connotation "caring for materially" is not supported by the Greek. Rather, it means to give recognition for the place and efforts of the Saints in Jerusalem in relation to

---

4. Gaebelein, *Volume 9: John–Acts*, 291.
5. Gaebelein, *Volume 9: John–Acts*, 310.
6. Joseph M. Spencer, *For Zion: A Mormon Theology of Hope* (Salt Lake City, UT: Greg Kofford Books, 2014), 84.
7. Dieter Georgi, *Remembering the Poor: The History of Paul's Collection for Jerusalem* (Nashville, TN: Abingdon Press, 1992).
8. Georgi, *Remembering the Poor*, 33–34.

the expected end times.[9] Georgi does indicate that "remembering" included financial support, but that was not the primary focus.[10]

Brian Capper and Fiona Gregson have argued that community property sharing was widely idealized in the Greco-Roman era and was actually practiced by the Essenes in Palestine.[11] Capper further argues that Luke's language for describing the sharing of property in the early Church uses many of the same phrases as those found among the Essenes. He points particularly to the Qumran community in the Dead Sea area, and their practice of donating all property to the common treasury. Capper suggests the first Christians in Jerusalem were following the Qumran community pattern.

Steve Walton[12] and Wedderburn[13] disagree with Capper on this point. Walton argues that outside the Dead Sea area, the Essenes followed a variety of practices regarding property and those practices would be better known in Jerusalem.

> The Damascus Document[14] portrays Essene communities which had a common fund to provide for widows and orphans without requiring compulsory pooling of possessions. For example, community members were expected to give at least two days'

---

9. Georgi also argues that the early Christians expected the Millennium to be ushered in during their lifetimes. See also Wedderburn, *A History of the First Christians*, 31.

10. Georgi, *Remembering the Poor,* 38, 41.

11. Brian Capper, "The Palestinian Cultural Context of Earliest Christian Community of Goods," in *The Book of Acts in Its Palestinian Setting*, ed. Richard Bauckham (Grand Rapids, MI: Eerdmans, 1995); Fiona Jane Robertson Gregson, "Everything in common? The theology and practice of the sharing of possessions in community in the New Testament with particular reference to Jesus and his Disciples, the earliest Christians, and Paul" (PhD Middlesex University/London School of Theology, 2014).

12. Steve Walton, "Sharing Possessions in Earliest Christian Communities An Exegetical Sketch of Acts 2:44–47; 4:32–5:11; 6:1–6" (British New Testament Society Acts seminar, 2019).

13. Wedderburn, *A History of the First Christians*.

14. "Damascus Document," *Encyclopaedia Britannica*, 1998, https://www.britannica.com/topic/Damascus-Document.

income per month to the 'Guardian and the Judges' to provide for people in need.[15]

Wedderburn also observes that Essenes pooled their income and shared their resources, but their practices differed from the early Christians.[16]

The *Expositor's Bible Commentary* also notes that the early Christians were not monastic.

> They lived in their own homes . . . and had their own possessions as any household would. In these ways the communal life of the early Christians differed from that of the Qumran covenanters. But though the Christians had personal possessions, they did not consider them private possessions . . . to be held exclusively for their own use and enjoyment. Rather, they shared what they had and so expressed their corporate life.[17]

All Things Common as Communal Ownership

Luke reports that early Christian converts had "all things common" (Acts 2:44, 4:32), but there are different views on what the author of Acts intended to convey with that phrase. Luke also reports that those early Saints sold their property and gave the proceeds to the Apostles (see Acts 2:45, 4:34–35), and he even includes two examples of this practice (see Acts 4:36–5:2). What is less clear is whether the practice was common and widespread, and what the expectations were of those early Christians regarding their land and property.

The passages in which Luke states the early believers "had all things common" have been interpreted by many to mean a form of communal living, especially when linked to (1) the assertion that no one lacked because the believers sold their lands and houses and gave the proceeds to the Apostles to be distributed as needed (see Acts

---

15. Walton, "Short Sharing Possessions in Earliest Christian Communities: An Exegetical Sketch of Acts 2: 44–47; 4: 32–5: 11; 6: 1–6." 10.
16. Wedderburn, *A History of the First Christians*, 32.
17. Gaebelein, *Volume 9: John–Acts*, 311.

4:34–35); (2) the example of Barnabas who sold his property and gave the proceeds to the Apostles (see Acts 4:36–37); and (3) the "daily ministration[s]" described in Acts 6:1. If not an early example of total pooling of possessions, at least this appears to have been an example of consecration as many early Latter-day Saints understood it.

Elder Bruce R. McConkie stated in his *New Testament Commentary*:

> In the early part of both this and the meridian dispensations, the Saints attempted to live the full law of consecration. That is, they consecrated their temporal means and spiritual abilities to the Lord's work. All of their talents, strength, time, properties, and monies were made available for use in the establishment of the Lord's earthly Church and kingdom. . . . The New Testament contains only passing allusions of how the system operated in that day.[18]

Further, Richard Holzapfel and Thomas Wayment argue that Luke was writing many years after the events he described. The summary Luke offers in Acts 2:42–47 "moves quickly, and in a single verse [44] details the revelation and implementation of the law of consecration. For Luke, the institution of the practice of the law of consecration may have been part of the distant past, an event for which he had only the sketchiest details."[19]

Regarding Acts 4:31–37, Holzapfel and Wayment acknowledge that "it is difficult to know exactly how the early Saints practiced the law of consecration." If all property was sold and the proceeds consecrated, "such a landless community would have little hope of long-term survival."[20] Holzapfel and Wayment go on to suggest that the incident with Ananias and Sapphira constituted "the end of the practice of the law of consecration among the members of the early Church. . . . The practice of the law of consecration was likely limited to the Jerusalem Saints and the ending of it, or at least the problem of

---

18. Bruce R. McConkie, *Doctrinal New Testament Commentary: Acts–Philippians*, Vol. 2 (Salt Lake City, UT: Bookcraft, Inc., 1971), 57.
19. Richard M. Holzapfel and Thomas A. Wayment, *Making Sense of the New Testament: Timely Insights and Timely Messages* (Salt Lake City: Deseret Book, 2010), 276.
20. Holzapfel and Wayment, 280.

corruption here detailed, foreshadows later internal issues that would rend the Church."[21]

Scholars have differing opinions on what Luke meant by "all things common." Some seem to favor an interpretation that private possessions were still the norm but believers held those possessions "lightly," meaning they were willing to sacrifice and contribute to the good of the community if called upon. Others do not seem to dwell much on the nuances of the phrase and simply accept that it meant the common pooling of assets.

Carl R. Holladay acknowledges that Luke's account in Acts "conflicts with what we know from other historical sources such as Josephus," and therefore, "we must be cautious against simply historicizing the Acts account, reading it as a historically accurate account of the events it reports."[22] Yet when Holladay translates and comments on "all things common" in Acts 2 and 4, he appears to do exactly what he cautions against.

Holladay focuses on the concept of sharing with each other (2:42) and rightly notes that the fellowshipping indicated "goes beyond meeting together and simply being in each other's presence." He mentions both tangibles (food, clothing, money, etc.) and intangibles (beliefs, ideas, encouragement, etc.). Then almost casually he inserts "solidarity of belief leads to community of goods" (2:44–45) without further discussion of what this means.[23]

In commenting on the passage in Acts 4:32–37, Holladay focuses on the "community of believers forming around the apostles and yielding to their authority." He wrote, "A community that claimed no private ownership of property but 'shared everything in common' . . . embodies ideals long valued in the Greek and Roman philosophical traditions. Community of goods was also practiced at Qumran."[24]

---

21. Holzapfel and Wayment, *Making Sense of the New Testament*, 280–81.
22. Carl R Holladay, *Acts: A Commentary (The New Testament Library)* (Louisville, KY: Westminster John Knox Press, 2016), 13.
23. Holladay, *Acts: A Commentary*, 108.
24. Holladay, *Acts: A Commentary*, 134.

After raising questions about how widespread common property ownership was, Johannes Munck and colleagues simply comment: "Those who attained the faith held everything in common. . . .
Nobody was in need, for those who owned anything sold it and gave
the money to the apostles to be shared by all, each man according to
his need."[25] Munck and colleagues were writing fifteen to fifty years
before the more current authors I cite, but I find it both puzzling
and worrisome that Holladay neither cites nor refutes the linguistic
and historical evidence provided by *The Expositor's Bible Commentary*,
Steve Walton, Fiona Gregson, and Brian Capper.

All Things Common as Consecration

Regarding Acts 4:34–35, *The Expositor's Bible Commentary* points
out: "The acts Luke alludes to here were extraordinary and voluntary
acts of Christian concern done in response to special needs among the
believers, and they involved both sharing possessions and selling real
estate. By separating these actions from those described in verse 32
and by the way he treats them, Luke suggests that they were exceptional and were not meant to be normative for the church."[26]

Fiona Gregson notes the similarity between the language in Acts
and the counsel the Savior gave to the rich man.[27] The account cited
here appears in Mark 10:17–26 (see also Matt 19 and Luke 18).

> And when he was gone forth into the way, there came one running,
> and kneeled to him, and asked him, Good Master, what shall I do
> that I may inherit eternal life? . . . Then Jesus beholding him loved
> him, and said unto him, One thing thou lackest: go thy way, sell
> whatsoever thou hast, and give to the poor, and thou shalt have
> treasure in heaven: and come, take up the cross, and follow me.

---

25. Johannes Munck, William F. Albright, and C. S. Mann, *The Acts of the Apostles*,
ed. David Noel Freedman, The Anchor Bible (Garden City, NY: Doubleday &
Company, Inc), 39.

26. Gaebelein, *Volume 9: John–Acts*, 311.

27. Fiona Jane Robertson Gregson, *Everything in Common?: The Theology and
Practice of the Sharing of Possessions in Community in the New Testament*
(Eugene, OR: Wipf and Stock Publishers, 2017).

And he was sad at that saying, and went away grieved: for he had great possessions.

And Jesus looked round about, and saith unto his disciples, . . . Children, how hard is it for them that trust in riches to enter into the kingdom of God! It is easier for a camel to go through the eye of a needle, than for a rich man to enter into the kingdom of God. And they were astonished out of measure, saying among themselves, Who then can be saved?

Peter then exclaims, "What about us? We have left everything to follow you!" (Mark 10:28). Is this what the Saints did when they "had all things common"—they sold all that they had and distributed it to the needy?

The rich man was not told to go and sell everything and give the proceeds to the Apostles (or the Church). He was told to give directly to the poor. This could have meant to give alms directly to those in need, though given Jewish traditions requiring anonymity, more likely it would mean giving to the synagogue or to the Essenes.[28] Later, the Saints "laid the proceeds of their sales at the feet of the apostles," and the Apostles or their appointees determined who qualified to receive aid and how much.[29]

What were the implications for the rich man? The rich man would recognize that even with his wealth, giving all that he had to the poor would not eliminate poverty. At best, it would either lift a

---

28. "Charity (Tzedakah): Charity Throughout Jewish History," American–Israeli Cooperative Enterprise, 2022, https://www.jewishvirtuallibrary.org/charity-throughout-jewish-history; Frank M. Loewenberg, *From Charity to Social Justice: The Emergence of Communal Institutions for the Support of the Poor in Ancient Judaism* (New Brunswick, NJ: Transaction Publishers, 2001), 39–40.
29. I should also point out that under rabbinical teachings, alms giving was not the best way to assist the poor because it does not foster self-reliance. "The highest form of charity is not to give alms but to help the poor to rehabilitate themselves by lending them money, taking them into partnership, employing them, or giving them work, for in this way the end is achieved without any loss of self-respect at all" (Jewish Virtual Library, "Charity (Tzedakah): Charity Throughout Jewish History."; See also Loewenberg, *From Charity to Social Justice*, 44).

small number of people out of poverty or it would defer the effects of persistent poverty for a slightly larger number of the poor.

The Savior did not say act alone. The rich man could have organized a group of wealthy friends and extended his impact to a larger group of the poor. He was asked to do all that he could personally do to alleviate poverty, even if his action would only be a partial remedy for a limited number of people and his sacrifice might appear to be orders of magnitude larger than the blessings received by the benefited poor. He was asked to place the well-being of others on an equal footing with his own. By doing so, he would be following the example of the Savior.

In 2019, Steve Walton presented a paper at the British New Testament Society on the sharing of possessions in the earliest Christian church. This piece drew on and updated his earlier work on a similar subject.[30] Walton argues that the Greek syntax, when read in the context provided by Acts 2:44–45, "indicate[s] periodic sale and distribution, as people were in need . . . , rather than a once-for-all sale of all possessions on entry into the community."[31]

Walton makes an important point regarding early Christian attitudes toward property.

> The believers' unity does not issue in people pooling all their possessions when they join the community, but rather portrays a transformed attitude to possessions. Instead of regarding their goods as their own . . . , they held them loosely and were ready to give to others as need required (vv 32, 34–35). This attitude reflects biblical passages which understand everything as belonging to God, and humans as functioning as stewards or trustees of God's good gifts (e.g. Ps 24:1; Gen 1:26–28).[32]

---

30. Steve Walton, "Primitive Communism in Acts?: Does Acts Present the Community of Goods (2:44–45; 4:32–35) as Mistaken?" *Evangelical Quarterly: An International Review of Bible and Theology* 80, no. 2 (2008).
31. Walton, "Short Sharing Possessions in Earliest Christian Communities: An Exegetical Sketch of Acts 2:44–47; 4:32–5: 11; 6:1–6," 2.
32. Walton, 4.

I find a footnote in the *Oxford Study Bible* helpful as well. It states, referring to the passage in Acts 5 on the sale of property, that Acts 5:4 "makes clear, such disposal of personal property was not mandatory, but was done at the promptings of the Spirit."[33]

Walton goes on to observe that laying the donor's gift at the feet of the Apostles broke the standard reciprocal arrangement of gifts. Traditionally, receiving a gift placed the recipient under obligation to the giver. The arrangement described in Acts emphasizes that the donation was to the community as a whole. Walton summarizes his argument as follows:

> In sum, Luke's portrait of the earliest believers is of a sharing of possessions which put others' needs at the centre of their life together. The principles at work were to regard 'possessions' as belonging not to oneself, but to God, and thus to place them at the disposal of God's people as needed (4:32, 34). . . . What is new is that this readiness to share flows from the coming of the Spirit on the entire believing community, initially at Pentecost and later as others join, for the expectation of the programmatic 2:38–39 is that they, too, would receive the Spirit. . . . The gift of the Spirit to all is transformative, and leads to holding goods lightly with an attitude of stewardship on behalf of God.[34]
>
> Luke's concern, then, may be summed up as regarding material goods and property as held in stewardship by believers; they are to be generous to those in need because and as God in Christ has been generous to them (cf. 2 Cor 8:9). The form of this generosity will vary from place to place and time to time, of course, but Luke wants believers' commitment to it to be steadfast.[35]

Fiona Gregson agrees with Walton and *The Expositor's Bible Commentary* on these points.

---

33. *The Oxford Study Bible: Revised English Bible with the Apocrypha*, ed. M. Jack Suggs, Katharine Doob Sakenfeld, and James R. Mueller (New York: Oxford University Press, 1992), 1399, note 34.
34. Walton, "Short Sharing Possessions in Earliest Christian Communities," 7.
35. Walton, "Short Sharing Possessions in Earliest Christian Communities," 19.

However, in Acts, it is clear that not all property was sold as while they had possessions and property that was held in common (4.32), later chapters in Acts show they still had property that they were using (12.12). Furthermore, the phrase about selling indicates an ongoing as opposed to one off selling (4.34).

While Luke is not describing a situation where everything is sold, his use of verbs which remind the reader of the rich ruler [Luke 18:22], suggests that he is communicating a significant shift in how individuals in the early church saw (and held) their own possessions and commending that shift to his readers. The specific description of what is sold and the examples of selling at the end of chapter 4 and beginning of chapter 5 may limit those who could contribute in this way. . . . However while only those who had fields or houses could contribute in this way, all could hold what they had, little or large, in common and consider it not just their personal possession.[36]

The record in Acts does report on two sales of land, one by Barnabas who sold his land and gave the money to the church (see Acts 4:36–37). The other and more startling example is that of Ananias and Sapphira who sold their land and gave only part of the proceeds to the Church. When Peter asked Ananias why he withheld part of the proceeds, Ananias "fell down, and gave up the ghost" (Acts 5:1–5). I use here a slightly different translation of the text to clarify Peter's questions and their significance for the discussion here:

> Peter said "Ananias, how was it that Satan so possessed your mind that you lied to the Holy Spirit by keeping back part of the price of the land? While it remained unsold, did it not remain yours? Even after it was turned into money, was it not still at your own disposal? What made you think of doing this? You have lied not to men but to God." (Acts 5:3–4)[37]

It appears from this reading of the text that Ananias's fault was in lying in order to appear more righteous than he really wanted to be. But Peter's questions also suggest that Ananias could have kept his land or even

---

36. Gregson, "Everything in Common?," 63.
37. *The Oxford Study Bible: Revised English Bible with the Apocrypha.*

kept the proceeds from the sale as indicated by Walton,[38] Gregson,[39] and the *Oxford Study Bible*. If these scholars are correct, Ananias could also have been forthright and told Peter that he was only giving part of the sale proceeds to the Church. Again, his sin seems to have been in lying rather than in withholding some of the money.

As noted earlier, Holzapfel and Wayment suggest this incident represented the end of efforts to live the law of consecration among the early Christians.[40] Given the efforts of the Saints in Antioch and Paul's repeated efforts to raise funds for the Jerusalem congregation, it seems more likely that efforts were rather transformed as the circumstances of the young church changed.

The church in Jerusalem clearly had significant need for resources to meet the needs of the local Saints. In Acts 6 we read that there was some murmuring among the Grecian members because they felt their widows were being shortchanged in the "daily ministration." So, a significant number of widows and perhaps the Apostles needed to be provided for on a daily basis.

Paul reports in his letter to the Romans that the Saints in Macedonia and Achaia were raising funds for the church in Jerusalem.[41] He was also clearly giving guidance to the believers in Corinth and Galatia to raise funds for Jerusalem but to do it without impoverishing themselves (see 1 Corinthians 16:1–4). Further, the disciples in Antioch were "every man according to his ability, determined to send relief unto the brethren which dwelt in Judea: Which also they did, and sent it to the elders by the hands of Barnabas and Saul" (Acts 11:29–30). Georgi questions whether Saul and Barnabas were in fact the couriers carrying the funds to Jerusalem,[42] but it appears that there was a collection and transfer from Antioch to Jerusalem.

When Paul returned from his travels, he brought "alms to [his] nation, and offerings" (Acts 24:17). These examples suggest that the

38. Walton, "Short Sharing Possessions in Earliest Christian Communities."
39. Gregson, "Everything in common?"
40. Holzapfel and Wayment, *Making Sense of the New Testament*, 280–81.
41. Romans 15:25–28, *The Oxford Study Bible: Revised English Bible with the Apocrypha*.
42. Georgi, Remembering the Poor: The History of Paul's Collection for Jerusalem, 44.

disciples in these other cities either had assets that could be liquidated or "surplus" income that could be forwarded to Jerusalem, though likely at some sacrifice.

At the same time, it is clear in the record that not all righteous Saints "sold all that they had." Simon the tanner had a house by the seaside in Joppa, and Peter "tarried many days" with him (Acts 9:43; 10:6–9). Mary, the mother of John, had her own house, large enough "where many were gathered together praying" (Acts 12:12). In Thessalonica, Paul and Silas stayed at the home of Jason (see Acts 17). In Corinth, Paul stayed for some time and worked with Aquila and Priscilla in their tent-making business (see Acts 18). Finally, when Paul went to Cæsarea, he and his party "entered into the house of Philip the evangelist, which was one of the seven; and abode with him" (Acts 18:3).

How, then, should we understand the repeated statement that the Saints had "all things common"? Viewing the accounts in Acts and the Epistles from the vantage point stated here bears a striking resemblance to the covenants Latter-day Saints make in the temple today. We commit all that we have for the building of the kingdom and the establishment of Zion. Most are not called upon to "sell all that they have," but some may be. The Prophet Joseph Smith prepared this remarkable statement on the principle of sacrifice for the *Lectures on Faith*: "Let us here observe, that a religion that does not require the sacrifice of all things never has power sufficient to produce the faith necessary unto life and salvation."[43]

I find the argument that the early Christians in Judea were encouraged to hold their possessions lightly, and to make them available to the community as needed, a compelling one. I also see that view as a plausible application of the law of consecration in a Zion society today.

Acts Passages: Unity and Circumcision

On the day of Pentecost, Peter taught thousands about the doctrine of Christ. "Then Peter said unto them, Repent, and be baptized

---

43. Joseph Smith, "Lectures on Faith: Lecture 6," in Doctrine and Covenants, 1835 (The Church of Jesus Christ of Latter-day Saints, 1835), 60.

every one of you in the name of Jesus Christ for the remission of sins, and ye shall receive the gift of the Holy Ghost" (Acts 2:38). Three thousand souls heeded the call and were baptized. Luke reports that, together with those who were already converted, "all that believed were together, and had all things common; And sold their possessions and goods, and parted them to all men, as every man had need" (Acts 2:44–45).

A subsequent passage in Acts 4:32 adds further details: "And the multitude of them that believed were of one heart and of one soul: neither said any of them that ought of the things which he possessed was his own; but they had all things common."

Luke reports the early Christians were of "one heart and one soul" (Acts 4:32). Thus it appears that at least some part of the first Christians worked to achieve two important components of a Zion people: unity and the elimination of poverty. Their efforts deserve our careful consideration, but it is also important that we recognize the limitations in those early efforts. For example, it is not clear what the unity implied by "one heart and one soul" means, given the contention among the first Christians over the issue of circumcision and other aspects of the Mosaic law.

Unity is one essential attribute of a Zion people. In considering the level and type of unity that existed among New Testament Christians, it is helpful first to recognize that there were multiple "types" of converts.[44] They included Jews who knew the Savior during His mortal ministry and who spoke Aramaic as their first language, Jews from other nations who spoke Greek or some other language as their native tongue, and Gentiles, non-Jewish people, some from Palestine and some from other regions. As happens today, all these new believers brought with them their own culture, understanding, and expectations.

When the Saints and the Apostles gathered to replace Judas as a member of the Twelve, only about 120 Jewish disciples assembled to participate and witness the selection of the new apostle (see Acts 1:15).

---

44. Raymond E. Brown, "Not Jewish Christianity and Gentile Christianity but Types of Jewish/Gentile Christianity," *The Catholic Biblical Quarterly* 45, no. 1 (1983).

On the day of Pentecost, "devote [Jews] from every nation under heaven" were staying at Jerusalem (Acts 2:5). When Peter addressed the crowd on that day, he spoke to his "Fellow Jews," regardless of native language or homeland (see Acts 2:14). Luke records that about 3,000 were "added to the number of believers" (Acts 2:41). Later, in Acts 4:4, we learn of an additional 5,000 converted souls.

Luke further reports that the disciples met together constantly to hear the Apostles teach, fellowship, break bread, and pray (see Acts 2:42). Luke asserts that "the multitude of them that believed were of one heart and of one soul" (Acts 4:32), qualities that partially define Zion.

We must remember that these were all devote Jews who joined the believers in Christ at this time. As *The Expositor's Bible Commentary* observes: "For both theological and practical reasons . . . as well as because of the inevitable tug of the traditional, the early Christians in Jerusalem sought to retain their hold on the religious forms they had inherited and to express their new faith through the categories of the old."[45]

For devout Jews, circumcision was an essential symbol of their covenant with God. Genesis 17:10–14 records the covenant with Abraham, made hundreds of years before Moses and millennia before Christ:

> This is my covenant, which ye shall keep, between me and you and thy seed after thee; Every man child among you shall be circumcised. . . . It shall be a token of the covenant betwixt me and you. . . . And my covenant shall be in your flesh for an everlasting covenant. And the uncircumcised man child . . . hath broken my covenant.

We often hear covenants described as a two-way promise, but they are not just a contract. Covenants establish an enduring relationship between the parties. Circumcision for the Jews was a token that they were accepted by God as part of His people.

While the coming of Christ did away with the covenant of circumcision (see Moroni 8:8), Wedderburn points out that belief in

---

45. Gaebelein, *Volume 9: John–Acts*, 291.

Jesus did not make the first Christians less Jewish.[46] They believed Jesus to be the fulfillment of the promises made to Israel. Indeed, in making his defense to the Sanhedrin, Stephen points to the covenant of circumcision as a central feature of the Abrahamic covenant (see Acts 7:8).

For perspective, all of the conversions took place before Saul's conversion (see Acts 9:1–9) or Peter's vision (see Acts 10:9–16). Indeed, even after Peter went to the Roman Cornelius and the Spirit fell on all those who heard his words (see Acts 10:44), "they of the circumcision which believed were astonished, as many as came with Peter, because that on the Gentiles also was poured out the gift of the Holy Ghost" with manifestations quite like those on the day of Pentecost (Acts 10:45–47). When Peter returned to Jerusalem, he was challenged for visiting and eating with the uncircumcised (see Acts 11:1–3).

The early believers in Jerusalem were Jews with a long history and very entrenched beliefs and practices, including the practice of circumcision. Among this relatively homogeneous group, it was possible to obtain a certain level of unity in their beliefs. But those beliefs included both an understanding that the gospel was only for the Jews and retention of the covenant of circumcision, in addition to other distinctly Jewish practices.

When Peter explained his vision and the experience with Cornelius's household, his listeners were willing to accept that God was extending repentance and salvation to the Gentiles (see Acts 11:18). But for these believers, extending repentance and salvation to Gentiles did not remove the requirement for circumcision.

This points out the need to carefully assess and distinguish between cultural practices and the universal truths of the gospel. But circumcision was not just a cultural practice; it was a sign of the covenant. We must also acknowledge that God changed many aspects of the covenant when Christ came. "All old things are done away." (See 3 Nephi 12:27; Hebrews 8:13; 2 Corinthians 5:17; Romans 7:6.) The teaching is implied in the Gospels but not stated succinctly. We must

---

46. Wedderburn, *A History of the First Christians*, 34.

also acknowledge that what God requires of us changes depending on our circumstances.

Before Christ's earthly ministry, circumcision was a symbol of a covenant that brought men closer to Christ. After His mortal ministry, circumcision was a roadblock that kept men from coming closer to Christ by focusing on abiding by an outward symbol rather than the new inward covenant (see Doctrine and Covenants 74:3–4). Before the Resurrection, it was good. After the Resurrection, the requirement was not of God. With the standard set forth in Moroni 7:15–19, requiring circumcision would be judged to be both from God and good, and not from God and evil, depending upon the time period.

This significant change simply points out the validity of Joseph Smith's teaching:

> That which is wrong under one circumstance, may be, and often is, right under another. God said, "Thou shalt not kill"; at another time he said, "Thou shalt utterly destroy." This is the principle on which the government of heaven is conducted, by revelation adapted to the circumstances in which the children of the Kingdom are placed. Whatever God requires is right, no matter what it is, although we may not see the reason thereof till long after the events transpire. If we seek first the kingdom of God, all good things will be added.[47]

With the conversion of Paul, and especially after the Jerusalem conference recorded in Acts 15, Paul and his companions actively proselyted among both Jew and Gentile, but throughout Paul's epistles we see the struggles he faced to overcome the influence of the "Judaizers" who continued to insist that new male converts be circumcised.

If Luke was not overstating the degree of unity among the first Christians, he was at best describing only Jewish converts during a limited time period. Paul consistently taught the need for unity (see 1 Corinthians 1:10; Romans 12:4–5; Ephesians 4:1–3; Philippians 1:27). Some portion of the early Church may have achieved

---

47. Joseph Smith Papers, *History, 1838–1856*, vol. D-1, *The Joseph Smith Papers*, (Salt Lake City, UT: Church Historian Press, The Church of Jesus Christ of Latter-day Saints, 1842), 3.

such unity, but the record seems clear that lack of unity became a serious problem for the Church.

Grace and Power

In the summarizing passage in Acts 4:32–35, Luke notes the power of the Apostles' witness and the grace that "was upon them all" without further comment or explanation. *The Expositor's Bible Commentary* makes an important observation about Acts 4:33, noting that the "great power" came not only from the powerful witness of the Resurrection borne by the Apostles but also from the "new life manifest in sharing possessions to meet the needs of others. It was this kind of power Jesus had in mind when he said, 'All men will know that you are my disciples if you love one another.' (John 13:35)" [48]

A common aphorism employed by many is the expression, "If you were accused of being a Christian, would there be enough evidence to convict you?" The phrase is used to encourage Christian behaviors, not just verbal assertions or historical connections. *The Expositor's Bible Commentary* does not employ the aphorism, but its citation of the Savior's teaching in John points to the type of "evidence" that should be expected.

As both Paul and Mormon teach, there is one spiritual gift that is both essential and to be desired above all others: the gift of charity, which "the Father . . . hath bestowed upon all who are true followers of his Son, Jesus Christ" (Moroni 7:48). As we "pray unto the Father with all the energy of heart, that [we] may be filled with this love," the gift of charity will manifest itself through the way we treat others.

The grace that attended the early Christians would be a manifestation of the spiritual gift of charity. *The Expositor's Bible Commentary* states earlier, "For Luke as well as for the early Christians, being filled with the Holy Spirit not only concerned proclaiming the Word of God but also sharing possessions with the needy because of believers' oneness in Christ."[49] The oneness with Christ leads to true unity in Zion.

---

48. Gaebelein, *Volume 9: John–Acts*, 311.
49. Gaebelein, *Volume 9: John–Acts*, 309.

Gleanings

When all is said and done, what we learn about Zion from the first Christians under the Apostles is quite different than I originally hoped and expected. The lessons are important, but they don't shed much light on the economic and governance practices that will prevail in Zion.

We can glean two important lessons from this discussion, however. First, believers in Jesus Christ should follow the Lord's prophet and be prepared for change, even in key elements of our traditions and practices. Second, the early Christians were taught to seek the gift of charity and to hold their property lightly, acknowledging God's ultimate ownership, and we should do the same. In April 1978, President Spencer W. Kimball gave this counsel to the Church:

> May I suggest three fundamental things we must do if we are to "bring again Zion," three things for which we who labor for Zion must commit ourselves.
>
> First, we must eliminate the individual tendency to selfishness that snares the soul, shrinks the heart, and darkens the mind. . . .
>
> Second, we must cooperate completely and work in harmony one with the other. There must be unanimity in our decisions and unity in our actions. . . .
>
> Third, we must lay on the altar and sacrifice whatever is required by the Lord. . . . We consecrate our time, talents, and means as called upon by our file leaders and as prompted by the whisperings of the Spirit.[50]

I see these principles at work among the early Christians, and those who "labor for Zion" will strive to follow them today as counseled by President Kimball.

Nephite Society After the Savior's Visits

With the Savior's death came great destruction and death on the American continent. Almost a year later, the Savior visited the

---

50. Spencer W. Kimball, "Becoming the pure in heart," *Ensign*, May, 1978, 81.

survivors and delivered His gospel to them. As a result of the more wicked part of the people being destroyed and the Savior's personal appearance and teachings, those who remained demonstrated great faith, repented, were baptized, received the gift of the Holy Ghost, and earnestly sought to live the Savior's teachings. Did they establish a Zion society in the Americas, and if so, how did it work?

A preliminary question to consider is what the Nephites thought about Zion. Did they seek to establish Zion? Did their prophets urge them in that direction? To answer these questions, it is helpful to begin with an overview of the use of "Zion" in the Book of Mormon.

Specific references to Zion occur 45 times in the Book of Mormon, compared to 277 times in the Doctrine and Covenants. Thirty-four of the Book of Mormon references occur in the first two books of Nephi. Of the total 45 mentions of Zion, 26 are quotations from Isaiah, again mostly by the first Nephi. The other 19 occurrences are prophecies and admonitions relating to the establishment of Zion in the last days, after the Gentiles receive the Book of Mormon and take it to the remnant of Lehi's seed. Just from a statistical perspective, it does not appear that the Nephites expected to establish Zion themselves. They looked forward to the establishment of Zion in the last days, in our time. The righteous Nephites were simply living the principles taught by Jesus and His prophets, which always leads God's people toward Zion.

One particular prophetic reference to Zion in the Book of Mormon is found in 2 Nephi 26:14, 30–31:

> But behold, I prophesy unto you concerning the last days, . . . wherefore, the Lord God hath given a commandment that all men should have charity, which charity is love. And except they should have charity they were nothing. Wherefore, if they should have charity they would not suffer the laborer in Zion to perish. But the laborer in Zion shall labor for Zion; for if they labor for money they shall perish.

This connection of charity to Zion's laborers in need is important. We will discuss it in more detail in chapter 4.

Eventually, those who survived the cataclysms at the death of the Savior were able to eliminate contentions, disputes, and "every man did deal justly one with another." But the change was not overnight, based on the record we have in 4 Nephi.

The Savior's visit occurred at the end of the thirty-fourth year. It wasn't until the thirty-sixth year that everyone was converted and contention was eliminated.

> And it came to pass that the thirty and fourth year passed away, and also the thirty and fifth, . . . And it came to pass in the thirty and sixth year, the people were all converted unto the Lord, . . . and there were no contentions and disputations among them, and every man did deal justly one with another. And they had all things common among them; therefore there were not rich and poor, bond and free, but they were all made free, and partakers of the heavenly gift. (4 Nephi 1:1–3)

Even among "the more righteous" and with multiple miraculous visits by the Savior Himself (see 3 Nephi 26:13) and the bestowal of the Holy Ghost, it still took well over a year to convert the people sufficiently to completely eliminate contention and disagreements. But they were successful.

In addition, in the thirty-sixth year they were able to achieve a condition in which "there were not rich and poor, bond and free, but they were all made free, and partakers of the heavenly gift." And significantly, they "had all things common among them" (4 Nephi 1:3).

I think the most immediate interpretation for "the heavenly gift" is the Atonement of Jesus Christ, surely the greatest gift we can receive. But I am not sure that in this context that interpretation fits. The logic is 1) they had all things common, 2) therefore there were no economic distinctions, but rather 3) they were all free and partakers of the gift. The gift seems to be related to having all things common and the elimination of class distinctions.

After the first day of the Savior's visit and before He arrived on the second day, the people "did pray for that which they most desired; and they desired that the Holy Ghost should be given unto them" (3 Nephi 19:9). After they were baptized, "the Holy Ghost did fall

upon them, and they were filled with the Holy Ghost and with fire"
(3 Nephi 19:13).

I believe that the heavenly gift they enjoyed came through the
Holy Ghost and was the gift of charity, as described by Mormon:

> Charity is the pure love of Christ, and it endureth forever; and
> whoso is found possessed of it at the last day, it shall be well with
> him. Wherefore, my beloved brethren, pray unto the Father with
> all the energy of heart, that ye may be filled with this love, *which he
> hath bestowed upon all who are true followers of his Son, Jesus Christ.*
> (Moroni 7:47–48; emphasis added)

Charity is the pure love that Christ has for each of us. If we can
become His "true followers," we can receive the gift of being filled
with the same love for others that the Savior has for us. It is truly
a heavenly gift, one that would eliminate contention and disputes
among those with this gift. If we have the gift of charity, we place the
interest of others on a level with our own.

After hearing the Savior's teachings, the Nephites started to implement the doctrine they had received. "And they taught, and did minister one to another; and they had all things common among them,
every man dealing justly, one with another. And it came to pass that
they did do all things even as Jesus had commanded them" (3 Nephi
26:19–20).

Had Jesus commanded them to abandon private land ownership
and pool their resources? Perhaps, since Mormon is clear that not all
that the Savior taught is contained in the record we have. But just as
with the Saints in Enoch's day, we should avoid imposing our understanding of land ownership on past societies. It was not necessary, or
perhaps even desirable, to abandon private land ownership, if they had
it, in order to achieve the desired outcome.

The result of the heavenly gift was that all those converted kept
the second great commandment and loved others as themselves. If that
can be achieved within a community, every man will deal justly with
others and the community will move quickly toward the elimination
of poverty. It won't happen overnight, since it takes time for people to
understand the implications of their conversion and to conform their

lives to the higher principles. But that seems to be the path. And it worked for the Nephite society for two hundred years.

As the people prospered and the population grew rapidly, they again found it advantageous to rebuild some of the cities (see 4 Nephi 1:7–8). Mormon does not specify what the advantages of city life were for a people with ready access to additional land, but it seems likely their reasons were similar to those that lead to the founding of the city of Enoch.

Mormon also provides no details on how land was assigned or on how the challenges of urban life were overcome. His focus is appropriately on how the people treated each other and what led to the destruction of his people. After two hundred years, prosperity again led to pride and vanity which in turn led people to place their own desires above those of their neighbors. With the reemergence of class distinctions, they started to build organizations that catered to and reinforced those distinctions. Eventually, the society split into the same old factions.

The Book of Mormon account is helpful in providing insight into the attitudes God's covenant people should foster and how they should implement gospel principles in their social relations. It doesn't provide much guidance on institutional or civic arrangements in an urban setting.

This chapter set out to explore two aspects of early Christian societies: having "all things common" and unity. What we have learned is that because of the gift of charity, the early Christians in both Judea and the Americas came to hold their personal possessions "lightly." Having "all things common" meant that all the converted loved one another and valued the welfare of all equally. They were willing to give all that they possessed if needed and called for. This foundational love for the Savior and for others led to the unity required in Zion and eliminated contention at least among the Nephites. Unity persisted until undermined by pride and tradition.

The lessons for Zion today seem clear. We must choose Jesus Christ as did the people in Enoch's day. And we must seek the gift of charity through the Holy Spirit as did the early Christians after hearing the teachings of the Savior.

CHAPTER 3

Latter-day Efforts to Establish Zion

As previously mentioned, "Zion" appears 277 times in the Doctrine and Covenants, which Steven Harper has described as a handbook for bringing about Zion. Instead of a selfish world, "the Lord offered an alternative he called Zion, and the work of building Zion became the work of the revelations."[1]

I do not intend to review all of the instructions received regarding Zion as contained in the Doctrine and Covenants. Professor Harper and others have done that in other places. In this chapter, I consider Latter-day Saint efforts to establish a Zion society. In some ways such a review is a daunting task. For one thing, a mountain of source material is available, ranging from an entire book of scripture, as noted, to all the historical documents that have been preserved and are now available. Other authors have spent decades in careful study of these

---

1. Steven C. Harper, *Making Sense of the Doctrine & Covenants: A Guided Tour Through Modern Revelations* (Salt Lake City, UT: Deseret Book, 2008).

sources and have produced entire volumes summarizing, reviewing, and commenting on what the Saints were supposed to do, what they were able to accomplish, where they fell short and why, and why we have yet to achieve the goal. Contributing to that conversation is beyond the scope of this chapter.

The purpose of this chapter is to identify the conclusions that Church leaders reached after three unsuccessful attempts to implement an economic order intended to alleviate poverty in the nineteenth century. In this brief review, I will draw heavily on the work of others, especially as they cite original sources, and add my analysis to a few key points. Interested readers are encouraged to refer to the sources cited here and to other works on early Church history. Establishing Zion remains a prime directive for Church members, and the more we learn about past efforts, the better prepared we will be for the future.

Perhaps a useful starting point for my purposes is an observation made by then-Apostle John Taylor in 1874. After hearing of Brigham Young's plan to create united order communities across the Utah territory, and listening to explanations and counsel on the subject at a meeting in Nephi, Utah, Elder Taylor still had misgivings about the practicality of the Order. He noted in his address: "The greatest embarrassment that we have to contend with at the present time is not in knowing what to do, but knowing how to do it."[2]

Ohio and Missouri

I will focus on three initiatives the Saints undertook to establish an economy for a Zion society as they understood it.

1. The establishment Zion in Jackson County, Missouri, in the 1830s
2. The Utah consecration movement by Brigham Young in 1854
3. The implementation of United Order principles in Utah in the 1870s

---

2. John Taylor, 19 April 1874, *Journal of Discourses* 17:48, as quoted in Leonard J. Arrington, Feramorz Y. Fox, and Dean L. May, *Building the City of God: Community and Cooperation among the Mormons* (Salt Lake City, UT: Deseret Book, 1976).

Again, my purpose is not an exhaustive treatment of these important efforts. I will only take time and space to touch on a few highlights, with occasional deeper looks into particular sources to understand and evaluate the reasoning behind these efforts. My discussion draws heavily on *Building the City of God: Community & Cooperation among the Mormons* by Leonard J. Arrington, Feramorz Y. Fox, and Dean L. May.[3] While this book was published nearly fifty years ago, and much excellent historical work has been done since, *Building the City of God* remains a classic that has the focus and sufficient detail to inform the discussion here.

Before the Book of Mormon was published and the Church was formally organized, those seeking divine direction through the Prophet Joseph Smith frequently received the same counsel. Oliver Cowdery, Hyrum Smith, Joseph Knight Sr., and David Whitmer were all told: "Keep my commandments, and seek to bring forth and establish the cause of Zion" (Doctrine and Covenants 6, 11, 12, 14).

In the era of Jacksonian individualism, the Saints were directed to create the city of Zion based on principles of consecration and cooperation, quite contrary to the mood of their neighbors in Missouri.

> The Law of Consecration and Stewardship, which Joseph Smith announced in February, 1831, . . . was intended to be a major instrument in reorganizing the social and economic patterns of life among his followers. Moreover, it was to provide the model upon which all human society would be organized when the Savior returned to the latter-day Zion in Missouri.[4]

In the face of social opposition, none of the Saints' three efforts proved successful. In Missouri, the Saints were persecuted and driven out of Jackson County, then out of the state altogether. In Utah, enemies and apostates were again active in undermining the Church's efforts. But as Arrington, et al., observe:

---

3. Arrington, et al., *Building the City of God.*
4. Arrington, et al., *Building the City of God,* 2.

It is interesting, however, that the Latter-day Saints rarely blamed their persecutors for the failure of communal experiments under Joseph Smith and Brigham Young. More often, they blamed themselves. Moral imperfection in the form of selfishness and greed kept them from living the high law of God. There is implicit in this self-condemnation an interpretation of the role of institutions in reform that sets Mormons apart from modern reform traditions. Living under ideal conditions is not, in the Mormon view, an experience that perfects man. Rather, it is an evidence that man has achieved perfection.[5]

Edward Partridge was called as the bishop for the Church in Zion (Jackson County). The bishop's efforts to implement consecration involved three initial steps. Those called to gather to Zion were instructed to consecrate all of their property to the Church through a formal deed to the bishop. As part of the consecration, the bishop and the family (or individual) would assess the needs and capacities of the family. The bishop would then transfer a stewardship to the family (or individual) including real and personal property sufficient to meet their needs. The transfer was also carried out by a written deed. According to Arrington, et al., "The system [the law of consecration and stewardship] aimed at equality in consumption but not in the capital controlled or managed by individuals. Men were to be given responsibilities proportionate to their needs, circumstances, and capacities."[6]

As Bishop Partridge envisioned, these stewardships were to be more long-term revocable leases that could be nullified by the bishop if the family failed to live up to the community's expectations and standards. Legal disputes soon made it necessary for the stewardship deeds to be non-revocable.

The direction given in Doctrine and Covenants 42 anticipated that stewards would manage their properties effectively and produce sufficient to meet their own needs and some surplus. This surplus was to be given to the bishop each year to provide for the poor, for those

---

5. Arrington, et al., *Building the City of God*, 8.
6. Arrington, et al., *Building the City of God*, 16.

still needing stewardships, and to purchase lands for the public benefit of the Church, including houses of worship, and building up the New Jerusalem (Doctrine and Covenants 42:34–35).

After several years of struggle and amid substantial persecution, the Lord gave His assessment of the effort in Zion in 1834:

> Behold, I say unto you, were it not for the transgressions of my people, speaking concerning the church and not individuals, they might have been redeemed even now. But behold, they have not learned to be obedient to the things which I required at their hands, but are full of all manner of evil, and do not impart of their substance, as becometh Saints, to the poor and afflicted among them; And are not united according to the union required by the law of the celestial kingdom; And Zion cannot be built up unless it is by the principles of the law of the celestial kingdom; otherwise I cannot receive her unto myself. (Doctrine and Covenants 105:2–5)

On all three critical dimensions of Zion, the Saints as a body fell short. They failed to consecrate their properties to provide for the poor, they lacked sufficient unity, and they fell short in their righteousness.

After the Saints were driven from Missouri, during the Nauvoo period (and while they were crossing the plains and becoming established in the Great Basin), there was substantial cooperation among Church members. Indeed, it proved essential for their survival. But it was not until 1854 that the Church again attempted to live the law of consecration and stewardship as it was understood during the Missouri era.

Consecration in Utah

In the April 1854 general conference, both Brigham Young and Orson Hyde addressed the topic of consecration. Following the conference, the First Presidency issued their eleventh general epistle summarizing conference. The epistle reiterates the original principle from Missouri that "all Saints should consecrate their substance unto the Church, and receive their inheritances at the hands of Bishop Partridge, who was then officiating in that office." The epistle further states: "The people seemed to feel a strong desire to comply with every commandment and requirement that had been given, and appeared to feel as though now there were no obstacles to a full and frank compliance with the law of consecration as first given to Brother Joseph."[7]

There followed encouragement that the Saints should come forward and consecrate their possessions to the Church. Arrington, et al., report that the first deeds of consecration were recorded in 1855 and that the general epistle issued following the April 1855 general conference indicates there had been a delay in receiving consecrations while the form of "a deed which should be legal in accordance with the laws of the Territory" was finalized.[8]

Over the next several years, Church leaders offered vigorous encouragement for the Saints to consecrate their properties. From England, Orson Pratt published a strong defense of consecration as essential to achieve equality among the Saints. His essay opens with "Be one: and if ye are not one ye are not mine."[9] In September 1854 after returning to Salt Lake, Elder Pratt spoke out in support of consecration.

> There is one subject that . . . gave me great joy when I learned that it was being established in our midst. What is it? It is the consecration of the properties of the whole Church, according to the written revelations, commandments, and laws of the Most High God. . . . It gave me great joy to learn that there was a prominent step taken at your last Conference to bring about and accomplish this object.[10]

Arrington, et al., review available documents and provide a discussion of both the rationale for initiating the movement in 1854 and an estimate of the relative success of the consecration movement.[11] Their research suggests that the movement was practically terminated in 1858. They further estimate that less than 40 percent of the families living in the Utah Territory at the time recorded deeds of consecration, and no property was ever actually transferred to the Church.

---

7. Quoted in Arrington, et al., *Building the City of God*, 68–69.
8. Arrington, et al., *Building the City of God*, 69.
9. Orson Pratt, "The Equality and Oneness of the Saints," *The Seer*, 1854.
10. Orson Pratt, "Consecration," in *Journal of Discourses* (Salt Lake City, UT: The Church of Jesus Christ of Latter-day Saints, 1854), 2: 21.
11. Arrington, et al., *Building the City of God*, chapter 4.

Equally important, a program for using consecrated property in adjusting and assigning stewardships was never set up by the Church. Arrington, et al., offer four possible explanations for Brigham's failure to set up such a program. Their third possibility is of particular interest:

> Any practicable program would have had to recognize the bishops as overseers of property, and President Young was quick to see what might happen under weak or incompetent management. His expressed intent of maintaining control over his own possessions on the ground of his superior ability to utilize it is consistent with the doctrine of stewardship, but points to a practical difficulty in its observance.[12]

Despite Orson Pratt's assertions to the contrary in the articles already cited, experience suggests that the capacity to serve as a spiritual shepherd to a ward does not necessarily translate into prudent and effective management of agriculture and industry. Whatever the motivations and intents of Church leaders and members, and despite a strong cooperative spirit, the Saints in the 1854–1858 period again failed to exhibit as a body the level of unity and willingness to consecrate needed to establish Zion.

Brigham Young never abandoned his aspirations to establish Zion, but the Saints' lack of commitment and the growing outside influences in the territory shifted his attention to other avenues for resisting those worldly incursions. The cooperative movement in Utah was initiated with the objective of protecting the Saints from those influences and speculators. The Saints were forced to cooperate throughout their early history in order to resist and overcome the impact of persecution, and to survive and thrive in the desert. By 1865, with the imminent arrival of the railroad and the emergence of non-LDS merchants profiting from the Saints and sending those profits out of the territory, Brigham Young found it necessary to adjust his position on trade among the Saints. The Saints responded by forming cooperative mercantile establishments. The most successful of these was started in Brigham City under the leadership of Lorenzo Snow in 1864.

---

12. Arrington, et al., *Building the City of God*, 77.

The cooperative movement asked participants to voluntarily contribute their capital to a common project. Often the initial project was a store that would purchase locally produced items for resale. As the venture grew, so too did the supply chain, and the cooperative would expand into production as well as simply purchasing for resale. The objective was to achieve local self-sufficiency to the extent possible and especially to "make them independent of Gentile stores."[13]

These cooperatives were essentially joint stock companies, and the amount of capital contributed varied significantly. Local leaders frequently were also the major stockholders even though an effort was made to price shares within the reach of most people. Further, labor and materials needed by the cooperative were furnished in exchange for capital stock, though in the case of Brigham City, at least one-fourth of wages paid could be taken in store merchandise.[14] The Brigham City cooperative was so successful that by 1874 "virtually the entire economic life of this community of 400 families was owned and directed by the cooperative association."[15]

In 1874, Brigham Young initiated the effort to establish the united order in communities across the territory. He observed that "Brother Snow has led the people along and got them into the United Order without their knowing it."[16] There was concern in Brigham City that the united order envisioned by Brigham would require changes in the Brigham City system. "In fact," according to Arrington, et al., "the term United Order of Box Elder County was superficially attached to the older community without effecting substantial change in the spirit or manner of its operations."[17]

But there was one fundamental difference between the cooperatives and the united order system. In the cooperatives, people pooled their capital and received shares of stock that paid dividends. In the united order, members were expected to pool both capital and labor for the support of the community. As Arrington, et al., put it, "On

13. Lorenzo Snow, as quoted in Arrington, et al., *Building the City of God*, 111.
14. Arrington, et al., *Building the City of God*, 112–13.
15. Arrington, et al., *Building the City of God*, 115.
16. Arrington, et al., *Building the City of God*, 120.
17. Arrington, et al., *Building the City of God*, 121.

coming into the Order, a member would transfer control of his economic property to the board and agree to assume such responsibilities and to perform such labors as might be decided upon by the central authority."[18]

Here again, the experience of Lorenzo Snow in Brigham City is relevant and insightful. Arrington, et al., describe the Brigham City order as "functioning beautifully" in 1877, but the prospect of further growth "would bring incalculable management problems." "The assumption by the corporation of responsibility for many decisions that are normally made by families and individual business units magnified the problems of the spiritual-temporal leader, Lorenzo Snow."[19]

A letter from Lorenzo Snow to Brigham Young in 1877 reveals the anxiety that Lorenzo felt at the additional responsibility. I quote only a few paragraphs here.

> A greater weight of responsibility comes upon us to supply necessities and conveniences by furnishing employment to those who have accepted the Order and classification (of labor) than we otherwise would feel if each pursued his own course, and this is expected by the people.
>
> When Israel left their leeks and onions by the direction of Moses they looked to him for their supplies, and became very quarrelsome and troublesome whenever they failed. This is a feature in the United Order which I contemplate with no small degree of anxiety, viz. concentrating a multitude of individual responsibilities upon one man or a few men. . . .
>
> I confess, in the solemn silence of the night, that I have sometimes inquired of myself, where are we drifting, in following this untrodden path for many generations, and in sailing upon a sea so little known and unexplored? Is there not danger of getting an elephant on our hands (to use a common phrase) that our wisdom and ability cannot manage or support? In other words, may we not drift into responsibilities that would be difficult or even impossible to discharge? I have sought to avoid such a

---

18. Arrington, et al., *Building the City of God,* 147.
19. Arrington, et al., *Building the City of God,* 124.

dilemma as much as I could consistently with a knowledge of what was required of me.[20]

While the united order saw some success, particularly in the southern part of the territory, the response in Salt Lake City and other communities was tepid at best. While votes of support in Church gatherings were generally unanimous, actual entry into the order was limited in many communities.

The general failure of the people of Salt Lake City and in scores of other communities to go actively into the order indicates that opposition was much more widespread than appeared when votes were taken in assemblies of the Saints.[21] Even Brigham Young proved reluctant to fully enter the order because of concerns about the ability of others to manage his property as effectively as he could. He said:

> I am laboring under a certain embarrassment and so are many others, with regard to deeding property, and that is to find men who know what to do with property when it is in their hands. . . . When this factory at Provo can go into the hands of men who know what to do with it, it will go; when my factory in Salt Lake County can go into the hands of men who know what to do with it, it will go.[22]

Arrington, et al., note that apparently such men were never found.

With the death of Brigham Young in 1877, John Taylor became the president of the Church. Elder Taylor joined the Church in 1836, was made an Apostle two years later, and was seriously wounded while with Joseph in Carthage Jail. He was well aware of the efforts to create Zion in Missouri, of the consecration movement in 1854 in Utah, the cooperative movement ten years later, and the united order efforts that followed in 1874. Elder Taylor was in St. George when Brigham first announced the 1874 united order initiative. He and others traveled

20. As quoted in Arrington, et al., *Building the City of God*, 125–26.
21. Arrington, et al., *Building the City of God*, 148.
22. Brigham Young, "The United Order Is the Order of the Kingdom Where God and Christ Dwell," in *Journal of Discourses* (Lehi, UT: Albert Carrington, 1874), 17:157–58.

north to meet President Young's party and participate in a public discussion of the new order in the Nephi, Utah, region. At the time, Elder Taylor said in part:

> We have heard a good deal since we have assembled, in relation to what is called the Order of Enoch, the New Order, the United Order, or whatever name we may give to it. It is new and then it is old, for it is everlasting as I understand it. I am sometimes asked—"Do you understand it?" Yes, I do, no, I do not, yes, I do, no, I don't, and both are true; we know that such an order must be introduced, but are not informed in relation to the details, and I guess it is about the same with most of you. . . . The greatest embarrassment that we have to contend with at the present time is not knowing what to do, but knowing how to do it.[23]

Under President Taylor's leadership, the Church stepped back from efforts to create or expand the united order and focused efforts on expanding cooperative efforts through boards of trade. In March 1879, President Taylor praised the cooperative efforts in Brigham City but, regarding the united order, observed: "Unless you can get the United Order in the hearts of the people, you can never plant it anywhere else; articles and constitutions amount to very little; we must have this law of God written in our hearts."[24]

The boards of trade promoted by the Church were intended to curb the worst ills of pure "hurtful" market competition. The boards of trade proved very successful at promoting economic development in the region until federal efforts to enforce the anti-polygamy laws increased in late 1884. Vestiges of these boards could be found into the twentieth century in the Utah sugar beet industry, the wool industry, and a few others.

"Barnabas" in the Latter-days

In telling the story of the efforts to establish a latter-day Zion, it would be wrong to omit some mention of the many Saints who acted

---

23. Arrington, et al., *Building the City of God*, 312.
24. Arrington, et al., *Building the City of God*, 316.

with a faith like that of Barnabas in Acts. In Luke's record, Barnabas sold his field and gave the proceeds to the Apostles. Whether Barnabas is noteworthy because he was unusual or because he was typical, the point is that, guided by the Spirit, he recognized a need and acted to help the Christian community in Jerusalem. There are similar examples of faithful Saints acting to support and build the kingdom in the latter days, some in dramatic fashion and others in simply pursuing a life of faithful service. I will briefly mention six examples here, though many others could be cited.

Martin Harris

One of the earliest and most dramatic examples of a Barnabas-like act was provided by Martin Harris (1783–1875). In 1827, Joseph Smith was a twenty-two–year-old man of modest means and little formal education who claimed to have seen an angel and to have found gold plates. Martin Harris was twice Joseph's age and was a prosperous and respected farmer. When Martin heard about Joseph's claims, he was intrigued but skeptical. Martin's struggles to gain and keep a testimony, his family problems, and his loss of the 116–page manuscript translation are well documented elsewhere.

Martin was the only acquaintance Joseph knew who had the financial capacity to publish the Book of Mormon.[25] Despite public ridicule, family objections, and financial risk, Martin mortgaged his farm to guarantee the three thousand dollars required by E. B. Grandin. Martin's original hope was that he could sell copies of the book to raise the money to satisfy the debt.

Even before the Book of Mormon was printed, the Lord counseled Martin in the summer of 1829 to "not covet thine own property, but impart it freely to the printing of the Book of Mormon. . . . Impart a portion of thy property, yea, even part of thy lands, and all save the support of thy family. Pay the debt thou hast contracted with the printer. Release thyself from bondage" (Doctrine and Covenants 19:26, 34–35). In April 1831, Martin sold 151 acres and paid off the mortgage to Grandin.

---

25. Susan Easton Black, *Martin Harris: Uncompromising Witness of the Book of Mormon* (Provo, UT: BYU Studies, 2018).

Despite his shortcomings and challenges, Martin Harris did as did Barnabas: he sold his field, and the proceeds enabled the printing of the Book of Mormon.

Vienna Jaques

Sister Vienna Jaques (1787–1884) worked in Boston as a laundress, nurse, and midwife.[26] She was baptized in July 1831 and moved to Kirtland in November 1832. In December 1832, the Church was commanded to build the Kirtland Temple but faced significant financial challenges throughout its construction. Vienna, through frugal living, hard work, and wise investment, had amassed significant savings. When the Saints were invited to donate to the temple, Vienna was one of the first to step forward and gave all of her savings to the Prophet. While the amount given cannot be verified, several sources suggest it was in the range of $1,400. In September 1833, Joseph wrote a letter to Vienna in which he states that her contribution "proved a Savior of the life as pertaining to [the Church's] pecuniary concerns."[27]

Vienna Jaques is one of only two women mentioned by name in the revelations contained in the Doctrine and Covenants (see Doctrine and Covenants 90:28). The instructions given in section 90 regarding the support for Vienna to relocate to Missouri and receive an inheritance there were given sometime after she donated her savings to the cause of Zion. Not long after she arrived in Missouri, the Saints were driven out of the state. She moved to Nauvoo and then to Salt Lake City, where she remained faithful and ministered to many until her death at the age of ninety-six.[28]

John Tanner

John Tanner (1778–1850) was a successful businessman in Lake George, New York, and part-time Baptist minister. When his leg was miraculously healed, he and Elizabeth Tanner were baptized in 1832. The Tanners helped their sons and other families move west

---

26. Brent M. Rogers, "The Fascinating Life of Vienna Jaques," *Mormon Historical Studies* 16, no. 1 (2015): 150–51.
27. Rogers, "The Fascinating Life of Vienna Jaques."
28. Rogers, "The Fascinating Life of Vienna Jaques."

to Kirtland. Then in December 1834, John had an impression that he was needed in Kirtland and his family should move immediately. He disposed of his farms, orchards, and a hotel and moved with his family and several other families to Kirtland in January 1835.

When they arrived, John found that the mortgage on the temple site was due within days and that the impoverished Church leaders had been praying for a way to pay the debt. He immediately loaned Joseph Smith the $2,000 needed to satisfy the debt, and loaned the temple committee $13,000. Leonard Arrington observed that there is no evidence any of these loans were repaid.[29]

John continued to contribute large sums of money to the building of the temple and assisted in the work until he exhausted his financial resources. When he moved with his family to Missouri to help build up Zion, he had a "borrowed team and one old broken down stage horse, and an old turn pike cart, a cag [keg] of powder, and $7.50 in cash."[30]

Joseph Toronto

Another striking example is that of Joseph Toronto (born Giuseppe Efisio Taranto [1818–1883]), the first Italian convert. He was raised in Palermo, Sicily, and worked as a fisherman and sailor. On one voyage to New York in 1843, he became concerned that someone would steal the money he was saving. That night Giuseppe had a dream that he should take the money he had saved over several years to "Mormon Brigham."

On arriving in the United States, Giuseppe began searching for Mormon Brigham. In Boston, he became converted to the gospel after listening to a missionary named George B. Wallace. After his baptism, he remained in Boston and adopted the anglicized version of his name, Joseph Toronto. Toronto worked as a shipping merchant for

---

29. Leonard J. Arrington, "The John Tanner Family," *Ensign*, 1979, 46.
30. George S. Tanner, *John Tanner and His family* (Salt Lake City, UT: John Tanner Family Association, 1974), 74–77.

more than a year, but following a boating accident in which he nearly drowned, he decided to move to Nauvoo, Illinois.[31]

Joseph arrived in Nauvoo shortly after the temple capstone was placed. On Sunday, July 6, 1845, President Brigham Young announced to the assembled Saints that work on the temple would have to stop. Tithing funds were depleted, and funds coming from newly arriving immigrants had not produced the hoped-for revenue.

Joseph was deeply moved, and he determined to do whatever he could to help. The next afternoon, Monday, July 7, President Young "had an interview with Bro. Joseph Toronto." President Young's journal entry for the next day states that he "went and lay at the feet of the Bishops Whitney and Miller $2600 in gold that I had received of Brother Toronto." When the manuscript history was compiled in the 1850s, the account read as follows: "Brother Joseph Toronto handed to me $2500 in gold and said he wanted to give himself and all he had to the up building of the church and kingdom of God; he said he should henceforth look to me for protection and counsel. I laid the money at the feet of the bishops."[32]

Martin Harris, Vienna Jaques, John Tanner, and Joseph Toronto are remarkable examples of doing precisely what Barnabas did. But there are other equally remarkable but less dramatic examples of consecrated behavior among the Saints.

Mary Twinberrow Wattis Bennett

Mary Bennett (1819–1896) joined the Church in 1842 in England. Two years earlier her father and stepmother had responded to Wilford Woodruff's teaching and were baptized with other members of the United Brethren. About the time of Mary's baptism, her father, stepmother, and siblings immigrated to Nauvoo. In the fall of 1843, Mary's desire to gather to Nauvoo led her to separate from her husband and

---

31. "Joseph Toronto," *Global Histories, The Church of Jesus Christ of Latter-day Saints,* 2021, https://www.churchofjesuschrist.org/study/history/global-histories/italy/stories-of-faith/it-07–joseph-toronto-bb?lang=eng.
32. James Toronto, "Joseph Toronto," *Pioneer,* 2014.

immigrate with her two children. As part of the separation, Mary received £400 from her husband.[33]

Mother and children sailed from Liverpool to New Orleans with other LDS immigrants. The plan was to travel from New Orleans to Nauvoo on the steamboat *Maid of Iowa*, partially owned by Joseph Smith. When the immigrants disembarked in New Orleans, they found that the *Maid* was embargoed, and they would not be able to continue their journey until the steamboat's deep financial woes were resolved and the embargo lifted.

Priscilla Mogridge, one of the immigrants, recorded in her journal: "A lady of fortune was in the company—a Mrs. Bennett—and out of her private purse she not only lifted the embargo, but also fitted out the steamer with all necessary provision, fuel, etc., and soon the company were again on their way."[34]

Mary's donation totaled $1,091.25, or about half of her settlement. She probably would have objected to being characterized as "a lady of fortune," but at the time she had the funds necessary to meet the immediate need. And she did not hesitate to "sell her field."

Recognizing that Mary's sacrifice seriously imperiled her financial future, the steamboat captain directed the boat's clerk to issue promissory notes for the sums advanced. Jay Burrup states that the notes were apparently never redeemed.[35] The steamboat finally arrived in Nauvoo on April 13, 1844, and was greeted by Joseph Smith. Joseph granted Mary 120 acres of farmland a few miles east of Nauvoo. The grant documents place the value of the land at $1,091.25.

Mary married William Kay, the elder who had baptized her. But given the persecutions and turmoil in Nauvoo following the death of Joseph Smith, the young family was never able to prosper on the land grant. In early 1846, the Kays sold the land for $370, outfitted their wagon, and moved west.

---

33. Jay Greaves Burrop, "Mary's Altar," *Pioneer* 47, no. 1, Spring (2000).
34. As quoted in Burrop, "Mary's Altar."
35. Burrop, "Mary's Altar."

Joseph Millet

Elder Boyd K. Packer quoted from the journal of Joseph Millet (1832–1911) in his conference talk in April 1980, and the Church has since produced a short dramatized video highlighting the incident Elder Packer referred to.

Elder Packer described Joseph as one of the "rank and file" of the Church.[36] Joseph, with his large family, was suffering through "very, very difficult times" in Iron County, Utah. He recorded in his journal that his children indicated one of his neighbors was out of flour. Joseph says in his journal simply, "I divided our flour in a sack to send to" Brother Newton Hall.

> Just then Brother Hall came
> Says I, "Brother Hall, are you out of flour?"
> "Brother Millett, we have none."
> "Well, Brother Hall, there is some in that sack. I have divided and was going to send it to you. Your children told mine that you was out."

Newton Hall had tried others without success. He had prayed and "the Lord told him to go to Joseph Millett."[37] Although not a dramatic event in the course of world history, this event was significant for both Newton Hall and Joseph Millett. Joseph also recorded in his journal, "You can't tell me how good it made me feel to know that the Lord knew there was such a person as Joseph Millett." Joseph's consecrated act in that single instance continues to shine for all those who hear of his example. But it appears to have been typical for Brother Millet. After his passing, his son paid this tribute to his father: "He lived a faithful life, was kind and benevolent to all, full of charity and sympathy, ever seeking who he might do good to the Poor & Fatherless, and to those in need."[38]

---

36. Boyd K. Packer, "A Tribute to the Rank and File of the Church," *Ensign*, May, 1980.
37. Packer, "A Tribute to the Rank and File of the Church," 63.
38. As quoted in Keith A. Erekson, "The Conversion of Artemus Millet and His Call to Kirtland," *BYU Studies Quarterly* 4, no. 2 (2001): 81.

These examples agree precisely with Steve Walton's interpretation of "all things common" in Acts. We see people who through consecrated actions blessed the lives of others, furthered the work of the Lord, and contributed in very meaningful ways to building Zion.

Gleanings from the Early Church

A number of valuable lessons and insights can be gleaned from the Missouri/Utah efforts to establish Zion. The Saints are expected to gather with other Saints, but the location for the gathering is flexible. Critically, the Saints must be pure in heart and live together in righteousness. They must also live together in unity and eliminate poverty with consecrated donations from those who have more and distribution to those who have less through short-term aid and work assignments or stewardships.

The Missouri/Utah model of consecration as implemented in Missouri and attempted in Utah created management challenges that were never overcome. The failure to understand the "how" of Zion was acknowledged by senior Church leadership at the time.

Cooperation, on the other hand, whether forced by persecution or voluntary, was successful in raising living standards and providing opportunities. Stock companies for joint enterprises were a successful mechanism for cooperative ventures. And voluntary cooperation could offset the worst ills of "hurtful" competition.

Finally, and very important, consecration must be in the hearts of the people. Any institutions or organizations that succeed will arise from that bedrock requirement, not the other way around.

More broadly, to endure, Zion must be in the hearts of the people, and there must be sufficient unity in understanding and purpose that that purity is passed on to future generations. With that purity of heart, short and even medium-term Zion-like society is possible. Permanence, however, requires more—a self-reinforcing social structure to encourage purity over time and in future generations. However, Zion is a choice, and people will always have their agency to make other choices.

PART 2
Principles

On the banks of the Fishing River in Missouri, the Lord gave His assessment of the efforts to establish Zion as of June 1834.

> Behold, I say unto you, were it not for the transgressions of my people, speaking concerning the church and not individuals, they might have been redeemed even now. But behold, they have not learned to be obedient to the things which I required at their hands, but are full of all manner of evil, and do not impart of their substance, as becometh Saints, to the poor and afflicted among them; And are not united according to the union required by the law of the celestial kingdom; And Zion cannot be built up unless it is by the principles of the law of the celestial kingdom; otherwise I cannot receive her unto myself. (Doctrine and Covenants 105:2–5)

The Lord calls His people Zion when they live together in righteousness, eliminate poverty, and are unified. This was the standard in Enoch's day, and this revelation makes clear that it remains the standard in our day.

CHAPTER 4

Foundation Stones for Organizing Zion

In the early 1970s, Barbara A. McConochie composed a simple children's hymn that was subsequently included as hymn number 303 in the 1985 edition of our hymnbook. The title and message of the hymn are the same: "Keep the Commandments." The inspiration for this hymn reportedly came from President Harold B. Lee's encouraging message to the Church that safety and peace come from keeping the commandments. Learning obedience to the things the Lord commands is essential for establishing Zion.

How many commandments are there? Are we expected to keep all of them, all the time? Is the list fixed, or does it change over time? Is it even possible to keep all the commandments, all the time? I am sure that someone, somewhere, has been developing a list of the commandments. If so, I expect that list must be regularly updated. But there may be a more productive approach to obedience.

President Russell M. Nelson spoke of his early studies of appropriate and inappropriate activities on the Sabbath. His conclusion was that there was a more helpful way to think about keeping the Sabbath. He learned from the scriptures that what he did on the Sabbath was an indication of his relationship with God. "My conduct and my attitude on the Sabbath constituted a sign between me and my Heavenly

Father. . . . When I had to make a decision whether or not an activity was appropriate for the Sabbath, I simply asked myself, 'What sign do I want to give to God?' That question made my choices about the Sabbath day crystal clear."[1]

Ultimately, I would like to identify the foundation truths—Zion's foundation stones—inherent in the gospel of Jesus Christ and that underpin the other relevant specific commandments and principles. The aspirational, idealistic principles and standards of behavior I seek are not specific do's and don'ts. Rather, with the foundation stones firmly in mind, I think most questions of what we should do or not do can be answered with the help of the Spirit. The foundation stones for Zion are captured in two commandments, two eternal gifts from our Father in Heaven, and one commandment that no individual can keep on their own. Stated simply, the foundation stones for Zion are:

- Thou shalt love the Lord thy God with all thy heart, might, mind and strength.
- Thou shalt love they neighbor as thyself.
- All men are endowed by their Creator with agency, the freedom to make choices that affect their future.
- All men are held accountable by their Creator for the choices they make.
- The law of the celestial kingdom requires unity among God's covenant people.

The Savior criticized the scribes and Pharisees for being careful to pay tithing on plants but omitting "the weightier matters of the law, judgment, mercy, and faith" (Matthew 23:23). Focusing on and aspiring to align our lives more fully with the "weightier" foundation stones of the gospel will both enrich our souls and guide our efforts to keep the commandments more faithfully. But we ought not to expect that our understanding of gospel principles is a fixed goal to be achieved once and then considered complete. There will always be greater depths to be plumbed.

---

1.   Russell M. Nelson, "The Sabbath Is a Delight," *Ensign*, May, 2015.

Love of God and Others

Nephi explains the doctrine of Christ as the choice to accept the Savior's invitation: "Follow thou me" (2 Nephi 31:10). Just as God instructed Enoch to invite "this people" to choose the Father and love each other, so Nephi calls on all who read his words to make the same choice and accept the Savior's invitation. Following the Savior's example begins with embracing His teachings and expressing a willingness to keep His commandments.

The Savior identified baptism as the physical act that manifests our spiritual willingness to keep the commandments and enter a covenant relationship with God and Christ. If we do this, if we accept and follow the example of Christ "with full purpose of heart" and "real intent" (2 Nephi 31:13), we are promised the gift and companionship of the Holy Ghost.

Choosing to accept the invitation and demonstrating our willingness to follow Christ's example is the beginning. We must then continue to learn to follow His example: pressing forward, "having a perfect brightness of hope, and a love of God and of all men" (2 Nephi 31:20).

During His mortal ministry, the Savior identified the first two foundation stones, and indicated their relationship to all other specific commandments: "Thou shalt love the Lord thy God with all thy heart, and with all thy soul, and with all thy mind. This is the first and great commandment. And the second is like unto it, Thou shalt love thy neighbour as thyself. On these two commandments hang all the law and the prophets" (Matthew 22:37–40).

These two overarching commandments are qualitatively different than other more specific commandments. "Thou shalt love the Lord thy God with all thy heart" is much more general than "Thou shalt have no other gods before me. Thou shalt not make unto thee any graven image. . . . Thou shalt not bow down thyself to them nor serve them" (Exodus 20:3–5). Similarly, "thou shalt love thy neighbor as thyself" is more general than "thou shalt not steal" or "thou shalt not kill." The lack of specific do's and don'ts in both provides each of us with the opportunity to ponder and reflect on whether our actions (or inaction) align with the two commandments.

To say that all the law and the prophets "hang" on these two commandments is to assert that all other commandments can be derived from the two great commandments. But the Lord has also made clear that His commandments are not comprehensive and all-inclusive.

> For behold, it is not meet that I should command in all things; for he that is compelled in all things, the same is a slothful and not a wise servant; wherefore he receiveth no reward. Verily I say, men should be anxiously engaged in a good cause, and do many things of their own free will, and bring to pass much righteousness; For the power is in them, wherein they are agents unto themselves. And inasmuch as men do good they shall in nowise lose their reward. But he that doeth not anything until he is commanded, and receiveth a commandment with doubtful heart, and keepeth it with slothfulness, the same is damned. (Doctrine and Covenants 58:26–29)

Elder Jeffery R. Holland pointed out:

> My brothers and sisters, the first great commandment of all eternity is to love God with all of our heart, might, mind, and strength— that's the first great commandment. But the first great truth of all eternity is that God loves us with all of His heart, might, mind, and strength. That love is the foundation stone of eternity, and it should be the foundation stone of our daily life.[2]

As we draw upon that foundation of God's love for us and learn to live by the two love commandments, we will develop an awareness of our surroundings. We are expected to increase our sensitivity to the guidance of the Spirit, to recognize the needs of individuals and our community, and to make the conscious choice to respond to those needs. As we become more Christlike, we will turn away from our self-centered behavior and "do many [good] things of [our] own free will, and bring to pass much righteousness" (Doctrine and Covenants 58:27).

---

2. Jeffrey R. Holland, "Tomorrow the Lord Will Do Wonders among You," *Ensign*, May, 2016.

Agency and Accountability

Our first parents were given several commandments while in the garden. One was positive (to have children) and another negative (don't eat the fruit of a particular tree). The reason for not eating the fruit was explained (thou shalt surely die). But then this great truth was given: "Nevertheless thou mayest choose for thyself, for it is given unto you" (Moses 3:17). Two foundation truths were thus revealed which flow from God's profound love for us: 1) we have agency and are able to choose our future and 2) choices have consequences, and when we exercise our capacity to choose we are also accountable, meaning accountable for the consequences.

Agency and accountability are thus the third and fourth foundation stones on which we can and must rely in building Zion. We are not commanded to be accountable agents. Agency and accountability are not commandments any more than hearts, lungs, and muscles are commandments. Agency and accountability are gifts from our loving Father and are quintessential aspects of human existence. The eternal importance of the gift of agency is clear as we consider one outcome of the council in heaven in which Satan challenged God to save us all.

> Wherefore, because that Satan rebelled against me, and sought to destroy the agency of man, which I, the Lord God, had given him, and also, that I should give unto him mine own power; by the power of mine Only Begotten, I caused that he should be cast down. (Moses 4:3)

Lehi taught his children that we were created to have joy (see 2 Nephi 2:25). Joseph Smith taught the same principle when he said that "happiness is the object and design of our existence."[3] But both Lehi and Joseph were clear that obtaining the happiness and joy God desires for us requires that we freely choose the path that leads to it. As Elder Neal A. Maxwell put it, "Yes, in the plan, God would have us be happy, but first we had to be free to choose. God's gift to us of

---

3. Joseph Smith Papers, *History*, 1838–1856, D-1, 3.

this moral agency tells us wonderful things about His beneficial and developmental purposes."[4]

Satan's plan would have destroyed God's "beneficial and developmental purposes" embodied in His work "to bring to pass the immortality and eternal life of man" (Moses 1:39). To achieve God's desires for us, we must choose to be like Him through successive developmental choices to become more like the Savior. Lehi spelled out the relationship between correct choices and happiness in his teachings to his sons:

> Adam fell that men might be; and men are, that they might have joy. And the Messiah cometh in the fulness of time, that he may redeem the children of men from the fall. And because that they are redeemed from the fall they have become free forever, knowing good from evil; to act for themselves and not to be acted upon, . . . Wherefore, men are free according to the flesh; and all things are given them which are expedient unto man. And they are free to choose liberty and eternal life, through the great Mediator of all men, or to choose captivity and death, according to the captivity and power of the devil; . . . And now, my sons, I would that ye should look to the great Mediator, and hearken unto his great commandments; and be faithful unto his words, and choose eternal life, according to the will of his Holy Spirit; . . . (2 Nephi 2:25–28)

This passage is particularly instructive because it identifies the three requirements for obtaining the happiness, joy, and eternal life that God desires for His children. First, we must freely choose to accept the good news of the gospel. Second, we must act on that decision and live the principles ("hearken unto his commandments; and be faithful" [2 Nephi 2:28]). Finally, it is essential that there be a Messiah to overcome death, the damaging consequences of poor choices by others, and the just consequences of our own prior poor choices.

The achievement of God's plan for His children requires that each have the capacity and the freedom to choose her own life path and how she will respond to life's challenges and opportunities. From the

---

4. Neal A. Maxwell, "The Great Plan of the Eternal God," *Ensign*, May, 1984.

creation, women and men have been instructed, given choices, allowed to choose between alternatives, and then act on their choices. In the garden, Adam and Eve were instructed: "Of every tree of the garden thou mayest freely eat, But of the tree of the knowledge of good and evil, thou shalt not eat of it, nevertheless, thou mayest choose for thyself, for it is given unto thee; but, remember that I forbid it, for in the day thou eatest thereof thou shalt surely die" (Moses 3:16–17).

Lehi taught that agency is based on law (see 2 Nephi 2:5). Satan had a plan to save us all. By far the easiest way to assure that all could qualify to be in the presence of God would be to eliminate sin by eliminating law. Where there is no law, there is no sin (see 2 Nephi 2:13, 9:25–26).

While this approach would assure that all God's children could return safely, it would have thwarted God's plan for our eternal development. None would be like God, for none would have developed the character of God. That development requires the free exercise of agency to choose righteousness. And agency exists only when there are opposing alternatives to choose between, when there is instruction and information about those alternatives, and when we have the power to act on our choice and the responsibility for the intended outcomes.

From the Creation, the choices people make and their ensuing actions are inextricably connected to consequences for the chooser, and very frequently for others. This connection between the choices we make, the actions we take based on those choices, and the consequences that result means that we are responsible for the consequences of our actions. Paul instructed the Galatians: "Be not deceived; God is not mocked: for whatsoever a man soweth, that shall he also reap" (Galatians 6:7). Elder Dieter F. Uchtdorf expressed a similar thought: "You have agency, and you are free to choose. But there is actually no free agency. Agency has its price. You have to pay the consequences of your choices."[5]

This repeated pattern of instruction, alternatives, choice, action, and consequences constitutes human agency and appears to be

---

5.   Dieter F. Uchtdorf, "On the Wings of Eagles," *Liahona*, July, 2006.

essential for human learning and development. It is worth stressing again that agency involves the full cycle. It is not simply choosing A over B. The exercise of agency involves taking informed action that changes the future, for better or for worse, and inescapably involves accountability for the consequences that result. We must each choose to "press forward with steadfastness in Christ, having a perfect brightness of hope, and a love of God and of all men" (2 Nephi 31:20).

The Unity Required in Zion

As the Lord revealed to Joseph Smith, the principle of unity is critical as a foundation stone for a Zion society. Unity is a commandment and therefore "hangs" on the first two commandments, but it differs from other commandments and has a special status in relation to Zion. Love of God and Christ and charity as Christlike love both spring from our heart and soul and can be sought after regardless of our condition or environment. Agency and accountability are very real aspects of our eternal existence. As President Oaks has indicated, our freedom may be constrained but never our agency.

On the other hand, we cannot achieve unity in Zion alone. Unity describes a relationship with other people, and achieving any degree of unity requires at least two people. Bringing together Saints who have made covenants with Christ, who share common goals and aspirations, who feel a level of trust and mutual respect, is called the gathering.

In the Church's infancy, the Lord directed the newly converted Saints to gather together for strength and mutual support. "Wherefore the decree hath gone forth from the Father that they shall be gathered in unto one place upon the face of this land, to prepare their hearts and be prepared in all things against the day when tribulation and desolation are sent forth upon the wicked" (Doctrine and Covenants 29:8).

Gathering to Zion implies more than simply relocating to be in proximity to other Church members. Even before the Saints gathered in Ohio, the Lord was clear on the need for unity among His people, reiterating a basic tenet and foundation stone of Zion. "And let every man esteem his brother as himself, and practice virtue and holiness before me. And again I say unto you, let every man esteem his brother as himself. . . . I say unto you, be one; and if ye are not one ye are not mine" (Doctrine and Covenants 38:24–25, 27).

Being of "one heart and one mind" was a critical feature of the city of Enoch. Failure to achieve unity among the Saints was one of the reasons the Lord identified for the failure to establish Zion in the 1830s: "And [they] are not united according to the union required by the law of the celestial kingdom" (Doctrine and Covenants 105:4).

The required unity lies along three interrelated dimensions. First, the Savior gave His life so that we could become one with Him and His Father. As He approached the final hours of His mortality, He prayed to the Father that we would achieve this unity: "And now I am no more in the world, but these are in the world, and I come to thee. Holy Father, keep through thine own name those whom thou hast given me, that they may be one, as we are" (John 17:11).

His infinite achievement made possible the unity with the Father that He prayed for: "I am Jesus Christ, the Son of God, who was crucified for the sins of the world, even as many as will believe on my name, that they may become the sons of God, even one in me as I am one in the Father, as the Father is one in me, that we may be one" (Doctrine and Covenants 35:2).

The second dimension of unity required of the Saints in Zion derives from our unity with Christ. Because the Saints in Zion are unified with and in Christ, they see His work as their work, and they see all God's children as Christ sees them. As a result, every saint "esteem[s] his brother as himself."

This was the standard Alma gave to the newly baptized Nephites: "And he commanded them that there should be no contention one with another, but that they should look forward with one eye, having one faith and one baptism, having their hearts knit together in unity and in love one towards another" (Mosiah 18:21).

This unity was the condition achieved by the Nephites following the appearances of the Savior. Through the influence of the Holy Ghost, they received the "heavenly gift" of charity and bore for each other a love similar to that of the Savior's. This is the essence of the second great commandment and the goal we are urged to strive for by both Paul and Mormon.

Unity with and in Christ does not imply sameness. From our premortal existence, there have been differences in callings and capacities. In mortality, God has given different spiritual gifts to different people. Yet as Paul taught the Ephesians, the various callings and gifts are given for one purpose: "For the perfecting of the Saints, for the work of the ministry, for the edifying of the body of Christ: Till we all come in the unity of the faith, and of the knowledge of the Son of God, unto a perfect man, unto the measure of the stature of the fulness of Christ" (Ephesians 4:12–13).

In a Zion society, differences in capacity, assignments, and situation do not result in differences in status or worth. Every member promotes the interest and well-being of others right along with his or her own interest. When pride and envy were allowed to enter the Nephite society after two hundred years of unity, their efforts to maintain a Zion-like society quickly fell apart.

Building this unity among the Saints takes time and practice. It requires each member of the group to listen to all other members actively and humbly. It requires transparency, unanimity, and cooperation in collective decision-making. It requires unanimous engagement and a commitment to action. Small wonder that this type of unity has been so rare among humans who share all the foibles of the natural man. But it has been achieved and will be achieved again as Zion continues to develop.

The third dimension of Zion's unity spans centuries. Joseph Smith taught:

> For we without them cannot be made perfect; neither can they without us be made perfect. Neither can they nor we be made perfect without those who have died in the gospel also; for it is necessary in the ushering in of the dispensation of the fulness of times, which dispensation is now beginning to usher in, that a whole and complete and perfect union, and welding together of dispensations, and keys, and powers, and glories should take place, and be revealed from the days of Adam even to the present time. (Doctrine and Covenants 128:18)

The unity required in Zion is first a unity with Christ. Second, and because of that first unity, it is a unity with the living Saints in

Zion ("one heart and one mind") that assures that the interests of the least will be valued equally with those of the greatest. Finally, it is a unity with all of the Church of the Firstborn from the days of Adam onward.

The Self-reliance Corollary

A corollary is a proposition or principle that follows logically from one that has already been demonstrated or proven. In that sense, the principle of self-reliance is a corollary that follows from the foundation stones, though the connection may not be immediately obvious. Self-reliance also implies action. The concept of self-reliance occurs repeatedly in discussions by Church leaders of Church aid to the poor. Work and self-reliance are often used as two key distinctions between Church programs and government assistance programs.

Self-reliance is interpreted to mean that one should work to the extent possible. Brigham Young shared this view:

> My experience has taught me, and it has become a principle with me, that it is never any benefit to give, out and out, to man or woman, money, food, clothing, or anything else, if they are able-bodied, and can work and earn what they need. . . . This is my principle, and I try to act upon it. To pursue a contrary course would ruin any community in the world and make them idlers.[6]

Self-reliance may seem a curious doctrine for the Church to espouse so thoroughly. Gospel doctrine emphatically teaches that a person cannot rely solely on his or her own efforts and attain exaltation. Beyond the most obvious need for a Redeemer, there are doctrines taught by Joseph Smith that:

1. We cannot be saved without our dead, nor they without us (see Doctrine and Covenants 128:15).
2. We must be married to receive the highest blessings (see Doctrine and Covenants 131:2–3).

---

6. Quoted in Dallin H. Oaks, *The Lord's Way* (Salt Lake City, UT: Deseret Book, 1991), 116.

3. The Saints must gather together (see Doctrine and Covenants 29:8).

Further, it is difficult to conceive of a completely self-reliant person or family if by self-reliance we mean a family that provides for all their own needs through their own labor. We are now and for the most part have always been interdependent beings. We rely on each other so much that total self-reliance seems both unattainable and undesirable.

President Marion G. Romney and Elder Alexander Morrison have clarified the role of self-reliance and have stressed that self-reliance is an essential contributor to personal freedom. Elder Morrison wrote:

> We cannot be free [to act] if we are not self-reliant. Put another way, self-reliance is a prerequisite for freedom, and dependence is the enemy of freedom. The scriptures (Doctrine and Covenants 29:24–35) tell us that man is intended by God to be "an agent unto himself." He cannot do so unless he is self-reliant. Independence and self-reliance thus are critical keys to spiritual growth. Whenever we are in a situation that threatens self-reliance, we will find that freedom is threatened too.
>
> Although self-reliance and freedom are tied together, there is nothing spiritual, in and of itself, in being self-reliant. In our laudable strivings to attain self-reliance, we must be careful not to rely too much on the arm of flesh and to remember that we are wholly reliant upon God for all of life's blessings, including life itself. One could be self-reliant—completely independent—and lack every other desirable attribute of character. . . .
>
> Self-reliance, then, is not an end but a means to an end. Self-reliance becomes a factor in spiritual growth only as we use the freedom it brings to make the right choices. In particular, those who are self-reliant are free to serve others.[7]

President Marion G. Romney stressed this link between self-reliance and service to others in the following words:

---

7. Alexander B. Morrison, *Visions of Zion* (Salt Lake City, UT: Deseret Book, 1993), 111–12.

The key to making self-reliance spiritual is in using the freedom to comply with God's commandments. The scriptures are very clear in their command that it is the duty of those who have, to give to those who are in need. . . .

We lose our life by serving and lifting others. By so doing we experience the only true and lasting happiness. Service is not something we endure on this earth so we can earn the right to live in the celestial kingdom. Service is the very fiber of which an exalted life in the celestial kingdom is made. . . . Can we see how critical self-reliance becomes when looked upon as the prerequisite to service, when we also know service is what godhood is all about?[8]

This connection between self-reliance and service to others may seem paradoxical. If everyone is self-reliant in the sense just related, who are the recipients of all the service being rendered? The resolution of the apparent paradox lies in understanding self-reliance as doing all that we can and contributing all that we can to our own well-being, that of our family, and to the society around us. But self-reliance does not mean reliance "on the arm of flesh" or trying to do everything alone. Cooperation and the acceptance of service from others often extends our own ability to do, to contribute, and to become. Accordingly, the reasoning and relationship to human development are summarized as follows:

1. A person cannot be free to act on their choices if she or he is not self-reliant, and reduced self-reliance reduces our freedom to act independently and contribute all that we might.[9]

2. Using our freedom to make correct choices and comply with heavenly commandments makes our self-reliance spiritual because we will choose to serve others.

3. Self-reliance as willing and loving service and contributions to the well-being of others as well as ourselves, to the full extent of our capacity, is "the very fiber of which an exalted life in the celestial kingdom is made."[10]

---

8. Marion G. Romney, "The Celestial Nature of Self-reliance," *Ensign*, November, 1982, 63, 65.

9. Romney, "The Celestial Nature of Self-reliance."

10. Romney, "The Celestial Nature of Self-reliance," 64.

Agency may be exercised in the pursuit of self-interest, or we may choose to serve others and place their well-being on an equal footing with our own. The concepts of agency and accountability extend beyond individual service rendered to other individuals.

Consecration and Eliminating Poverty in Zion

The five foundation stones for a Zion society are thus love of God and Christ, charity or Christlike love for others, individual agency, individual accountability, and unity. One inevitable outgrowth of these five foundation stones will be the elimination of poverty in Zion. But I do not see consecration and the elimination of poverty as a foundation stone of Zion. Rather, it is a natural byproduct of the five foundation stones and the self-reliance corollary identified here.

Throughout the revelations given to Joseph Smith are directions and commandments to look after the poor and the needy. The revealed principles include the law of consecration and stewardship, canonized in Doctrine and Covenants section 42. As many have noted previously, critical language in this revelation was modified by Joseph Smith between its earliest recording in 1831 and eventual publication as accepted scripture in 1835. While no manuscript of the original revelation as dictated by the Prophet has been found, from the multiple copies made by others, it is possible to piece together the original with some degree of confidence. Joseph Spencer includes in his book "the earliest extant version of what is now Doctrine and Covenants 42:29–37."[11] The excerpt I quote here from the 1831 text is taken from the *Joseph Smith Papers*:

> If thou lovest me thou shall serve & keep all my commandments & Behold thou shalt consecrate all thy properties that which thou hast unto me with a covenant and Deed which cannot be broken & they Shall be laid before the Bishop of my church & two of the Elders such as he shall appoint & set apart for that purpose & it shall come to pass that the Bishop of my church after that he has received the properties of my church that it cannot be taken from you he shall appoint every man a Steward over his own property or that which

---

11. Spencer, *For Zion: A Mormon Theology of Hope*, 96.

he hath received in as much as shall be sufficient for him self and family & the residue shall be kept to administer to him that hath not that every man may receive according as he stands in need & the residue shall be kept in my store house to administer to the poor and needy as shall be appointed by the Elders of the church & the Bishop & for the purpose of purchaseing Land & building up of the New Jerusalem which is here after to be revealed that my covenant people may be gathered in one in the day that I shall come to my temple & this I do for the salvation of my people.[12]

As noted, historical events[13] and divine guidance prompted Joseph to edit this passage rather heavily for publication in the 1835 edition of the Doctrine and Covenants. Again, the following passage from the 1835 edition is taken from the *Joseph Smith Papers*. The key language changes are in bold:

8 If thou lovest me thou shalt serve me and keep all my commandments. And behold, **thou wilt remember the poor**, and consecrate **of** thy properties **for their support**, that which thou hast **to impart unto them**, with a covenant and a deed which cannot be broken—**and inasmuch as ye impart of your substance unto the poor, ye will do it unto me**—and they shall be laid before the bishop of my church and his counsellors, two of the elders, **or high priests**, such as he shall **or has** appointed and set apart for that purpose.

9 And it shall come to pass, that **after they are laid before** the bishop of my church, and after that he has received **these testimonies concerning the consecration of** the properties of my church, that they cannot be taken **from the church, agreeable to**

---

12. Joseph Smith Papers, *Revelation Book 1*, The Joseph Smith Papers, (Salt Lake City, UT: Church Historian Press, The Church of Jesus Christ of Latter-day Saints, 1831), 64. https://www.josephsmithpapers.org/paper-summary/revelation-book-1/48.

13. For an excellent discussion of the historical events during the intervening years, see Spencer, *For Zion: A Mormon Theology of Hope* and Underwood, "The Laws of the Church of Christ (Doctrine and Covenants 42): A textual and Historical Analysis," in *The Doctrine and Covenants: Revelations in Context*, ed. Andrew H. Hedges, J. Spencer Fluhman, and Alonzo L. Gaskill (Provo, UT: Brigham Young University 2008).

my commandments, every man shall be made accountable unto me, a steward over his own property, or that which he has received by consecration, inasmuch as is sufficient for himself and family.

10 And again, **if there shall be properties in the hands of the church, or any individuals of it, more than is necessary for their support, after this first consecration, which is a residue, to be consecrated unto the bishop, it shall be** kept to administer to those who have not, **from time to time,** that every man **who has need may be amply supplied, and receive according to his wants. Therefore,** the residue shall be kept in my store house, to administer to the poor and the needy, as shall be appointed **by the high council of the church,** and the bishop **and his council,** and for the purpose of purchasing lands for the public benefit of the church, **and building houses of worship,** and building up of the New Jerusalem which is hereafter to be revealed, that my covenant people may be gathered in one in that day when I shall come to my temple. And this I do for the salvation of my people.[14]

These are important changes, but do they reflect a change in the basic principles of consecration or our responsibility to the poor? I don't think so, but in order to support this conclusion, let me share how others view these changes.

First, both versions begin with the same admonition: "if ye love me, thou shalt serve me and keep all my commandments." Regarding this allusion to John 14:15, Joseph Spencer has observed:

Thus the law of consecration as originally given—and this is still the case in the present version of the text as well—began with a poignant allusion. Consecration is the "one thing" the Saints of every age continue to "lack" (Mark 10:21), the thing to which all attention should turn once a basic morality is established. If one truly loves God, then it is necessary to keep all his commandments,

---

14. Joseph Smith Papers, *Doctrine and Covenants, 1835*, The Joseph Smith Papers, (Salt Lake City, UT: Church Historian Press, The Church of Jesus Christ of Latter-day Saints, 1835), 122. https://www.josephsmithpapers.org/paper-summary/doctrine-and-covenants-1835/130.

and that means it is necessary to get serious about consecration. What, though, does the law of consecration itself look like?[15]

For the discussion here, that is a vital question. Later Spencer makes this important point:

> It seems clear to me that we make a mistake when we understand the law of consecration as either a naïve economic project whose relevance dissipated with its failure in the nineteenth century or a divine economic system whose relevance will dawn when the Saints are purged of their worldly investments. Instead, we would do well to understand the law of consecration as an outline of exactly how we as Saints are to live right now, wherever we are, and in company with the Saints.[16]

Robert Couch has observed that the change in Doctrine and Covenants 42 regarding consecration increases reliance on individual agency by making the amount consecrated a matter of individual choice rather than a fixed requirement that "all" is to be deeded to the Church.[17]

Jeremiah John and colleagues note that "with the 1831 text, consecration entailed giving one's properties to God and then letting the Church care for the poor. However, with the 1835 text, Church members came to share more directly in this responsibility for the poor."[18] This is consistent with the adjustment in emphasis seen in the Church over the years as increasing emphasis has been placed on members and families to accept responsibility for not only poverty alleviation but all aspects of living the gospel. (See the chapter on the Church in Zion.)

---

15. Spencer, *For Zion: A Mormon Theology of Hope*, 97.
16. Spencer, *For Zion: A Mormon Theology of Hope*, 105.
17. Robert Couch, "Consecration, Holy War, and the Poor: An Apocalyptic Approach to Doctrine and Covenants 42," in *Embracing the Law: Reading Doctrine and Covenants 42*, ed. Jeremiah John and Joseph M. Spencer (Provo, UT: Neal A. Maxwell Institute for Religious Scholarship, Brigham Young University, 2017).
18. Jerimiah John et al., "Summary Report," in *Embracing the Law: Reading Doctrine and Covenants 42*, ed. Jeremiah John and Joseph M. Spencer (Provo, UT: Neal A. Maxwell Institute for Religious Scholarship, Brigham Young University, 2017), xix.

John, et al., also propose that Doctrine and Covenants 42:33, in referring to a "first consecration," suggests that this may be "the first step of a larger, more demanding law."[19] However, consistent with what we observed about the believers in Jerusalem, and with Doctrine and Covenants 119, it may be that the first consecration is the first in an ongoing program of consecration for the poor.[20]

Other scriptures could, of course, be cited to establish that the Lord's commandments to the Saints in the early years of the Church created the same expectations that have always existed for God's people, most especially for those directed to establish Zion.

My careful research has led me to summarize the law of consecration as follows:

- We must work hard and improve our stewardships to provide sufficiently for ourselves and our families, but
- We should restrain our consumption and assure that there is also a surplus to be consecrated for the poor and the building of the kingdom.
- We must minister to the poor by consecrating our time, talents and also our means.
- Our consecration is to be ongoing and lifelong.
- We must hold all our possessions "lightly" and keep them available to the kingdom as needed.
- We should engage in frequent self-reflection and ask ourselves how we are doing regarding our consecrated efforts.

Consecration is a covenant and follows naturally from our love for and devoted service to God and Christ, our Christlike love for all God's children, our freedom to choose service to others, and our desire to be united according to celestial laws.

---

19. John et al., "Summary Report," xix.
20. See also Harper, *Making Sense of the Doctrine & Covenants: A Guided Tour Through Modern Revelations*, 141.

Where to Start?

This chapter has focused on five foundation stones for building a Zion society:

1. **Devotion to God and Christ:** "Thou shalt love the Lord thy God with all thy heart, with all thy might, mind, and strength; and in the name of Jesus Christ thou shalt serve him" (Doctrine and Covenants 59:5).

2. **Charity:** "Charity is the pure love of Christ, and it endureth forever; and whoso is found possessed of it at the last day, it shall be well with him. Wherefore, my beloved brethren, pray unto the Father with all the energy of heart, that ye may be filled with this love, which he hath bestowed upon all who are true followers of his Son, Jesus Christ" (Moroni 7:47–48).

3. **Agency:** "Verily I say, men should be anxiously engaged in a good cause, and do many things of their own free will, and bring to pass much righteousness; For the power is in them, wherein they are agents unto themselves. And inasmuch as men do good they shall in nowise lose their reward" (Doctrine and Covenants 58:27–28).

4. **Accountability:** "That every man may act in doctrine and principle pertaining to futurity, according to the moral agency which I have given unto him, that every man may be accountable for his own sins in the day of judgment" (Doctrine and Covenants 101:78).

5. **Unity:** "I say unto you, be one; and if ye are not one ye are not mine" (Doctrine and Covenants 38:27).

Some of us may be tempted to look at the requirements for Zion and conclude that we will never qualify. However, all of us are capable if we put in the time and effort. For example, my son-in-law is an Air Force officer and has always been fascinated with airplanes. To walk through the Smithsonian Air and Space Museum with him is a stunning experience. He explains the history and use of each plane, including which variations were made in which factory and in what sequence. He can even tell if the paint on the exhibited plane is true to the original color. I come away thinking I could never master that much information. But, of course, that is not true. I could if I put in the time, effort, and passion that my son-in-law has invested.

Malcolm Gladwell made famous the observation that true expertise in any field takes 10,000 hours of deliberate practice.[21] Gladwell bases his claim on a study by K. Anders Ericsson. But Ericsson's study finds that true expertise is actually the result of another important factor in addition to 10,000-plus hours of deliberate practice. It also requires teaching and coaching by others, on feedback and accountability.[22]

So it is with the establishment of Zion. The Lord has clearly stated the requirements to engage in the work of establishing Zion:

> If ye have desires to serve God ye are called to the work; For behold the field is white already to harvest; . . . And faith, hope, charity and love, with an eye single to the glory of God, qualify him for the work. Remember faith, virtue, knowledge, temperance, patience, brotherly kindness, godliness, charity, humility, diligence. Ask, and ye shall receive; knock, and it shall be opened unto you. Amen (Doctrine and Covenants 4:3–7)

The Lord requires a willing heart, a passion for Zion, and a focus on developing the key virtues of godliness. He does not require immediate perfection. Achieving Zion is a developmental process. It is a process, however, that requires our best efforts and consistent practice in conjunction with other Saints. We have superb coaches, called the Holy Ghost and the prophets, to provide guidance on where we should be placing our current emphasis, and in what ways we need additional practice. When we find that we lack in any area, if we will ask in faith, we will receive the help and guidance we need.

Neither these foundation truths nor any other foundational principles are innate in our nature even though we are children of God

---

21. Malcolm Gladwell, *Outliers: The story of success* (Little, Brown, 2008).
22. K. Anders Ericsson, "Deliberate Practice and Acquisition of Expert Performance: A General Overview," *Academic Emergency Medicine* 15, no. 11 (2008).

(see Mosiah 3:19). Whatever "foundation stones" we base our lives on must be nurtured, first in the home and in other socialization processes as children mature. But the foundations of our lives are elaborated, and can be completely replaced, through our life experiences and through our interactions with others.

Importantly, especially in the current context, alternative values and the behaviors they imply are elaborated, tested, gained, lost, adapted and adjusted through social interaction and public discourse.[23] Consider, for example, the experience of converts to The Church of Jesus Christ of Latter-day Saints. Such conversions are often the result of deep and meaningful spiritual experiences. But that does not imply that newly baptized members fully understand the foundation stones of the gospel associated with Church membership. It is not just the unique LDS vocabulary they need to learn. Even lifelong members spend their lives striving to fully comprehend the foundation stones of service derived from devotion to God, charity, agency, accountability, and unity inherent in the gospel of Jesus Christ.

The religious tradition we come from can affect our initial attitudes toward Church attendance even after we embrace the gospel and are baptized. New converts coming from a Protestant tradition often view baptism as joining a community and active participation in the community is part and parcel of membership. They actively and regularly attend Church meetings and social events in their newfound faith because that is what belonging to a community means for them.

Missionaries who have served in countries with a strong Catholic tradition may have observed a very different pattern, as I did. As missionaries in Brazil, we often encountered the attitude "I was born a Catholic and I will die a Catholic." But this strong allegiance to the Catholic faith did not translate into regular church attendance. Attending Mass once or twice a year on holidays and the occasional wedding or funeral was viewed as adequate and was not in any way a reflection of a lack of dedication. The two traditions tend to produce a very different pattern of attendance among new converts.

---

23. Robert B. Reich, *The Power of Public Ideas* (Cambridge, MA: Harvard University Press, 1988).

The five foundation stones underlie the more specific commandments enumerated in the "law and the prophets" and the guidance we receive from living prophets. The central point is that as we focus our efforts on understanding and embracing these five foundation stones, we will find the guidance and peace promised to those who keep the commandments. And, we will become better qualified to live in a Zion society.

Achieving Zion is fundamentally a collective effort. When the Lord rejected the efforts to establish Zion in the 1830s, He made it clear that it was the collective effort of the Church as a body that was insufficient, not just the righteousness of the Saints in Missouri.

> Behold, I say unto you, were it not for the transgressions of my people, *speaking concerning the church and not individuals,* they might have been redeemed even now. . . . But I speak *concerning my churches abroad*—there are many who will say: Where is their God? Behold, he will deliver them in time of trouble, otherwise we will not go up unto Zion, and will keep our moneys. Therefore, in consequence of the transgressions of my people, it is expedient in me that mine elders should wait for a little season for the redemption of Zion. (Doctrine and Covenants 105:2, 8–9; emphasis added)

How these five foundation stones impact the organizations and institutions of a Zion society is an important domain of practice. Before we can turn to practices, however, there is much to be learned from the guidance provided by the Lord regarding the "cornerstone of Zion," Nauvoo. We must also consider principles related to the role of the Church and the place of the family in Zion.

CHAPTER 5

Nauvoo—
The Cornerstone of Zion

The first canonized revelation Joseph Smith received after the Saints were driven out of Missouri in October 1838 is recorded in Doctrine and Covenants 124. The revelation was received in January 1841, after the Saints had purchased land in Commerce, Illinois, renamed it Nauvoo, and secured a favorable city charter from the state of Illinois.

Alex Smith emphasizes the importance of section 124 by noting how few revelations from the Nauvoo period were canonized during Joseph's lifetime:

> Of the 110 sections canonized during Joseph Smith's lifetime (those that were included in the 1844 edition of the Doctrine and Covenants), only three date from the Illinois period. . . .
>
> It was widely known among Church members almost immediately upon its reception. It was the first text inscribed by general Church clerk Robert Thompson in the Book of the Law of the Lord, a record designed to contain Joseph Smith's revelations and which also became the first tithing book of the Church. It was read before the Saints at the April 1841 general conference of the Church in Nauvoo—the first conference following the receipt of the revelation.[1]

---

1. "Organizing the Church in Nauvoo," The Church of Jesus Christ of Latter-day Saints, ND, accessed 12 Oct 2022, 2022, https://www.

The Gathering, Temples, and Church Structure

I start with the presumption that everything in section 124 is there for a purpose and contributes to our understanding of how Zion should be organized. The revelation opens with a commandment to Joseph to proclaim to the world the truth of the gospel of Jesus Christ, and that the Nauvoo stake is to serve as the cornerstone of Zion: "Make a solemn proclamation of my gospel, and of this stake which I have planted to be a cornerstone of Zion" (Doctrine and Covenants 124:2).

The status of the stake in Nauvoo as the cornerstone of Zion is reiterated three more times in section 124:

- In describing the function of the Nauvoo House, the revelation states: "The weary traveler may find health and safety [in the Nauvoo House] while he shall contemplate the word of the Lord; and the cornerstone I have appointed for Zion" (v. 23).
- The Nauvoo House is to be "a resting-place for the weary traveler, that he may contemplate the glory of Zion, and the glory of this, the cornerstone thereof" (v. 60).
- In naming the high council to serve in the Nauvoo Stake, the Lord states, "I give unto you a high council, for the cornerstone of Zion (v. 131).

With such Divine emphasis on the status of the stake in Nauvoo, it is well worth considering the nature of that cornerstone. The first consideration is how Church leaders understood the concept of a stake in early 1841. Church organization was beginning to solidify, but understandings and vocabulary were still very much under development. The concept of a stake came from Old Testament language that described Zion as a tent supported by stakes and cords (see Isaiah 33:20, 54:2; 3 Nephi 22:2). Zion was the center place and stakes were the surrounding gathering places for the saints.

On May 18, 1838, Joseph Smith, Sidney Rigdon, and a number of others left Far West and traveled north "for the purpose of Laying off

---

churchofjesuschrist.org/study/manual/revelations-in-context/organizing-the-church-in-nauvoo?lang=eng.

stakes of Zion, marking Locations & laying claims for the gathering of the saints for the benefit of the poor, and for the upbuilding of the Church of God."[2] They were not establishing ecclesiastical units; they were surveying and laying out land for future communities.

In June 1838, Joseph Smith presided at a conference to organize a stake at Adam-ondi-Ahman. *The Joseph Smith Papers* provide a historical introduction to this event and make it clear that, at this time, Church leaders used the term "stake" to describe "multiple places of gathering in Missouri."

> In 1833, [Joseph Smith] explained that when growth necessitated expansion beyond the original plat of the city of Zion in Jackson County, Missouri, the Saints could develop another plat "in the same way and so fill up the world in these last days." By 1837 it was time to expand, and in September church leaders in Kirtland selected [Joseph Smith] and Sidney Rigdon to go to Missouri and "appoint other Stakes or places of gathering" in addition to Far West.[3]

The term "stake" as used in Doctrine and Covenants 124 referred to the community of Nauvoo, not just the ecclesiastical structure of a stake as we think of the term today. Stakes were equated with places for the saints to gather.[4]

The stake/community in Nauvoo is designated the cornerstone of Zion. And Zion is described in scripture as a physical location and a city (see Doctrine and Covenants 57:1–2 and Moses 7:19), and it is described as the condition of the Lord's people (see Doctrine and Covenants 97:21 and Moses 7:18). While the community in Nauvoo certainly had a physical dimension, the designation as a cornerstone of Zion seems to go well beyond the location of Nauvoo. Cornerstones

---

2. "Journal, March–September 1838," *The Joseph Smith Papers*, 42, accessed March 7, 2024, https://www.josephsmithpapers.org/paper-summary/journal-march-september-1838/28.

3. https://www.josephsmithpapers.org/paper-summary/minutes-28-june-1838/2#historical-intro

4. "Minutes, 17 September 1837–B," *The Joseph Smith Papers*, 243, accessed March 7, 2024, https://www.josephsmithpapers.org/paper-summary/minutes-17-september-1837-b/1.

in the twenty-first century are often decorative and are no longer included in temple construction.[5] In the nineteenth century, they were the principal stone that determined the layout and direction of the entire edifice.

The cornerstone of Zion certainly includes a temple. But the revelation also details an organizational structure for the stake and the larger Church, and it outlines the organizational structure for what is essentially a commercial venture. It also provides guidance on how the Saints in Zion should act. In combination with a strong civic governance structure, these components make Nauvoo the cornerstone of Zion.

The Lord poses a question in verse 10: "Where shall be the safety of my people, and refuge for those who shall be left of them?" In this instance, "them" refers to the survivors of a wicked world that are left after "[the Lord] shall unveil the face of [His] covering, to appoint the portion of the oppressor among hypocrites, where there is gnashing of teeth" (v. 8). The Lord proceeds to answer His question in verses 27–28. The Saints are to send out messengers and gather "all [the] Saints" to Nauvoo, to bring with them their wealth and to build a temple: "Build a house to my name, for the Most High to dwell therein. For there is not a place found on earth that he may come to and restore again that which was lost unto you, or which he hath taken away, even the fulness of the priesthood."

The Lord accepted baptisms for the dead outside the temple when the Saints were poor, but "it is ordained that in Zion, and in her stakes [gathering places], and in Jerusalem, those places which I have appointed for refuge, shall be the places for your baptisms for your dead" (Doctrine and Covenants 124:36).

So it is in Zion and in her stakes/gathering places that the Saints will find refuge, and in Jerusalem for the remnants of Israel. That refuge is to center around the temple, as I suggested was the case in the cities of Enoch and Melchizedek.

---

5. Scott Taylor, "First Presidency: Temple cornerstone ceremonies discontinued," *Church News*, June 17, 2023.

Therefore, verily I say unto you, that your anointings, and your washings, and your baptisms for the dead, and your solemn assemblies, and your memorials for your sacrifices by the sons of Levi, and for your oracles in your most holy places wherein you receive conversations, and your statutes and judgments, for the beginning of the revelations and foundation of Zion, and for the glory, honor, and endowment of all her municipals, are ordained by the ordinance of my holy house, *which my people are always commanded to build unto my holy name.* And verily I say unto you, *let this house be built unto my name,* that I may reveal mine ordinances therein unto my people; For I deign to reveal unto my church things which have been kept hid from before the foundation of the world, things that pertain to the dispensation of the fulness of times. (Doctrine and Covenants 124:39–41, emphasis added)

And again, verily I say unto you, I command you again to build a house to my name, even in this place. (Doctrine and Covenants 124:55)

The temple is an essential feature of the pattern the Lord set forth for the creation of a Zion society. If the Saints are now to gather to stakes worldwide, small wonder the Lord is directing the construction of temples across the globe. Temples are fundamental for strengthening the stakes of Zion.

We often cite Nephi's confident statement that when the Lord gives a commandment, He always prepares a way that we can accomplish the thing commanded (see 1 Nephi 3:7). In section 124, however, the Lord acknowledges that there are times when the enemies of the kingdom "hinder" us from performing a task we are commanded to undertake. In such cases, "it behooveth [the Lord] to require that work no more at the hands of those sons of men, but to accept of their offerings" (Doctrine and Covenants 124:49).

The catch is that men must first "go with all their mights, and with all they have, to perform that work, and cease not their diligence." This speaks to the need for freedom of worship and a government that protects freedom of religion and other rights. If Zion is to be built up, we must work with all our might and diligence to accomplish that goal, and that will require that we work to assure the freedom and protection of our right to establish a Zion society. Nauvoo had by this time secured a strong city charter from the state that gave them broad leeway to act in their own defense.

In an 1838 revelation, the Lord made clear that in order for a local branch of the Church to become a stake, that local unit had to acknowledge the authority of the First Presidency by a vote of the people.[6] Section 124 sets out the offices and officeholders in the local Nauvoo Stake and in the Church. Similar to Paul's explanation to the Ephesians, the Lord gave these offices and keys "for governments, for the work of the ministry and the perfecting of [His] Saints" (Doctrine and Covenants 124:143).

The offices identified in section 124 include:

- A bishop for the Church as a whole (v. 21)
- A patriarch (vv. 91–94, 124)
- A president (v. 125) and two counselors (vv. 91, 103, 126)
- A president of the Quorum of the Twelve Apostles (v. 127) and twelve Apostles (v. 128)
- A stake high council (v. 131)
- A stake president (v. 133–134) with two counselors (v. 136)
- At least one elder's quorum presidency (v. 137)
- Seven presidents of the seventy (vv. 139–140)
- Local bishops (v. 141)
- Aaronic priesthood quorum presidents (v. 142)

While the Lord identifies specific individuals to fill these offices, as a pattern for Zion, it is the offices themselves that offer direction on how the Church should be organized. The same basic structure continues to be employed in Church administration today. Additional offices involving first assistants to the Quorum of the Twelve and refocused and expanded Quorums of Seventy have been added over the years to meet the needs of the expanding Church. But it is not difficult to see the pattern set out in section 124 in contemporary Church organization.

---

6. "Revelation, 12 January 1838–B," *The Joseph Smith Papers*, 1, accessed March 7, 2024, https://www.josephsmithpapers.org/paper-summary/revelation-12-january-1838-b/1

Organization of the Nauvoo House as a Model for Collective Action

An important precursor to Nauvoo was the first stake organized in Kirtland. On April 26, 1832, Joseph received a revelation which (1) created the united firm which joined the mercantile and publishing efforts in Kirtland and Missouri into a single jointly managed stewardship; and (2) consecrated the land of Kirtland as the first stake "to" Zion. The profits of the united firm were to be cast into the Church storehouse for the benefit of the whole church. Every man was to seek the interest of his neighbor, doing all things with an eye single to the glory of God (see Doctrine and Covenants 82:11–19).

Section 124 also contains extensive direction regarding the purpose, organization, funding, and initial management of a commercial boarding house to be built in Nauvoo. What purpose does this extended discussion serve as part of the "cornerstone of Zion"?

The organization of the Nauvoo House was as a stock company. Shares were to be priced at $50 each (at the time, farm laborers earned about $0.50 a day, carpenters about $1.20 a day, and blacksmiths about $1.50 a day).[7] The maximum investment allowed was 300 shares, or $15,000 ($510,000 in today's currency). Setting a maximum on allowable shares per investor was insightful.

One of the challenges cooperative stock ventures in Utah faced was the gradual concentration of stock holdings as time went by. The shares frequently provided significant dividends, and there apparently was no shortage of current shareholders in the communities willing to buy shares from those with a need to liquidate their holdings. Eventually, there was very little "cooperative" about the venture other than the name. Limiting the maximum holdings of any individual would help maintain broad-based participation. Since the shares in the Nauvoo House were heritable and transferrable, it is not clear how the long-term breadth of shareholders could be assured other than by limiting the number of shares any one owner could hold. At least initially the intent was to have many small shareholders.

---

7. For more detail, see "Prices and Wages by Decade: 1840–1849," University of Missouri Libraries, 2022, no. 30 Dec (2022).

Additional operating funds, if needed, were to be obtained proportionally from the shareholders. Should there be a surplus (profit), it was to be reinvested or distributed to shareholders.

Governance was to be provided by a small board with the express directive to pursue the good of Zion over profit. The Nauvoo House was to offer rest that "the weary traveler may find health and safety while he shall contemplate the word of the Lord; and the cornerstone I have appointed for Zion" (Doctrine and Covenants 124:23). Verse 24 suggests that the Lord would be willing to "dwell" in this house as well, if it is kept pure. The clear intention in the revelation is that the Nauvoo House was to approach the sanctity of a temple, except it was built for strangers: "As pertaining to my boarding house which I have commanded you to build for the boarding of strangers, let it be built unto my name, and let my name be named upon it" (Doctrine and Covenants 124:56).

Finally, the Lord instructs that stock shares should only be sold to faithful believers.

> And again, verily I say unto you, let no man pay stock to the quorum of the Nauvoo House unless he shall be a believer in the Book of Mormon, and the revelations I have given unto you, saith the Lord your God; For that which is more or less than this cometh of evil, and shall be attended with cursings and not blessings, saith the Lord your God. Even so. Amen. (Doctrine and Covenants 124:119–120)

The vision of the cornerstone of Zion includes cooperative ventures similar to those eventually started in Utah. Cooperative efforts of this sort are effective and important extensions for individuals and families, expanding their range of choices, as the Saints in Utah discovered in the 1860s and 1870s.

- They can be a means of providing the capital necessary to create a boarding house, retail store, or manufacturing facility that would generally be beyond the means of small investors.
- They can provide the information needed by individuals and families to make better choices.
- Ventures such as the Nauvoo House provide a mechanism for an expanded range of action. As was demonstrated in Utah, pooling

capital in a cooperative venture potentially creates choices for individual action that would not otherwise be possible.

- Accountability in cooperative ventures is to the shareholders and to the customers/clients.

Cooperative firms (co-ops) are entities created and owned by members. Their purpose is to benefit the members through risk sharing, pooled capital, joint marketing, and the like. Control of the firm is generally democratic with one vote per shareholder, regardless of the amount of capital contributed. Profits are returned to members in proportion to the level of their investment. Examples include agricultural co-ops such as Sunkist, marketing co-ops such as REI, and mutual insurance firms such as State Farm. One of the largest cooperatives in the world is the Spanish firm Mondragon Corp. Section 124 seems to favor the cooperative model.

The revelation lays out a framework that can be applied to a range of cooperative ventures. Some will be commercial such as the Nauvoo House or the cooperative stores in Utah. Others will likely be educational, philanthropic, or mutual insurance ventures. As the Saints in Zion see needs beyond the capacity of any one family, section 124 provides a model for joining together with other families to exercise their agency and accountability in new and expanded domains.

This discussion leaves some questions unanswered. For example, in our society we restrict cooperation within an industry out of concern that those cooperating do not place the interest of customer and community on an equal footing with their own interests. Competition is seen as "efficient" in terms of maximizing the well-being of both producers and consumers. But much of the practical business regulation we have imposed over the years is intended to correct or mitigate against market failures, when uncontrolled competition may be harmful to society. How will innovation and efficiency be fostered in Zion if all ventures are cooperative? Will a focus on the good of Zion rather than profit be sufficient to promote innovation?

Cooperation does not imply that planning and coordination in industry should be centrally controlled and planned. The Saints in Utah demonstrated the challenges of such an approach even when implemented by righteous leaders. There will be active markets in

Zion, and those markets will serve to enhance individual agency and accountability because market participants will put the interests of all—shareholder, employee, competitor, and customer—on an equal footing. But innovation can at times be disruptive and even destructive of existing patterns. How will Zion promote creative and contributive innovation while managing its impact on existing patterns of practice?

It seems unlikely that economic growth will enter the equation unless society demands more in order to assure that all have enough. We know "there is enough and to spare" (Doctrine and Covenants 104:17). And we know how the Lord would like us to address the distribution to the poor through voluntary contributions of opportunity, time, and means. But at least as implemented among the Nephites, the approach laid out in section 124 produced significant increases in the standard of living for all. Will a similar outcome result in a more industrialized society?

Council to Those Who Seek to Live in a Zion Society

Toward the end of the verses discussing the stock financing system to be used to build the Nauvoo House, there is what might seem a digression into individualized counsel addressed to those "who wish to know [the Lord's] will concerning them." I puzzled for some time over what to make of these passages as part of the cornerstone of Zion and researched what happened to each of the fifty-four people mentioned by name in the section.

In addition to Joseph and Hyrum, ten of the men died before the Saints left Nauvoo. All twelve were named in the revelation in positions of leadership. Of the remaining forty-two, it is difficult to discern a pattern based on personalities. Most made it to Utah and apparently were faithful members. But eighteen of those mentioned eventually left the Church either to join one of the splinter groups following the death of Joseph and Hyrum, or simply through disaffection.

Oliver Cowdery was readmitted in 1848 and died in 1850 in Missouri. Even some who were praised by the Lord in the 1841 revelation fell away. George Miller, who the Lord says is "without guile" and he "may be trusted because of the integrity of his heart," became a Strangite and was excommunicated in 1848. Four named Apostles or members of the First Presidency left the Church. Indeed, it seems the more frequently a brother was mentioned in the revelation, the more likely he was to fall away. William Law is mentioned in seven verses, Lyman Wight in four, and George Miller in four. The majority of those mentioned, however, went on to live faithful lives.

Following the principle that what the Lord says unto one He says unto all, these passages can be seen as a restatement or cornerstone for how the Saints should act in relation to their commercial relationships as well as other areas of their lives. The counsel includes:

- Nine individuals are counseled specifically to buy stock in the Nauvoo House. Interestingly, none of the Church leadership other than Joseph and Hyrum were counseled in the revelation to buy stock (vv. 74, 77, 78, 80–82).
- In four instances, the Lord chastens those who ignore or undermine the prophet.
    - o "Henceforth hearken to the counsel of my servant [the prophet]" "and unto the authorities which I have called to lay the foundation of Zion" (v. 89).
    - o The Lord is not pleased when someone "aspireth to establish [his] counsel instead of the council which I have ordained, even the presidency of my church" (v. 84).
    - o "Stand by . . . my servant [the prophet] in the hour of affliction" (v. 16).
    - o "Await patiently and diligently for further instructions at my general conference" (v. 88).
- In three instances, the Lord instructs individuals to "go and proclaim my everlasting gospel, with a loud voice, and with great joy," including the direction to "publish the new translations of my holy word unto the inhabitants of the earth" (vv. 18, 88, 89).
- Three times the Lord directs individuals to "lift up [your] voice, long and loud, in the midst of the people, to plead the cause of the poor and the needy," or similar language (vv. 21, 75, 89).

- Once people gather with the Saints, "let no man go from this place who has come here essaying to keep my commandments" (three individuals) (v. 85).
- "Arise and come up and stand in the office of [your] calling" (v. 103).
    o "Prove faithful in all things that shall be entrusted unto [your] care" (v. 55, 113).
    o "Go with my servant . . . to accomplish the work that my servant [the prophet] shall point out to them" (v. 79).
- "Put [your] trust in me, and cease to fear concerning [your] family" (v. 87).
- "If you love me, keep my commandments" (v. 87).
- "Labor with [your] own hands that [you] may obtain the confidence of men" (v. 112).
- "Be humble before me, and be without guile" (v. 97, 103).
- "Repent of all [your] folly, and clothe [yourself] with charity" (v. 116).
- "Cease to do evil, and lay aside all [your] hard speeches" (v. 116).

In other words, live together in righteousness and unity, eliminate poverty, take the gospel to the world, and endure to the end.

My reading of section 124 provides great insight into how a Zion society will be structured. Zion and her gathering places (stakes) will be centered around the temple. The structure of the Church will be similar to the structure we see today, though organizational adjustments will likely be needed to meet the needs of a worldwide Church. There will be commercial, humanitarian, and other organizations initiated by the Saints as they exercise their agency and cooperate with other families to expand and implement their choices. And the Saints will live together in harmony, unity, and righteousness. There will be neither rich nor poor because keeping the second great commandment will fill the hearts of all with the same love that the Savior has for each of us.

While the structure of the Church is outlined in section 124, given the changes in the Church over the decades, the next chapter considers the role the Church will play in Zion.

CHAPTER 6

The Role of the Church in Zion

In contemplating the organization and establishment of Zion, it would be a mistake to overlook the changes that have taken place in The Church of Jesus Christ of Latter-day Saints. The spiritual purpose of the Church of Jesus Christ has been articulated at least since Paul taught the Ephesians about priesthood leadership:

> And he gave some, apostles; and some, prophets; and some, evangelists; and some, pastors and teachers; For the perfecting of the Saints, for the work of the ministry, for the edifying of the body of Christ: Till we all come in the unity of the faith, and of the knowledge of the Son of God, . . . speaking the truth in love, may grow up into him in all things. (Ephesians 4:11–15)

In this dispensation, the Lord has again specified His spiritual purpose in restoring the Church through Joseph Smith:

> Wherefore, I the Lord, . . . called upon my servant Joseph Smith, Jun., . . . and gave him commandments; And also gave commandments to others, that they should proclaim these things unto the world; and all this that it might be fulfilled, which was written by the prophets . . . that every man might speak in the name of God the

Lord, . . . That faith also might increase in the earth; That mine everlasting covenant might be established; That the fulness of my gospel might be proclaimed by the weak and the simple unto the ends of the world. (Doctrine and Covenants 1:17–23)

Prepare ye the way of the Lord, and make his paths straight, for the hour of his coming is nigh. (Doctrine and Covenants 133:17)

President David O. McKay gave a succinct statement of the purpose and mission of the Church:

The mission of the Church is to prepare the way for the final establishment of the Kingdom of God on earth. Its purpose is, first, to develop in men's lives Christ-like attributes; and, second, to transform society so that the world may be a better and more peaceful place in which to live.[1]

And Joseph F. Smith framed the "work of the ministry" and articulated the approach the Church should take in "perfecting the Saints":

We are governed by law, because we love one another, and are actuated by long-suffering and charity, and good will; and our whole organization is based upon the idea of self-control; the principle of give and take, and of rather being willing to suffer wrong than to do wrong. Our message is peace on earth and good will towards men; love, charity and forgiveness, which should actuate all associated with the Church of Jesus Christ of Latter-day Saints. Ours is a Church where law is dominant, but the law is the law of love. There are rules which should be observed, and will be observed if we have the spirit of the work in our hearts; and if we have not the spirit with us, we have only the form of godliness which is without strength.[2]

---

1. David O. McKay, *Teachings of the Presidents of the Church: David O McKay* (Salt Lake City, UT: The Church of Jesus Christ of Latter-day Saints, 2011), 22.
2. Joseph F. Smith, as quoted in John A. Widtsoe, *Priesthood and Church Government* (Salt Lake City, UT: Deseret Book , 1939), 184.

The Church Before 2009

The Church is made up of mortals, with all the mundane needs of mortal women, men, and children. As such, the Church has always been concerned about helping individuals and families live together in peace, harmony, and reasonable comfort. But the approach the Church takes to address these needs has changed over time, and there has been an important shift in just the past few years.

In the early Nauvoo period, the Church was the government, carrying out all the functions of a city government. The city sought recognition and a broad charter from the state in an attempt to protect the rights of Church members, not from any perceived need to either combine or separate church and state. James L. Kimball explained:

> From the inception of the Nauvoo Stake in October 1839, the Saints considered its officers to be the equivalent of a civil government of the area. Not only did the Nauvoo High Council pass resolutions regarding ferry usages, but it set standards and procedures for the cost and sale of town lots in Nauvoo (subject to the First Presidency's approval), contracted to erect a stone schoolhouse in the city, supervised the work of poor relief, and approved the establishment of businesses such as a water mill operated by Newel K. Whitney.[3]

In the first seventy years or so of the Church's existence, Church members were pioneers, settling new territory, establishing new settlements, and homesteading, often in fairly large groups in inhospitable areas. Orderly development of those early communities required centralized planning and coordination. There really was no other organization or institution available to shoulder the planning and coordination tasks other than the Church.

The Saints arrived in the Great Basin in 1847 in the hopes of escaping officially tolerated persecution and governmental neglect in the United States. The war with Mexico and the annexation

---

3. James L. Kimball, "Protecting Nauvoo by Illinois Charter in 1840," in *Sustaining the Law: Joseph Smith's Legal Encounters*, ed. Gordon A. Madsen, Jeffrey N. Walker, and John W. Welch (Provo, UT: BYU Studies, 2014), 297.

of the Great Basin region into the United States made any such hope unrealistic. By 1849, Utah began to petition for entry into the United States as the state of Deseret. The thinking was that a state would have more control over the laws and practices within its borders. Utah was made a United States territory in 1851 with Brigham Young as the first territorial governor. Even after the Utah war when Brigham Young was replaced as governor, and throughout the nineteenth century, the Church played a major role in settling new communities under the direction and often personal guidance of Church leaders.

Early in the twentieth century, the Church was still a major force in the growth and development of the region. The following passage is taken from a course of study for young priests, used between 1906 and at least 1912, and illustrates the breadth of active Church initiatives.

> What then, it might be consistently asked, are the promises, blessings and benefits vouchsafed under Church government, to the citizens of the kingdom, and actually possessed by them here, and now? . . . [A number of spiritual blessings are listed.]
>
> Nor is this all: like worldly governments, it [Church government] also furnishes many temporal blessings. The cause of education is promoted by the establishment of academies, colleges, and universities; with buildings, furnishings, and the employment of teachers. Lands are purchased and homes and farms brought within the reach of many worthy people. The poor and destitute are clothed, fed, and housed; the sick and the afflicted are cared for. Assistance is rendered in various ways, in the laying out of new towns and villages; public industries and enterprises are started, and fostered by Church government.[4]

By the 1930s, if not before, the Church began to narrow the focus of its attention. In 1937, the Church's Department of Education published a volume entitled *Program of The Church of Jesus Christ of Latter-day Saints* written by Elder John A. Widtsoe. Under the heading "Duties of the Church: The Threefold Obligation," Elder

---

4. Joseph B. Keeler, *First Steps in Church Government: What Church Government Is and What It Does* (Salt Lake City, UT: Deseret News, 1906), 80–81.

Widtsoe states that the "organized body of believers in the plan of salvation are under three heavy obligations."[5] Note that while it is "believers" who are under "heavy obligations," it is the Church which "must" act.

> First, the Church must care for its members. . . . The members of the Church must receive constant, intelligent care.
>
> Second, the Church must vigorously and incessantly spread the knowledge of the Gospel over the earth. . . . The Church as the earthly agent of the Lord must, therefore, attempt with all its might to teach the Gospel to the nations of the earth . . . Finding, teaching, converting, must be constant activities of the Church.
>
> Third, . . . the ordinances of earth must be performed for the dead. . . . To give the dead such opportunities is a heavy responsibility of the Church.
>
> These are three duties, carrying with them tremendous obligations, which require a perfected organization for their performance.[6]

The focus on a three-fold mission for the Church remained for decades and was a notable focus under President Spencer W. Kimball.

The Church in 2009 and Beyond

While caring for the poor has always been a concern for the Church, it wasn't added as a fourth dimension of the mission or purpose of the Church until 2009.[7] This four-fold purpose of the Church continued to be articulated through 2019. The May 2019 *General Handbook* of the Church stated:

> In fulfilling its purpose to help individuals and families qualify for exaltation, the Church focuses on divinely appointed

---

5. John A. Widtsoe, *Program of The Church of Jesus Christ of Latter-day Saints* (Salt Lake City, UT: Department of Education, The Church of Jesus Christ of Latter-day Saints, 1936), 123.

6. Widtsoe, *Program of The Church of Jesus Christ of Latter-day Saints*, 123–24.

7. Peggy Fletcher Stack, "New LDS emphasis: Care for the needy," *The Salt Lake Tribune* (Salt Lake City, UT), December 9, 2009.

responsibilities. These include helping members live the gospel of Jesus Christ, gathering Israel through missionary work, caring for the poor and needy, and enabling the salvation of the dead by building temples and performing vicarious ordinances.[8]

The more succinct statement of these "divinely appointed responsibilities" that I often heard was that the mission of the Church was to perfect the Saints, proclaim the gospel, redeem the dead, and care for the poor.

This adjustment in focus during the twentieth century was in part due to the expansion of the Church outside the United States. When the Church divested itself in the 1970s of the hospital chain that it owned, the rationale given was that the resources were needed more outside the United States. "Explaining the decision to divest the Church of its 15 hospitals in Utah, Idaho, and Wyoming, the First Presidency said that 'the growing worldwide responsibility of the Church makes it difficult to justify provision of curative services in a single, affluent, geographical locality.'"[9]

Education has long been an emphasis of the Church, but here again the competing demands of an expanding Church have nudged the Church to sharpen its focus on its core mission. The closure of the Church College of New Zealand in 2009 and Benemerito De Las Americas in Mexico in 2013 are recent examples.

The Church continues to maintain a large welfare production and distribution system. From the members' point of view, however, even the welfare production system seems to have become a professionally managed and operated, vertically integrated system that relies less and less on member volunteers.

A major adjustment and focusing of the Church's mission occurred again in recent years as reflected in the 2020 and subsequent editions of the *General Handbook*. The adjustment reflects increased emphasis on individuals and families to accept the

---

8. General Handbook, *General Handbook* (Salt Lake City, UT: The Church of Jesus Christ of Latter-day Saints, 2019), 9.
9. News of the Church, "Hospitals dropped as health services expands total worldwide program," *Ensign*, November 1974.

divinely appointed responsibilities of discipleship. This shift does not imply that families ought not to cooperate in seeking to discharge these responsibilities. On the contrary, the Church continues to encourage and provide opportunities for such cooperation. But the responsibility to act is more clearly defined as an individual and family obligation, with the Church playing a subordinate and supportive role.

Section 1.3 of the 2020 *General Handbook* states: "Jesus Christ established His Church to enable individuals and families to do the work of salvation and exaltation (see Ephesians 4:11–13; see also 2.2 in this handbook). To help accomplish this divine purpose, the Church and its leaders provide:

- Priesthood authority and keys.
- Covenants and ordinances.
- Prophetic direction.
- Scriptures.
- Gospel learning and teaching support.
- Service and leadership opportunities.
- A community of Saints."[10]

Section 2.2 states: "The First Presidency said, 'The home is the basis of a righteous life' (First Presidency letter, Feb. 11, 1999). In their homes, individuals and families engage in the work of salvation and exaltation. This work consists of four divinely appointed responsibilities:

- Living the gospel of Jesus Christ (see 1.2.1)
- Caring for those in need (see 1.2.2)
- Inviting all to receive the gospel (see 1.2.3)
- Uniting families for eternity (see 1.2.4)

To support members in doing the work of salvation and exaltation at home, Church leaders encourage them to establish a home where the Spirit is present."[11]

---

10. *General Handbook*, 5.
11. *General Handbook*, 10.

The implications of this adjustment are significant for the establishment of a Zion society. The obligations articulated by earlier leaders still exist, but the responsibility to discharge those obligations is now placed squarely on individuals and families. The role the Church is to play is vital as a resource for families to draw upon, but it is a supporting role rather than a leadership role.

This adjustment moves the membership one step closer to a community of Saints established on the foundation stones of Zion: families earnestly striving to obtain the divine gift of charity and consecrated to give their all for the establishment of Zion, including the elimination of poverty. It also defines the role of the Church in Zion: providing spiritual guidance and sacred opportunities that members can choose to draw upon as they choose to establish a Zion society. Zion is a choice, and our leaders are earnestly and repeatedly pleading with us to choose it. In his October 2022 general conference address, President Russell M. Nelson said:

> As I have stated before, the gathering of Israel is the *most* important work taking place on earth today. One crucial element of this gathering is preparing a people who are able, ready, and worthy to receive the Lord when He comes again, a people who have already chosen Jesus Christ over this fallen world, a people who rejoice in their agency to live the higher, holier laws of Jesus Christ.
>
> I call upon you, my dear brothers and sisters, to become this righteous people. Cherish and honor your covenants above all other commitments. As you let God prevail in your life, I promise you greater peace, confidence, joy, and yes, *rest*.[12]

The implications of this progressive sharpening of focus, especially the most recent adjustments, seem to me quite striking. President Nelson admonished the Saints to "cherish and honor [their] covenants above all other commitments." That would include the covenants to take upon us the name of Christ, to strive earnestly to love as the

---

12. Russell M. Nelson, "Overcome the world and find rest," *Liahona*, November 2022; emphasis in original.

Savior loves, and to keep all temple covenants, including the law of consecration.

As the Church expands internationally, its resources will increasingly be focused on providing individuals and families with the eight spiritual opportunities listed in the 2020 *General Handbook*. The opportunities and blessings associated with the four obligations enumerated in earlier years will fall to individuals and families. This will both strengthen and challenge families, but the Lord appears to have confidence that we as a Church are ready for this next stage in bringing about Zion.

CHAPTER 7

The Family as the Fundamental Unit in Zion

How Are Families Fundamental?

It is now commonplace to speak of the family as the fundamental unit of society. But what does that mean? In particular, what does it mean that the family is the fundamental unit of a Zion society?

In our western culture, the individual has replaced the family as the fundamental focus in most instances. Families have become little more than an administrative unit to facilitate the gathering of statistics and the efficient delivery of services. Consistent with our cultural emphasis on individuals, we see constant adjustments in the definition of family, most of which depart from a unit consisting of father, mother, children, and multi-generational connections. To be sure, some of these adjustments are to acknowledge the challenges the traditional family faces in today's world. For example, the Pew Research Center reported in 2015:

> Family life is changing. Two-parent households are on the decline in the United States as divorce, remarriage and cohabitation are on

the rise. And families are smaller now, both due to the growth of single-parent households and the drop in fertility. . . .

As a result of these changes, there is no longer one dominant family form in the U.S. Parents today are raising their children against a backdrop of increasingly diverse and, for many, constantly evolving family forms.[1]

In 1995, the First Presidency and the Quorum of the Twelve issued a proclamation to the world reaffirming the centrality of the family in the Creator's plan. If we are to establish Zion, we must do it based on the five foundation stones and the laws of the celestial kingdom. Those laws include temple covenants as a central component. Eternal marriage is the crowning covenant of the temple. Therefore, the marriage covenant solemnized in the temple is critical for launching a family unit enabled to participate in establishing Zion. Indeed, the covenant to engage in the establishment of Zion is an important prerequisite for eternal marriage.

The 1995 family proclamation focuses on husbands, wives, and their responsibilities to bear and rear children. The proclamation states that "the family is ordained of God. Marriage between man and woman is essential to His eternal plan. . . . Fathers and mothers are obligated to help one another as equal partners."[2]

The Proclamation does not give a definition of "family." It does note that "disability, death or other circumstances may necessitate individual adaptation. Extended families should lend support when needed." It further warns of the calamities that will follow "the disintegration of the family." However, the Church's Guide to the Scriptures offers a definition of family: "As used in the scriptures, a family consists of a husband and wife, children, and sometimes other relatives living in the same house or under one family head. A family can also be a single parent with children, a husband and wife without children, or even a single person living alone."[3]

---

1. Pew Research Center, "The American Family Today," 2015, https://www.pewresearch.org/social-trends/2015/12/17/1–the-american-family-today/.
2. "The Family: A Proclamation to the World," *Ensign*, November 1995, 102.
3. Guide to the Scriptures, "Family," Gospel Library.

This flexibility in defining a family is important, since more than half of the U.S. adult population is single. While Utah ranks the lowest among states in the percentage of the adult population that is single, the percentage is still nearly 44 percent. The Utah figure has increased steadily from about 36 percent in 1980. Among young adults ages 20 to 34 in Utah, more than 60 percent of men and nearly half of women are single. Across all age groups over age 34, about a quarter of Utah adults are single. (The percentage is higher among women 65 and over.)[4]

Single adults are not left out of Zion. As Liz Stitt points out, single adults have parents, a family heritage, and heavenly parents.[5] I would add, they often have siblings, nieces, nephews, and cousins as well, and the bond with others on the same covenant path cannot be overlooked.

None of God's children are excluded by the concept of family because family is so central to God's plan for all His children. The establishment of Zion will require an increased emphasis on the family. As Julie Beck put it, "The plan of happiness, also called the plan of salvation, was a plan created for families. The rising generation need to understand that the main pillars of our theology are centered in the family."[6]

The clarification in the current *General Handbook* that families have the responsibility to perfect the Saints, preach the gospel, redeem the dead, and care for the poor—and not the institutional Church per se—suggests that the significance of families as the fundamental unit in Zion goes well beyond the important task of bearing and rearing righteous children.

Families are fundamental units in a Zion society on at least six dimensions:

1. Families are the fundamental social unit providing love, nurturing, connection, and a sense of "home" to children,

---

4. Heidi Prior, "Utah's Single Population," Demographic Research, Kem C. Gardner Policy Institute, The University of Utah, August, 2022.

5. Liz Stitt, "The Family Proclamation: How Do I Fit in as a Single Adult?" [digital-only article], *Ensign*, September 2020.

6. Julie Beck, "Teaching the Doctrine of the Family," *Ensign*, March 2011.

parents, and all family members. Simply "growing up" does not mean a person no longer needs love, nurturing, connection, and "home."

2. Families are the fundamental productive unit in society, taking materials and combining family labor to produce consumables and care used by the family and others. In a Zion context, properties are not held by individuals, but by families. Family assets are used to produce sufficient to sustain the family and to generate a surplus which can be consecrated to the poor. Family production is also used to assist extended family members and others in times of need. Even economists started recognizing the centrality of the home as a productive unit in the 1970s and developed a sub-branch around what was termed "household production theory."

3. The family is a fundamental unit for social action and self-reliance. It is vital that we recognize the family as a locus of action in society. In our premortal existence, the Father organized His spirit children, proposed a plan of action to help them progress as the family of God, and then set them to act on the plan. Families in Zion should follow a similar pattern identifying needs, organizing, and rendering service to all.

Robert Coles has written extensively on this topic. One of his more poignant stories is that of Tessie, a six-year-old Black girl in New Orleans being escorted to school each day by four armed federal agents when schools were desegregated. When Tessie walked into the school, the white parents would taunt and threaten. This went on day after day. Her parents always left for work before Tessie got up in the morning. It was her grandmother, Martha, who made her breakfast and got her off to school. One morning Tessie decided not to go to school. Martha said that was okay if Tessie was sick, but if she was more discouraged than sick, that was another matter. Martha went on to teach Tessie about the great service being rendered to God and to the community through this daily effort.

"You see my child," Martha told Tessie, "you have to help the good Lord with His world. He puts us here—and He calls us to help Him out. . . . You're one of the Lord's people; He's put His Hand on you. He's given a call to you, a call to service—in His Name"[7]

Tessie squared her shoulders, picked up her lunch, and went to school. She was able to face the daily challenge because she was taught and supported in her service by her family.

Similar stories of personal initiative to improve the world could be told all around the globe. While it may appear that it is individual action, such actions generally involve a family base.

In my professional life, I have written for and taught international audiences seeking to bring about change in their communities. One of the basic concepts that I have taught repeatedly is the oft-quoted observation attributed to the anthropologist Margaret Mead: "Never doubt that a small group of thoughtful, committed citizens can change the world. Indeed, it's the only thing that ever has."[8] Families are often the point of origin for such world-changing action.

4. Families are the fundamental historians. The Church History Department takes as its prime directive the revelation given in the earliest days of the Church: "Behold, there shall be a record kept among you" (Doctrine and Covenants 21:1). Much of the material in the Church History Library comes from journals, diaries, and personal histories kept by families. President Spencer W. Kimball urged the Saints to keep their histories: "Again, I urge you to be diligent in recording your personal and family histories. . . . In this, let us be an example to others and reap the benefits of stronger family units as we preserve our heritage."[9]

The brass plates contained scripture and family history. They kept a nation from dwindling in unbelief and preserved

7. Robert Coles, *The Call of Service: A witness to Idealism* (Boston, MA: Houghton Mifflin, 1993), 2–3.
8. There is no evidence that Margaret Mead actually made this statement. There are, however, a number of other sources expressing a very similar sentiment. See https://quoteinvestigator.com/2017/11/12/change-world/.
9. Spencer W. Kimball, "Families Can Be Eternal," *Ensign*, November 1980.

a knowledge of a particular language and writing system (see 1 Nephi 5). The Book of Mormon itself is, for the most part, family history (see 1 Nephi 1:1, 16). The scriptures make frequent references to books of remembrance which I understand to be family histories, genealogies, and records of the righteous followers of Christ.

5. The family is the most fundamental schoolhouse. As stated in "The Family: A Proclamation to the World," "Parents have a sacred duty to rear their children in love and righteousness, to provide for their physical and spiritual needs, and to teach them to love and serve one another, observe the commandments of God, and be law-abiding citizens wherever they live."

   "Goodly parents" see that their children are taught in "all the learning of [their] fathers" (1 Nephi 1:1).

6. The family is the fundamental citizenship unit in Zion. After Lehi's initial recorded vision, he "went forth among the people and began to prophesy" (1 Nephi 1:18), and the Lord blessed Lehi because he did so (see 1 Nephi 2:1).

   Families in Zion will be actively involved in perfecting the Saints who live in their own household, but they will also reach out through Church and community collaborations to lift and encourage others, to teach and proclaim the good news of the doctrine of Christ, and to put in place the welding family links across generations.

This is a daunting list, especially for families that are just trying to cope with the challenges thrown their way by life in our contemporary society. Given the changes in family structure noted above and the challenges of children who suffer from depression and anxiety, let alone ADHD, autism, and other life-altering conditions, how are we supposed to build families capable of shouldering these responsibilities effectively?

Parents and Their Children

In 1833, the Lord gave instructions to the First Presidency and Bishop Newel K. Whitney to put their houses in order (see Doctrine and Covenants 93:38–50). In this passage the Lord again says, "What I say unto one I say unto all."

The instruction begins by teaching that human spirits are innocent in the beginning and that because all are redeemed from the Fall of Adam, we are all innocent before God in our infancy. We lose that innocence through our own choices to be disobedient. But we also lose it "because of the tradition of [our] fathers. But I [God] have commanded you bring up your children in light and truth" (Doctrine and Covenants 93:39–40).

Frederick G. Williams is then told that the cause of his affliction was that he had not taught his "children light and truth, according to the commandments" (Doctrine and Covenants 93:41–42). Frederick and Rebecca had four children at that time, ranging in age from ten to seventeen. Sidney Rigdon is also admonished: "in some things [Sidney] hath not kept the commandments concerning his children" (Doctrine and Covenants 93:44). Sidney and Phebe had nine living children, ranging from one to twelve years old. Bishop Newel K. Whitney is charged to "set in order his family, and see that they are more diligent and concerned at home, and pray always" (Doctrine and Covenants 93:50). Newel and Elizabeth had four living children between one and ten years of age.

Even Joseph was told that his "family must needs repent and forsake some things, and give more earnest heed unto your sayings" (Doctrine and Covenants 93:48). Joseph and Emma's only biological child at the time was Joseph III, who was a year old. Their adopted daughter, Julia, was about two years old. The admonition may have been mostly for Emma. However, both of Joseph's parents and seven of his siblings were living in Kirtland at the time, and we ought not to presume that the Lord limits His view of the family to simply parents and their children.

The commandment to teach children light and truth dates from our first parents. Enoch, the prophet and founder of the first Zion, taught that after Adam and Eve were cast out of the garden, the Lord instructed them to repent and be baptized. Adam responded with a very reasonable question: Why? (Moses 6:51–53). Adam was then given essentially the same instruction in Doctrine and Covenants 93 regarding the original innocence of children. By virtue of the Atonement, Adam's original sin "cannot be answered upon the heads of the children, for they are whole from the foundation of the world" (Moses 6:54).

But children grow up in a sinful world and are given their agency to choose between good and evil (see Moses 6:55–56). In Moses 6:57 Adam was counseled, "Wherefore teach it unto your children, that all men, everywhere, must repent, or they can in nowise inherit the kingdom of God." By commandment, Adam, and presumably all parents, are to "teach these things freely unto your children." Then follows a three-verse summary of the plan of salvation and the doctrine of Christ. By reason of the Fall, death came into the world. Mortals must repent and be born again into the kingdom of heaven, of water and the Spirit, and be cleansed by the blood of Christ. If they do so, the companionship of the Comforter and profound spiritual blessings will follow, including eternal life and immortal glory (see Moses 6:58–62).

The doctrine of Christ was introduced in the days of Adam. Enoch notes that Father Adam was not totally successful in leading his children to accept and act on this doctrine. "Behold, our father Adam taught these things, and many have believed and become the sons of God, and many have believed not, and have perished in their sins" (Moses 7:1).

The commandment to teach our children the doctrine of Christ is still very much in place today.

> And again, inasmuch as parents have children in Zion, or in any of her stakes which are organized, that teach them not to understand the doctrine of repentance, faith in Christ the Son of the living God, and of baptism and the gift of the Holy Ghost by the laying on of the hands, when eight years old, the sin be upon the heads of the parents. For this shall be a law unto the inhabitants of Zion, or in any of her stakes which are organized. (Doctrine and Covenants 68:25–26)

As taught in the scriptures, parents are obligated to teach the doctrine, but children are agents and must and will make their own choices.

Our Father in Heaven is the perfect parent, and yet one-third of the heavenly host exercised their agency and chose to follow Satan (see Doctrine and Covenants 29:36–37). We have multiple accounts in scripture of valiant priests and powerful prophets whose children chose not to embrace the doctrines of the kingdom.

Perhaps the most detailed account we have is of Laman and Lemuel, the sons of Lehi and Sariah. They were also "born of goodly parents" (1 Nephi 1:1). Despite heavenly visitations and warning voices, and despite witnessing miracles, Laman and Lemuel chose to walk away from the inspired and profound teachings of their father in preference for what the world had to offer.

From the record that we have in 1 Samuel, Eli was a devoted high priest and judge who served Israel faithfully for forty years. He was conscientious in teaching the child Samuel. Eli's sons were instructed sufficiently that they too became priests and served in Shiloh, the equivalent of the temple prior to the construction of the temple in Jerusalem. But Eli's sons chose to abuse their position and to become quite immoral. Eli warned them but failed to remove them from their priestly duties, with dire consequences for both him and his sons.[10]

Mosiah and Alma were both righteous, committed followers of Christ and spiritual leaders among their people. Nevertheless, "the sons of Mosiah were numbered among the unbelievers; and also one of the sons of Alma was numbered among them, he being called Alma, after his father; nevertheless, he became a very wicked and an idolatrous man" (Mosiah 27:8). These men eventually repented and became spiritually powerful in their own right, but it took the prayers of many people and divine intervention to bring about their conversion.

Once converted, Alma the Younger eventually became the spiritual leader of the Church in his day. But he too had a son who went astray. We have Alma's teachings in Alma 39–42 to his adult son Corianton, instructing him again on the doctrine of Christ and the plan of salvation. After chastising Corianton for his immorality while on a mission, and attempting to answer any lingering doubts about the plan of salvation, Alma offers these encouraging words: "Therefore, my son, see that you are merciful unto your brethren; deal justly, judge righteously, and do good continually; and if ye do all these things then shall ye receive your reward; . . . For that which ye do send out shall

---

10. Paulo R. Grahl, "Eli and His Sons," *Ensign*, June 2002.

return unto you again, and be restored" (Alma 41:14–15). Corianton was called again to preach to the people and bring souls to repentance (see Alma 42:31).

The examples of Alma, the sons of Mosiah, and Corianton all demonstrate that however powerful the teachings of parents, children make their own choices. They also demonstrate that repentance is possible and effective.

Concerning teaching children in our day, President Spencer W. Kimball taught: "We do not rear children just to please our vanity. We bring children into the world to become kings and queens, priests and priestesses for our Lord."[11] He then sites the passages from Doctrine and Covenants 93 directed at Frederick G. Williams and Sidney Rigdon, including Doctrine and Covenants 93:49:

> And then the Lord said, "What I say unto one I say unto all; pray always lest that wicked one have power in you, and remove you out of your place." (Doctrine and Covenants 93:49.)
>
> How sad if the Lord should charge any of us parents with having failed to teach our children. Truly a tremendous responsibility falls upon a couple when they bring children into the world. Not only food, clothes, and shelter are required of them, but loving, kindly disciplining, teaching, and training. Of course, there are a few disobedient souls regardless of training and teaching, but the great majority of children respond to such parental guidance. The scripture says, "Train up a child in the way he should go: and when he is old, he will not depart from it." (Prov. 22:6.) And if he departs, he will probably return if he has been brought up in the right way.[12]

What Should We Do?

When Douglas D. Holmes served as the first counselor in the Young Men General Presidency, he reflected on his prior service as a mission president. He and his wife wanted to change attitudes and behaviors among their missionaries. As they pondered and prayed,

---

11. Spencer W. Kimball, "Train Up a Child," *Ensign*, April 1978.
12. Kimball, "Train Up a Child."

they determined to focus on teaching the doctrine of Christ. Over time, they saw a significant change in their mission. The Holmes knew that President Boyd K. Packer had frequently taught: "True doctrine, understood, changes attitudes and behavior. The study of the doctrines of the gospel will improve behavior quicker than a study of behavior will improve behavior."[13] President Holmes said:

> I knew this before, but following this experience with my missionaries, I had a much greater appreciation for the power and virtue of the word of God to change hearts (see Alma 31:5). As our mission progressed and we continued to focus on teaching doctrine, their hearts changed and so did ours. Because we understood doctrine, we understood the "why" of obedience, not simply the "what" and "how."[14]

This is the same principle that led Alma to resign the judgment seat and focus on teaching the word of God. He knew that "the preaching of the word had a great tendency to lead the people to do that which was just—yea, it had had more powerful effect upon the minds of the people than the sword, or anything else, which had happened unto them" (Alma 31:5).

The doctrine of Christ and the power of the gospel will not change all hearts, as Alma found among the Zoramites. But as Douglas Holmes points out:

> The Book of Mormon is a powerful witness that "true doctrine, understood, changes attitudes and behaviors." Here are just a few examples:
>
> King Benjamin taught the words he received from an angel to his people, and the Spirit brought a mighty change to their hearts that they had "no more disposition to do evil, but to do good continually" (Mosiah 5:2).
>
> As Alma the Elder taught the people, "their souls were illuminated by the light of the everlasting word," and they were saved (Alma 5:7; see also verse 9).

---

13. Boyd K. Packer, "Little Children," *Ensign*, November 1986, 17.
14. Douglas D. Holmes, "The Power of Teaching Doctrine," *Ensign*, March 2017.

The sons of Mosiah, "because of the power of his word" (Alma 26:13), helped bring about a complete change of heart in thousands of the Lamanites (see Alma 17:14–17; 53:10).[15]

President Holmes goes on to urge us to first treasure up and live by the word ourselves, then teach only true doctrine, and to teach by the Spirit. I would add that our understanding of true doctrine changes as we live by the word and mature in our relationship with the Spirit.[16]

Focusing on true doctrine may not be as simple as it seems. Our understanding may change over time and as further light is revealed. I worry greatly that there are "traditions of the fathers" perhaps within the Church and even in my own view of the gospel that impede my ability to embrace the light and truth needed to establish Zion. Are there "truths" we accept in our North American Latter-day Saint culture that are in fact merely "traditions" that might not apply in other settings or times? Even more concerning, do we make assumptions based on those truth-traditions that impede others from accessing and embracing the light and power of the gospel?

In my mind, the safest course forward is to focus on the five foundation stones of Zion and the gospel as we strive to lead our families.

- Cultivate our personal devotion for and service to the Father and His Son and teach our family to do likewise.
- Seek the spiritual gift of charity toward others. We must strive to love each member of our family as the Savior loves them, and treat their interests and concerns equally with our own.
- Act always with a profound respect for the agency of others, including our family members in making their own life choices.
- Hold ourselves accountable for the choices we make and the resulting consequences, and seek righteous ways to help our family be accountable.

---

15. Holmes, "The Power of Teaching Doctrine."
16. Brigham H. Roberts, "Interesting Correspondence on the Subject of the Manual Theory," *Improvement Era*, June 1906, 713.

- Counsel together within the family and strive for unity in decision-making, then act cooperatively to implement the decisions reached.

Families would also be well advised, I believe, to apply the advice that President Spencer Kimball gave to the Church in 1978 specifically to the family.

- We must eliminate the individual tendency to selfishness that snares the soul, shrinks the heart, and darkens the mind.
- We must cooperate completely and work in harmony one with the other. There must be unanimity in our decisions and unity in our actions.
- We must lay on the altar and sacrifice whatever is required by the Lord.[17]

If we act with this motivation and build our families around these foundations and prophetic advice, we will enlarge our capacity to shoulder the expectations of families in Zion.

In 1980 President Spencer W. Kimball prophesied: "The time will come when only those who believe deeply and actively in the family will be able to preserve their families in the midst of the gathering evil around us. . . . We know that when things go wrong in the family, things go wrong in every other institution in society"[18] because the family is indeed the fundamental social unit in Zion.

---

17. Kimball, "Becoming the Pure in Heart," 81.
18. Kimball, "Families Can Be Eternal."

PART 3
Practices

With the foundation of the principles of Zion firmly in mind, we can consider how those principles can be applied. Part 3 considers three domains of practice: the elimination of poverty, the place of land in Zion, and how organizations and institutions will function in Zion.

CHAPTER 8

Addressing Poverty

O ne of the three characteristics of Zion is that there are "no poor among them" (Moses 7:18). In this chapter I want to consider what it means to be poor and how poverty can be eliminated in a society. Poverty has long been a global issue and remains the focus of important international organizations. Both the meaning of poverty and the best way to deal with it are well represented in debates among domestic and international development professionals and policymakers, and a detailed evaluation of their work is beyond the scope of this chapter. Rather, I would like to focus on principles with selected examples to illustrate those principles in practice.

For the sake of clarity, I first observe that the "daily ministrations" spoken of in Acts did not mean that true poverty was eliminated.[1] Even though there were none "among them that lacked," alleviating short-term and immediate suffering does not lift people out of poverty. Such short-term assistance is essential, but long-term solutions must address the causes of poverty.

---

1. Georgi suggests that "the poor" was a self-selected title by the Jerusalem congregation, so it is difficult to assess the full extent of poverty among early Christians at the time (Georgi, *Remembering the Poor: The History of Paul's Collection for Jerusalem*).

What Is Poverty and What Causes It?

To recognize the principles that can lead to the elimination of poverty, it is important to recognize that poverty has several dimensions. In the Book of Mormon, King Benjamin speaks of three economic classes:

- "Those who are rich as pertaining to the things of this world" (Mosiah 4:23)
- "The poor, ye who have not and yet have sufficient, that ye remain from day to day" (Mosiah 4:24)
- "Beggars," those who need immediate aid (Mosiah 4:16)

Benjamin also acknowledges that poverty takes a toll both physically and mentally when he urges the rich to give in proportion to their capacity, both in "substance" and ministering support. "Impart of your substance to the poor, every man according to that which he hath, such as feeding the hungry, clothing the naked, visiting the sick and administering to their relief, both spiritually and temporally, according to their wants" (Mosiah 4:26).

More broadly, Benjamin urged his people to "succor those that stand in need of your succor; ye will administer of your substance unto him that standeth in need; and ye will not suffer that the beggar putteth up his petition to you in vain, and turn him out to perish" (Mosiah 4:16).

Benjamin draws a parallel between the poor and his people on the one hand, and his people and God on the other. He asks, "Are we not all beggars?" He then observes that God is the source of both our temporal and spiritual well-being. Given that relationship, "O then, how ye ought to impart of your substance that ye have to one another" (Mosiah 4:19–22; see also Mosiah 18:29, Alma 16:16).

The "beggars" among the Nephites certainly stood in need of immediate assistance as Benjamin urged, but what of the poor who had sufficient but "stand in need of [our] succor"? When Alma and Amulek went to the Zoramites, they encountered a class of poverty that would seem to fit Benjamin's description of those who are poor but have sufficient.

For behold, they were cast out of the synagogues because of the coarseness of their apparel—Therefore they were not permitted to enter into their synagogues to worship God, being esteemed as filthiness; therefore they were poor; yea, they were esteemed by their brethren as dross; therefore they were poor as to things of the world; and also they were poor in heart. (Alma 32:2–3)

The poverty of the poor among the Zoramites included both limited worldly goods and social exclusion. These were not people on the verge of starvation, but they had been excluded from important social connections and rituals because of their poverty. One of their complaints was that they were excluded from the very synagogues "we have labored abundantly to build with our own hands" (Alma 32:5).

Another dimension of poverty is identified in the practices of ancient Judaism. As Frank Loewenberg puts it, "Avoiding poverty and not becoming dependent on others was a central axiom of ancient Judaism. This belief was so basic that it was held to be of biblical origin."[2] The passage Loewenberg cites is from Deuteronomy 15:4, which he quotes as "May there be no poor among you." The phrasing obviously presents a different insight in the interpretation of conditions in Enoch's Zion, suggesting the importance of self-reliance as we consider both the nature and elimination of poverty.

Both deficiency in worldly goods and social ostracism are recognized aspects of poverty found in current discussions about poverty and poverty reduction. Armando Barrientos defines poverty as "a state in which individuals or households show significant deficits in wellbeing." These deficits can be either in terms of material means or "exclusion from cooperative activity; those in poverty are not 'able to participate in the social life of a community at a minimally acceptable level.'"[3]

Barrientos observes that many development professionals recognize the multi-dimensional nature of poverty.

---

2. Loewenberg, *From Charity to Social Justice*, 43.
3. Armando Barrientos, *Social Protection and Poverty*, United Nations Research Institute for Social Development (Geneva, Switzerland: UNRISD, March 3, 2010), 5, https://www.unrisd.org/en/library/publications/social-protection-and-poverty.

There is a broad consensus among poverty researchers around the view that poverty is multidimensional. Households in poverty show consumption deficits often linked to restricted access to basic services, limited networks and access to economic opportunity. Typically households in poverty show deficits along many dimensions of well-being at the same time.[4]

To put the reality of the multi-dimensional nature of persistent poverty more prosaically, Ruth Lister provides a sampling of responses researchers received when they asked people living in persistent poverty to complete the statement "poverty is . . ."

- Having all the same dreams for the future that everyone else has, but no way on earth to make them come true.
- Saying no to my kids every day of their lives.
- Sleeping in a bed that used to be someone else's, wearing cast-off clothes, and being expected to be grateful.
- Being just one crisis away from collapsing—every day.
- Being treated like nothing, less than nothing, and accepting it.
- Having no hope left in me at all.[5]

Lister goes on to cite the work of the economist Amartya Sen. Rather than focusing on income or living standards, Sen asks why those things matter. His answer is that they are important to the extent that they help an individual achieve what really matters, namely the kind of life a person is able to lead and the choices and opportunities open to her in leading that life. As Lister puts it:

What is at issue here are the nonmaterial as well as the material manifestations of poverty. This changes the angle of vision so that poverty is understood not just as a disadvantaged and insecure economic *condition*, but also as a shameful and corrosive social *relation*. . . . At the heart of this psychic landscape of poverty lies social suffering.[6]

---

4. Barrientos, *Social Protection and Poverty*, 6.
5. Ruth Lister, *Poverty*, 2nd ed. (Medford, MA: Polity Press, 2021), 5.
6. Lister, *Poverty*, 8; emphasis in original.

This multi-dimensional approach to understanding poverty is consistent with the developmental approach embedded in the gospel which seeks to maximize human improvement. And it seems to capture what Alma saw among those who were "poor as to things of the world; and also they were poor in heart," people who were "despised of all men because of their poverty" (Alma 32:5).

The first question to consider is, What causes poverty? Why do people become poor or stay in poverty? Not all those who are poor stay poor, some of the non-poor become poor, and some families cycle in and out of poverty. To begin to understand what a Zion society must do to eliminate poverty, the causes of poverty must first be understood. As we should expect, there are multiple causes. There is an extensive debate among development specialists regarding the causes of poverty. Ruth Lister's book is a good place to start to understand the debates.[7]

My reading of the poverty literature and my own observations suggest that a number of factors may interact to push people into poverty and keep them there. These factors include at least the following:

- Some are poor because they lack economic opportunities.
- Some are poor because they lack the skills or social skills needed to take advantage of available opportunities.
- Some may see opportunities and may have the requisite skills, but they lack access to the resources (social connections, land, capital, and/or infrastructure) needed to take advantage of opportunities.
- Otherwise functioning households may be pushed into poverty because of the impact of unforeseen shocks such as natural disasters, health crises, and the like.
- Unstable governments and dysfunctional public policies have contributed to the poverty of millions.

If the problem of poverty were easily solved, the many organizations and thousands of people working to reduce it would have solved the problem.

---

7. Lister, *Poverty*.

How Is Poverty Overcome?

I find value in turning to the scriptures for strategies to overcome poverty. In particular, I would like to consider the case of the Zoramite poor. Alma and Amulek's approach is found in Alma 32–35. These chapters are often cited for their discussion of faith and the Atonement, both of which are clearly important. However, they also include important guidance on addressing poverty.

As noted previously, the Zoramite poor wanted Alma to teach them how they could worship God since they were excluded from the synagogue. Alma explained that it was possible to worship outside the synagogue, as well as on days other than "the Lord's day." He urged them to experiment with the "word" he was teaching and simply desire to believe. He promised they would begin to see a change in themselves. It would begin to enlarge their souls and enlighten their understanding. When that happened they would recognize the seed/word was good. If they then nourished it with faith, it would grow and eventually bear fruit. Alma said, "[Your] understanding doth begin to be enlightened, and your mind doth begin to expand" (32:34).

Alma urged the Zoramites to look forward with faith. "Nourish the tree as it beginneth to grow, by your faith with great diligence, and with patience, looking forward to the fruit" (32:41). And Alma promised his listeners, "Ye shall reap the rewards of your faith, and your diligence, and patience, and long-suffering, waiting for the tree to bring forth fruit unto you" (32:43).

The Zoramites then asked how they should begin to exercise their faith. Alma urged them to plant "the word," a desire to believe in Christ, in their hearts and then nourish it with their faith.

Amulek then spoke and said that Alma "hath spoken somewhat unto you to prepare your minds; yea, and he hath exhorted you unto faith and to patience—Yea, even that ye would have so much faith as even to plant the word in your hearts, that ye may try the experiment of its goodness" (Alma 34:3–4). Next he taught of the Atonement of Christ, the need for repentance, of justice and mercy, and the reality of a final judgment. Then he urged continual prayer, with the expectation that those prayers would be answered (see vv. 19–27). In verses 27 and 28 he taught:

Cry unto the Lord, let your hearts be full, drawn out in prayer unto him continually for your welfare, and also for the welfare of those who are around you.

After ye have done all these things, if ye turn away the needy, and the naked, and visit not the sick and afflicted, and impart of your substance, if ye have, to those who stand in need—I say unto you, if ye do not any of these things, behold, your prayer is vain, and availeth you nothing, and ye are as hypocrites who do deny the faith. (Alma 34:27–28)

This last admonition to pray for others and care for the poor seems to assume that the prayers identified in the earlier passages would be answered, that the people would begin to be lifted out of poverty and would have sufficient that they can render aid and minister to others.

The gospel taught by Alma and Amulek offers hope, not just of an eventual salvation in some future life but hope for more immediate tomorrows. It lifts the soul, expands the mind, and helps people look with optimism to the future. The gospel prepares the mind for both spiritual and temporal improvement.

Alma and Amulek first addressed the lack of hope among the Zoramites. They offered a vision for the future, with the promise that if the Zoramites would even "desire to believe," that desire would begin to change their way of thinking. Their minds would be expanded, their understanding enlightened. This is the effect of the gospel on people who hear the word and honestly try the experiment. However, the principle has greater application. What the poor often lack is hope, as expressed in Ruth Lister's list defining poverty. The beginning of leaving poverty is the seed of hope and the seedling of faith that a better future is possible.

All of those who accepted the teachings of Alma and Amulek were driven out of their land and into deeper poverty by the Zoramite leaders. The impoverished Zoramites turned to their neighbors in the land of Jershon and the converted Lamanites, now called the people of Ammon. "[The people in Jershon] did receive all the poor of the Zoramites that came over unto them; and they did nourish them, and did clothe them, and did give unto them lands for their inheritance; and they did administer unto them according to their wants" (Alma 35:9).

Realization of temporal improvement for the poor will come fully and completely only if the poor have access to the knowledge and resources they need to act on their new aspirations. Both require the willingness of those who have more to "impart of their substance" to educate and to provide opportunities to the poor. The people of Ammon demonstrated this principle by their willingness to provide short-term and immediate aid (food and clothing), access to resources so the Zoramites could become self-reliant (land), and other (unspecified) mentoring and support "according to their wants," meaning according to their needs. (See 3 Nephi 6:12 for the same principle acting in reverse.) Eventually, it even became necessary for the Nephites to defend the newly converted Zoramites from the anger of the community from which they had been expelled.

Where to Start in Eliminating Individual Poverty

Drawing on the Zoramite experience, and the broader anti-poverty work around the world, eliminating poverty requires that we take the following actions:

1. Feed the hungry, clothe the naked, and administer to their immediate needs.
2. Give them hope for the future (including security and an expectation they will reap the rewards from their efforts to provide for themselves).
3. Provide opportunities for education and personal development as needed.
4. Encourage those who have to provide access to resources needed by the poor to become self-reliant and fully engaged with the community.
5. Encourage the poor, as they become more self-reliant, to choose to serve and lift others in the same way they were lifted.

And as discussed below:

6. Communities must establish networks for support to overcome the effects of disasters, large and small, natural and man-made.

7. Stable and reasonably efficient governments must assure peace and the security of equitable and effective administration.

This pattern will not lift everyone out of poverty. Some who struggle with disabilities may never be able to take advantage of opportunities. We must continue to feed, clothe, and minister to them in charity.

If poverty is to be eradicated, effective solutions must focus on both the physical and social aspects of poverty. Residents of Zion must have access to adequate material goods and economic opportunities, and they must feel part of the community, empowered to pursue their dreams and engage with their neighbors as equals.

Because poverty and its causes are multi-dimensional, a single strategy will not succeed in eliminating poverty from a society. But several successful approaches can be highlighted.

First, immediate deprivation and suffering must be addressed. Whether it be food, clothing, shelter, or urgent medical needs, systems must be put in place to address the immediate and hopefully short-term needs. The welfare system of The Church of Jesus Christ of Latter-day Saints provides one example of such a system. That system includes food production, storage, and distribution. Food supplies are augmented by donation and distribution centers for used clothing and other household goods that are offered to the needy without charge and to the public at low cost. And Church members make regular cash contributions which are used by local authorities to meet other needs.

However, the Church's welfare system is not designed or intended to provide long-term assistance, except in rare circumstances. The immediate relief of suffering does not lift people out of poverty. To achieve that goal, longer-term strategies are required that address the root causes of poverty. Such strategies will require the creativity and energy of all the residents of Zion in a concerted effort to achieve the goal. And there is a massive mountain to climb: the challenge of scale.

Global Poverty and Individual Action

When the solutions to poverty appear to be most effective at the level of individuals and families, how can poverty be eliminated when there are many millions in poverty? In even the wealthiest countries,

5 to 10 percent of the population is considered poor. In the developing world, 75 to 80 percent of people live in poverty. The World Bank estimates that about 8 percent of the world's population lives in poverty. That translates into hundreds of millions of people. What can be done on such a scale?

Aid programs struggle just to meet the most immediate needs for food, shelter, and emergency medical needs, and they often fail while tens of thousands suffer and die. Such aid efforts are essential, but as I noted at the outset, providing food does not in itself lift someone out of poverty.

At the scale of world poverty and given the unique contexts of each culture and the individualized challenges each family faces with only their current knowledge and resources, there is no universal program that will address poverty on a global basis.

I believe the answer is for individuals and families to take what action they can at the scale available to them. A single family may have only a limited effect on global poverty, but they can have a noticeable effect on many lives. We can look to exemplars who have acted on a local scale initially but who have also had a much broader impact on their communities. By small and simple means—in this case ordinary people inspired to do good—the Lord works miracles and brings about His purposes, including the elimination of poverty.

By the early 1980s, China had implemented a nationwide policy limiting couples to one child per family. The objective was to reduce the growth rate of the country's population. But because of the cultural preference for male children, the policy also resulted in a sharp increase in children placed in orphanages, in children abandoned, and even infanticide of baby girls.[8]

What do you do if you find an abandoned baby? In 1972, Lou Xiaoying of Zhejiang Province was surviving by collecting and recycling rubbish. She came across a baby girl lying in the rubbish piled on the street. Not only did she rescue the baby, but she also took the child home and raised her. This was the first of more than thirty babies she found and rescued. A number of the children were given to friends

---

8. Kenneth Pletcher, "One-child Policy: Chinese Government Program," in *Encyclopaedia Britannica*, 2022, https://www.britannica.com/topic/one-child-policy.

and family. But Lou Xiaoying, her husband, and their one biological daughter devoted their lives to caring for abandoned babies. The last was a baby boy she rescued when she was eighty-two.

Even in her extreme poverty, she said, "I realized I had a real love of caring for children. I realized if we had strength enough to collect garbage how could we not recycle something as important as human lives?"[9]

Julia Nompi Mavimbela, born in 1917, was a native of South Africa, living most of her life in Soweto. She fought hard to obtain an education and was a noted teacher and principal. In 1955 her husband, John, was killed in an automobile accident. Evidence at the scene suggested that the other person involved, a white man, had veered into John's lane. The white police officers said that Blacks are poor drivers, so John was responsible for the crash. One of Julia's greatest trials was to overcome the bitterness and anger toward the man who had caused the accident, the policemen who had lied, and the court system that had deemed her husband responsible.[10]

Julia was a trained and effective teacher. Her subject was English, but when the government forbad teaching, speaking, or reading English, she was out of work. Further, the 1970s ban aggravated the unrest in Soweto. When Julia saw children loitering in the streets aimlessly, she thought, "What can I do to help this situation?" She couldn't open a school without running afoul of the authorities. She determined instead to train children to use their hands, eyes, and minds. In an effort to seek healing for herself and her community, Julia decided to teach children to love working in the soil and established a community garden.

She taught them: "Let us dig the soil of bitterness, throw in a seed of love, and see what fruits it can give us. . . . Love will not come without forgiving others. I knew deep in my heart I was breaking up the soil of my own bitterness as I forgave those who had hurt me."[11]

---

9. Daily Mail, "The Truly Inspiring Story of the Chinese Rubbish Collector Who Saved and Raised Thirty Babies Abandoned at the Roadside," DailyMail.com, 2012, https://www.dailymail.co.uk/news/article-2181017/Lou-Xiaoying-Story-Chinese-woman-saved-30–abandoned-babies-dumped-street-trash.html.
10. Matthew Heiss, "Healing the Beloved Country: The Faith of Julia Mavimbela," *Ensign*, July 2017.
11. Heiss, "Healing the Beloved Country: The Faith of Julia Mavimbela."

Her first challenge was to find a piece of ground. She was granted permission to use a parcel filled with old cars and negotiated to have the cars removed. After an initial tilling of the ground, she and the children started to work the garden. The poor soil and drought caused challenges, but each was in turn overcome.

Julia began to have the children bring notebooks and pencils. Everything planted in the garden had to be written down in the books, so after working for a few hours, the children sat and practiced writing while Julia introduced them to English words.

At harvest time, the children took home food to their families but also took a portion to a center that cared for white disabled children. The children were taught that self-reliance includes service.

People began to notice Julia's efforts, and other communities called on Julia to help them establish gardens. Eventually, her garden-literacy program included 783 branches through independent churches.

Julia went on to join The Church of Jesus Christ of Latter-day Saints, founded a women's club and a youth group, and became the president of the National Council of African Women. She was co-national president of Women for Peace, an organization with 15,000 women of all racial backgrounds. In 1991, she was elected vice-president of the National Council of Women for South Africa.[12]

The recognition she received was well-deserved, but the truly valuable contribution was the example she set. Despite her personal pain and loss, she asked, "What can I do to help this situation?" And she took action, initially on a very small scale, to make a difference. Teaching a handful of children self-reliance through gardening and literacy may not have seemed like much in the beginning. But through one individual's effort, great things were accomplished, and great examples touched and lifted hundreds.

Another powerful example is José María Arizmendiarrieta, a journalist during the Spanish Civil War. Following the war he became a Catholic priest, and in 1941 at the age of twenty-six, he was assigned to the Basque village of Mondragón, Spain. The community and surrounding area were deeply impoverished and fractured by civil war. José's

---

12. "Julia Numpi Mavimbela," Obituary, *Church News* (Salt Lake City, UT), August 12, 2000.

first efforts to lift the community included civic and cultural initiatives, including a soccer field, a medical clinic, and a housing complex for workers. He also began to educate young workers through study circles.

In 1943, José created a technical school. He worked with a small group who began pursuing long-distance degrees in engineering. By 1956, five members who had finished their degrees joined together to launch a cooperative company that produced kerosene heaters. More industrial co-ops were started in the region, drawing workers from the technical school and collaborating with one another to share expertise. This was the beginning of the Mondragon cooperative, now one of the largest cooperatives in the world.[13]

Nick Romeo observes that the growth of the co-ops followed a pattern.

> An obstacle would confront local workers, and a new co-op would be created to overcome it. When, in 1958, the Spanish Ministry of Labor excluded the new worker-owners from the national social-security system, arguing that they were not eligible for workers' benefits because they were also part-owners, Arizmendiarrieta created an internal pension and health-care system that was itself organized as a coöperative. . . . To meet the need for affordable financing, Arizmendiarrieta organized a coöperative bank.[14]

The Mondragon Corporation now exists as a voluntary association of ninety-five autonomous cooperatives. Much has been written about Mondragon, although not all of it is positive. In recent years, criticisms suggest that in expanding internationally, it is moving away from its cooperative roots.

Latter-day Saint authors have before pointed to Mondragon and other cooperatives as potential models for economic organization in a Zion society. Dean May, for example, mentioned Mondragon in his

---

13. Nick Romeo, "How Mondragon Became the World's Largest Co-op," *The New Yorker*, August 27, 2022, https://www.newyorker.com/business/currency/how-mondragon-became-the-worlds-largest-co-op.
14. Romeo, "How Mondragon Became the World's Largest Co-op."

essay on the economics of Zion.[15] Lucas and Woodworth devote an entire chapter to a discussion of Mondragon.[16]

I wish to emphasize two points from this example. First, a lone individual who recognized a need, and took action to address the need, made a monumental difference in the lives of those in the Mondragón region. The economic effects were not realized overnight. It took over a decade for his initial efforts to result in the first cooperative. The human effects were realized more quickly in bringing hope and a vision of future possibilities to those he worked with.

The second point worth serious attention is the potential for cooperative ventures to raise people out of poverty. In this, I agree with Lucas and Woodworth. Cooperative ventures, based loosely around the example of the Nauvoo House organization (see Doctrine and Covenants 124), are unlike common businesses. These ventures are owned and operated with the intent of lifting cooperative members. Their purpose is not to focus on profits and growth, but to build self-reliance and improvement among the members of the co-op.

There are many examples of cooperatives created to meet different needs, ranging from agricultural cooperatives with well-known names including Sunkist Growers, Inc.,[17] and Land O'Lakes.[18] The latest annual report of the National Cooperative Business Association reports 238 cooperative members in the United States, in industries ranging from agricultural production to electric utilities, and from banking and credit unions to housing. As with Mondragon, some of the largest cooperatives are not in the United States.

Yet another exemplary model comes from India. Ela Ramesh Bhatt was born September 7, 1933, in Ahmedabad, India. After graduating from law school, she joined the legal department of India's largest labor union for textile workers. But that union represented workers employed by textile-producing firms, and in India at the time, many textile workers were self-employed and not eligible to join the

15. Dean L. May, "The Economics of Zion," *Sunstone* 1990, no. August (1990).
16. James W. Lucas and Warner P. Woodworth, *Working Toward Zion: Principles of the United Order for the Modern World* (Salt Lake City, UT: Aspen Books, 1996).
17. "About Us," www.sunkist.com.
18. "Our Company," www.landolakes.com.

union. The traditional union simply did not address the needs of such indigent workers. In 1972, Bhatt started a new labor union: the Self-Employed Women's Association (SEWA).

> SEWA's primary goals included full employment and self-reliance of its members. The union considered local-level organizing by its members to be the primary means of achieving those goals, which helped alleviate poverty and facilitate development. As a result, SEWA members were organized locally into workers' cooperatives, producers' groups, rural savings and credit groups, and social security groups. Although many of the groups were organized by occupation, they also addressed other issues, including education, housing, health care, childcare, and violence against women.
>
> SEWA provided training to its members and ran a bank that provided access to savings and credit for members. Because of their poverty, employment status, and illiteracy, members had been unable to gain access to such services in other ways.[19]

SEWA grew to include hundreds of thousands of members in a variety of occupations.

Here again, Ela Bhatt went on to receive numerous recognitions and opportunities to serve her country and the world. But it is her example of individual action I wish to emphasize. She saw a need and recognized that she could join with others to address that need. Two quotes from interviews she granted serve to reinforce some of the points I am trying to make:

> I would say that the basic needs and problems of the poor will not be solved by the government, any government. They will have to be solved by the people themselves.[20]

---

19. Risa Whitson, "Self-Employed Women's Association," in *Encyclopaedia Britannica*, 2018, https://www.britannica.com/topic/Self-Employed-Womens-Association.

20. Ela Bhatt, "Interview with Ela Bhatt," interview by Geoffrey Jones, *Creating Emerging Markets—Oral History Collection*, 2017, https://www.hbs.edu/creating-emerging-markets/Documents/transcripts/Bhatt_Ela.pdf.

Poverty is powerlessness. Poverty cannot be removed unless the poor have power to make decisions that affect their lives.[21]

My final example is more recent. Scott Miller grew up in a suburb of Rochester, New York. When he was in college, his friend asked him to volunteer at a homeless shelter. Scott was shocked by what he experienced there. He had never realized there were people in his community who struggled for food and shelter.

After graduating from Kent State University, he worked for a social services agency in Ohio. However, he became increasingly frustrated by the lack of a long-term plan for poor families. "They would get financial assistance and maybe, if they were lucky, 30 minutes of counseling and then be referred somewhere else," he says. "It was a Swiss cheese system."[22]

Scott wanted to develop long-term solutions for people in poverty. In 1992 he co-founded Move the Mountain Leadership Center. Scott and his colleagues spent ten years listening to people in poverty and experimenting with programs. Eventually, with the help of community and state agencies, as well a grant from the Annie E. Casey Foundation, they established Circles USA. According to their website, "The term Circles was coined to represent the relational approach of getting people off welfare and into jobs through peer support from middle-income volunteers."[23]

The essence of the Circles USA approach is mentoring. Middle and upper-income volunteers (called allies) are teamed with low-income families (called leaders) seeking to leave poverty for good. Two or three allies are matched to each leader family. One ally may provide tutoring in budgeting and family financial management, while another may help make connections to community groups. The needs of each leader family are assessed and appropriate mentoring links

---

21. "Ela Bhatt," 2022, accessed February 4, 2023, https://theelders.org/profile/ela-bhatt.

22. Phuong Ly, *Personal Attention Reduces Poverty* (Palo Alto, CA: Stanford Social Innovation Review, 2012), https://ssir.org/articles/entry/personal_attention_reduces_poverty#.

23. "Circles USA Is the Result of More than 20 Years of Research," CirclesUSA.org, 2022, accessed February 4, 2023, https://www.circlesusa.org/about/history/.

established. These relationships will endure for twelve to eighteen months or longer.

President Gordon B. Hinckley taught that new members of the Church need three things: sound doctrine, a calling and a friend.[24] Circles USA is demonstrating that a similar pattern is needed to help families exit poverty: good principles, a purpose and a friend that can be called on for advice and support.

Circles USA is growing. At this writing it has seventy affiliates in twenty-two states. Mentoring is a demonstrated success story for supporting families seeking to leave poverty behind.

These examples of individual action in response to perceived community needs demonstrate that a small group of dedicated individuals can initiate significant change in many lives. Zion consists of the pure in heart, Saints committed to the five-fold foundation of Zion. As they cooperate and act together based on the principles of Zion, poverty will be eliminated.

Where to Start in Eliminating Global Poverty

We can draw a number of lessons from these examples. Again, let me stress that I am not offering any silver bullets. But that does not reduce the importance of these lessons

1. Individuals who see a need in their community and take action can make a meaningful difference.
2. As the effect of their efforts is recognized, others will be influenced to join them.
3. Collaboration and cooperation can have large impacts.

Poverty has multiple dimensions, including both inadequate material means and the emotional harms that result from social exclusion and isolation. Similarly, poverty has multiple causes, depending on the cultural and economic environment of the family and their unique life experiences.

There is no single "program" that will lift all people out of poverty, but there are principles which, when applied creatively to a given

---

24. Gordon B. Hinckley, "Converts and Young Men," *Ensign*, May 1997.

context, have demonstrated a powerful connection to poverty reduction and elimination.

The first principle is to inspire hope for the future. Ideally, that hope comes from an understanding and acceptance of the gospel of Jesus Christ. But hope also comes from seeing realistic opportunities for education and improvement.

I am reminded of the account given by one of my university colleagues of an evaluation he did of a program targeting recently divorced women in the western United States. In that context and time period, divorce nearly always resulted in women becoming instantly poor, with limited means to support themselves and any children still at home. In many instances, these women either had never been in the workforce or had been out of it for many years. The program was intended to give them minimal job skills in order to qualify them for entry-level employment.

The evaluation revealed that the participants were staying in the program much longer than anticipated. Interviews with participants revealed the reason. Their exposure to educational opportunities had given them hope and a broader vision for their future. They no longer wanted entry-level positions; they wanted to be the boss. They stayed in the educational program to gain additional skills to make higher opportunities possible.

The beginning of poverty elimination is hope for the future grounded in recognizing real opportunities. Building on this foundation of hope, the second principle is to provide an alternative life model, a vision and understanding of how people who are not poor live their lives. That alternative life model is not a single image. It might involve developing household financial management skills for some households, resumé preparation, or work-related behavior expectations. In other contexts it may include basic sanitation practices, acquisition of a second language or other formal education, or development of a technical skill. The alternative life model will vary with the culture and context.

This is not a quick-fix solution for poverty. As with the Mondragón community and Circle USA participants, this is a long-term investment that may take years to fully lift people out of poverty. But it is an essential step in the process.

The third principle that I see in many successful efforts to reduce or eliminate poverty is cooperative action by the poor themselves, often in concert with non-poor individuals and organizations. Whether it be pooling resources to buy goods on a larger scale and lower price, or actually forming cooperative ventures to create a store or manufacturing firm, recognizing the benefits of cooperative action is vital for poverty elimination.

The fourth principle addresses the social integration of the poor. Circle USA assigns a group of "allies" to befriend the "leader." For the Zoramite poor, it was the converted Lamanites in Jershon who "did administer unto [the Zoramites] according to their wants [needs]" (Alma 35:9). To fully escape poverty, people need to be integrated into and fully participating in the broader society as equals. The principle is that the non-poor segments of society will welcome those emerging from poverty and grant them equal status within the community.

Some might call it social mobility. The scriptures represent it as the elimination of class distinctions. As Jacob taught the Nephites, "Think of your brethren like unto yourselves, and be familiar with all and free with your substance, that they may be rich like unto you" (Jacob 2:17).

In combination, these four principles require that if poverty is to be eliminated, the rich must open their hearts and their pocketbooks and lift the poor by making resources and social connections available to those who have less. This does not imply an obligation to sell all that we have and donate to the poor, but it does imply that we "be familiar with all and free with [our] substance" (Jacob 2:17).

Luke recounts the Savior's parable of a rich man who had an exceptional harvest. With no place to store his bounty, he tore down his barns and built larger ones, planning to live for years on his wealth. The Lord called him a fool because that very night he died (see Luke 12:13–34). I don't think the Savior was condemning saving for the future. He was condemning "saving" more than we need when others around us are in want.

Under normal circumstances, these principles will effectively eliminate poverty over time. However, they are insufficient in the face of personal or widespread disasters. Disease and death can devastate a family and push otherwise self-reliant families into poverty. Natural disasters can wreak havoc on whole communities. War and civil strife have destroyed the security and livelihoods of millions. Zion cannot ignore the remaining two causes of poverty identified earlier: personal disasters and ineffective government.

Planning and Preparing for Personal Disasters

Families can be pushed into poverty by personal disasters. Some crises are very particular, such as the illness or death of family members, especially breadwinners. Others are more widespread, such as flooding, earthquakes, or tornados. Still others are man-made, such as industrial plant closures or economic recessions. Whatever the cause, the immediate result is that otherwise self-reliant families are forced into poverty at least temporarily.

If poverty is to be eliminated in Zion, there must be systems in place to address personal crises that overwhelm the capacity of the family or individual to respond and weather such challenges. While a Zion society may be able to avoid most, or even all, the man-made disasters (a rather questionable assumption), there is no reason to expect all natural disasters and personal health challenges to be eradicated.

Following the pattern set forth in the welfare program of The Church of Jesus Christ of Latter-day Saints, families are expected to be self-reliant to the extent possible. This implies forethought and preparation to deal with potential challenges. As discussed previously, such prior preparations may require teaching and mentoring to help families understand both the why and the how of prudent methodical preparation.

Thus, the first line of defense in responding to a crisis is the family itself. If adequate response is beyond their means or immediate capacity, the extended family in Zion provides the next level of support, whether it be food, shelter, or financial or emotional support.

Depending on the nature of the crisis, the capacity of extended families may be overwhelmed as well. Consequently, prudent advance preparation will involve joining together with other families in mutual insurance pools. Such pooling and risk sharing may be based on geography as in the county-level mutual property and casualty insurance ventures in North Dakota and other parts of the Midwest. Or the pooling may be based on the type of risk such as marine insurance, one of the oldest forms of insurance.

Individuals and families seeking to protect themselves from potential losses join together to create an insurance pool, owned by the members of the venture. The objective is not profit, but protection against significant loss as specified in the membership documentation. Such firms are common in today's world (such as mutual insurance companies). However, they are often so large that the connection between individual members and overall management may seem quite remote.

Insurance may also seem like a poor investment. By paying a premium, it may seem that the family is betting there will be a crisis that will require them to file a claim, while the insurance company is betting there will be no significant loss. If the company has the policy priced appropriately, the company nearly always appears to win.

A more productive way to approach insurance in Zion is to view insurance as loving neighbors pooling their resources to share life's risks. A given family may never experience a loss that results in a significant claim. In such a case, that family can view with gratitude the opportunity they have to help their neighbors in need.

One recent interesting approach to insurance is provided by Laka.co, a cooperative bicycle insurance venture. Laka characterizes its operations as "a team that looks out for each other." Laka does not charge a fixed "premium." According to their website, "We calculate your monthly contributions—up to a max capped amount—based on the collective's claims." Eighty percent of the "contributions" are paid out in claims.[25] The remainder is used for administrative costs. There is an expectation that members will care for themselves and their equipment appropriately and that people will act to minimize the burden placed on other team members. So far, this cooperative team approach is receiving high praise from participants. Whether the approach can be scaled or transferred to other risk domains is worth exploring.

Even large insurance companies can at times face losses that threaten their financial stability. Major natural disasters such as

---

25. "It pays to be part of the pack" (Laka.co, 2023, https://laka.co/gb).

hurricanes or the type of widespread wildfires seen in Canada, the western United States, and Australia in recent years offer examples. To protect themselves from such events, insurance companies buy insurance from other insurance companies. This practice is known as reinsurance and is quite common. It is also common for companies to appeal to the largest pool for ultimate protection: the tax-paying public through government programs.

Insurance is a complex undertaking, and the discussion here has undoubtedly glossed over important considerations. My point is simply that avoiding poverty induced by disasters requires prior preparation in terms of planning and the formation of mutual alliances that can respond quickly and effectively when the need arises. Self-reliant families will take precautions. When disasters occur, help should be available from the extended family in Zion. In the event of larger crises, neighbors may be called upon for immediate labor and resources (such as sandbags to stave off flooding). Cooperatives may pitch in to help their members or other cooperatives with whom they have a reciprocal support agreement. Mutual insurance ventures may spread the risks even more widely.

Safety nets to support families in times of crisis can be designed and implemented, but families need to take action to prepare in advance and to the extent possible. More problematic are the effects of ineffective and even destructive government policies.

Good Governance and Poverty Reduction

Scriptural accounts linking government and poverty generally focus on the personal righteousness of rulers and the resulting impact on their subjects. When kings and rulers are righteous (such as Benjamin and Mosiah in the Book of Mormon and Hezekiah and Jehoshaphat in the Bible), the rights of the people are protected, and a significant proportion of the population is also righteous.

When the wicked rule, the people mourn (see Doctrine and Covenants 98:9). The pattern that unrighteous rulers follow is repeated multiple times in scripture. Unrighteousness is grounded in pride on the ruler's part, which spreads to the ruling class. This pride leads to greater class distinctions, increased taxes to support a more lavish lifestyle, and greater oppression, especially of the poor. Examples of this pattern are found in the accounts of King Noah in the Book of Mormon and King Ahab in the Bible.

Scriptural admonitions regarding the poor focus on individual acts of generosity and ministering, not on public policies. To be sure, humility and righteousness among the ruling class influence all of society, including the poor. But it is also the case that government policies and practices affect poverty levels and the persistence of poverty more directly.

Much of the research on poverty reduction has focused on sub-Saharan Africa because such a high percentage of the world's poorest countries are in Africa. For example, Jeffrey Sachs's research on poverty reduction in Africa has identified five key elements for reducing rural poverty. He calls for international donors to achieve these elements. While the resources to meet these needs may come from outside a country, their lack reflects a fundamental failure on the part of the existing government to formulate and carry out effective policies that impact the poor. The five key elements include:

- Agricultural inputs such as fertilizer, improved seeds, green manures, and cover crops, etc.
- Investments in basic health
- Investments in education
- Improved power, transport, and communications services
- Safe drinking water and sanitation[26]

In their book *Why Nations Fail*, Daron Acemoglu and James Robinson argue that the root cause of extensive poverty is institutional. From their perspective, to overcome poverty social institutions must be inclusive, meaning that they allow and encourage participation by the great mass of people in economic activities that make best use of their talents and skills, and enable individuals to make the choices they wish.

To be inclusive, economic institutions must feature secure private property, an unbiased system of law, and a provision of public services that provides a level playing field in which people can exchange and contract. They also must permit the entry of new businesses and allow

---

26. Jeffrey D. Sachs, *The End of Poverty: Economic Possibilities for Our Time* (New York, NY: Penguin, 2006).

people to choose their careers.[27] Wayne Grudem and Barry Asmus also include "Laws that give protection and positive economic incentives to stable family structures" as one of the factors that help nations overcome poverty.[28]

Economic institutions and a country's poverty levels are influenced by the quality of governance. Djeneba Doumbia examined the connection between the quality of governance in sub-Saharan Africa and poverty reduction. She reached four conclusions:

1. The combination of political, economic, and institutional features of good governance, especially the control of corruption and regulatory quality, improves the income of the poor and decreases poverty. Good governance, as embodied, for example, in the control of corruption and the design and implementation of effective regulatory policies, significantly improves the ability of the poor to participate in and benefit from economic growth.

2. As countries improve the control of corruption in government, the impact on poverty reduction accelerates.

3. Two aspects of governance quality are particularly important for fostering inclusive economic growth: the ability of governments to adopt and implement effective policies and the rule of law. Fostering inclusive growth requires the effective implementation of government policies and the existence of institutions that make possible a fair distribution of the benefits from economic growth.

4. Enhancing human capital development through improved access to health care, education, and nutrition (especially for children); developing infrastructure; and advancing the financial sector are all key drivers for both poverty reduction and inclusive growth.[29]

---

27. Daron Acemoglu and James A. Robinson, *Why Nations Fail: The Origins of Power, Prosperity, and Poverty* (New York, NY: Crown Business, 2012), 74–75.
28. Barry Asmus and Wayne Grudem, *The Poverty of Nations: A Sustainable Solution* (Wheaton, IL: Crossway, 2013), 256–57.
29. Djeneba Doumbia, "The Quest for Pro-poor and Inclusive Growth: The Role of Governance," *Applied Economics* 51, no. 16 (2019), https://doi.org/10.1080/

Based on a literature review of more than 400 academic papers, a recent study by the UNDP[30] Oslo Governance Centre and the German Development Institute found empirical evidence from across the globe that investing in accountable, transparent, and inclusive governance will facilitate the reduction of poverty and inequality.[31]

Good governance is essential, but government policies, however well designed and implemented, are not enough to eliminate poverty. Jindra and Vaz surveyed households in seventy-one countries and found that while good governance is an important factor in reducing poverty, it is not sufficient.[32]

Eric Beinhocker argues that there is a significant cultural component to widespread poverty. He defines culture as "the emergent product of the micro rules of behavior followed by individuals. . . . In the case of nations, the rules or norms of behavior aren't merely acted out by thousands, but are acted out by millions."[33]

While acknowledging that there is no one cultural formula for economic success, Beinhocker places cultural norms that promote poverty reduction into three broad categories.

- Norms that relate to individual behavior. Economically successful cultures, in this view, support a strong work ethic, individual accountability, and a belief that each person is the protagonist in their own life. They also strike a balance between optimism that improvement is possible, and realism about the current situation.
- Norms that relate to cooperative behavior. Foremost is the

00036846.2018.1529392.

30. United Nations Development Programme.
31. Cameron Allen, *Connections that Matter: How the Quality of Governance Institutions May Be the Booster Shot We Need to Reduce Poverty and Inequality* (Oslo, Norway: United Nations Development Programme, Oslo Governance Centre, 2022).
32. Christoph Jindra and Ana Vaz, "Good Governance and Multidimensional Poverty: A Comparative Analysis of 71 Countries," *Governance* 32, no. 4, 2019.
33. Eric D. Beinhocker, *The Origin of Wealth: Evolution, Complexity, and the Radical Remaking of Economics* (Boston, MA: Harvard Business Press, 2006), 429.

belief that there is a positive payoff for all in cooperation. Such cultures also value generosity and fairness while sanctioning those who cheat and take advantage.

- Norms that relate to innovation. Cultures that look to rational scientific explanations of the world rather than religious or magical explanations tend to be more innovative, in Beinhocker's view. He argues that overly egalitarian cultures reduce incentives for risk taking and therefore are less innovative.[34]

I question Beinhocker's conclusion that norms supporting innovation require a rejection of religion. I place my hope in human curiosity, the five foundation stones of Zion, and Zion's commitment to the well-being of all.

Beinhocker also suggests that one norm is important for all three categories: how people view time. "Cultures that have an ethic of investing for tomorrow tend to value work, have high intergenerational savings rates, demonstrate a willingness to sacrifice short-term pleasures for long-term gain, and enjoy high levels of cooperation."[35]

Government policies are nearly always an outgrowth of culture, not the other way around. Changing attitudes and behaviors on a wide-scale basis will only happen if it is approached on a micro, or individual household, basis as described above.

Based on the five foundation stones in a Zion society, people will live together in righteousness and unity. To achieve such a condition, especially as it relates to the elimination of poverty, it is important to remember that policies adopted and implemented by government affect the range of choices available to individuals and families, and their ability to make and act on those choices. We ought not to wait for the establishment of Zion to pursue public policies and institutional improvements that will support the reduction of poverty and inequality in our communities.

---

34. Beinhocker, *The Origin of Wealth*, 430.
35. Beinhocker, *The Origin of Wealth*, 431.

Summary on Poverty Elimination

In this chapter I have attempted to sketch the basic outlines of what a Zion society must do to eliminate poverty. The elements I have suggested arise from the five foundation stones of Zion and are consistent with an overall plan to promote human development and happiness.

1. The poor are children of God with the same aspirations, needs and rights as all other members of Zion. Their poverty is rooted in causes specific to their unique situation. Creating a pathway out of poverty requires adaptation to their specific needs.

2. "The poor shall be exalted in that the rich are made low" (see Doctrine and Covenants 104:16). I take this to mean that those who have more must voluntarily and willingly share their knowledge, connections, and means to make available to the poor the full range of resources needed to escape all aspects of poverty.

3. Success in eliminating poverty will require cooperative action from all inhabitants of Zion.

4. Universal government programs cannot eradicate poverty, but effective governance is essential to create a stable, enabling environment as the poor take the actions necessary to change their lives.

CHAPTER 9

Land in Zion

In Margaret Mitchell's *Gone with the Wind*, Scarlett O'Hara's father, outraged when Scarlett rejects the idea of owning a plantation, shouts: "Land is the only thing in the world that amounts to anything, for 'tis the only thing in this world that lasts, and don't you be forgetting it! 'Tis the only thing worth working for, worth fighting for—worth dying for."[1]

This chapter considers the place of land in Zion and contrasts two viewpoints on land. The first is reflected in Gerald O'Hara's outraged shout and in a short story by Leo Tolstoy. The second offers an alternative view that places land at the center of many of God's covenants with His children but requires quite a different perspective.

In Robert Ardrey's 1966 book, *The Territorial Imperative*,[2] Ardrey argues that humans have an innate drive to acquire land and defend their territory. He cites examples from many studies of animal behavior involving territoriality and extends these findings to humans. Ardrey seemed to support Gerald O'Hara when he wrote:

---

1. Margarett Mitchell, *Gone with the Wind*, Macmillan and Co., Ltd., 1957 (Originally published 1936), 39.
2. Robert Ardrey, *The Territorial Imperative: A personal inquiry into the animal origins of property and nations* (New York: Atheneum, 1966).

Man is as much a territorial animal as is a mockingbird singing in the clear California night. We act as we do for reasons of our evolutionary past, not our cultural present. . . . If we defend the title to our land or the sovereignty of our country, we do it for reasons no different, no less innate, no less ineradicable, than do lower animals.[3]

Long before Ardrey wrote his book, Leo Tolstoy wrote a short story entitled "How Much Land Does a Man Need?"[4] In the story, a Russian peasant named Pahom overhears a conversation between his wife and his sister-in-law. Pahom's wife defends the life of the peasant farmer, while her sister praises the advantages of life in the city. Pahom concludes that if he just owned land, his life would be secure and he would not fear even the devil himself. The devil listens in on the same conversation, perceives Pahom's boast, and takes up the challenge.

Through substantial sacrifice and no small risk, Pahom is able to purchase a small farm and is initially very happy. Soon his relationships with his neighbors deteriorate, he becomes dissatisfied with his situation, and he reasons that if he just had more land, things would be better.

At the suggestion of a passing peasant (the devil in disguise), Pahom travels some distance from his home to verify that land is cheaper in this new location. He returns home, sells all that he has, and moves his family to the new community where he can control significantly more land. Again, for a variety of reasons, his initial enjoyment erodes, and he becomes dissatisfied. Once more, he concludes that if he just owned more land, his life would be better. At the suggestion of a passing trader (again the devil in disguise), he travels hundreds of miles to where the locals are nearly giving land away.

The local chief agrees to sell Pahom as much land as he can walk around in a day for a comparatively small sum. Pahom sets out at dawn from the agreed starting point, with minimal rations and a spade for marking the land he wants. He walks quickly and soon finds himself quite a distance from the starting point. The sun is hot, his

---

3. Steven Levingston, "Meanwhile: Does Territoriality Drive Human Aggression?" *New York Times,* April 14, 1999, https://www.nytimes.com/1999/04/14/opinion/IHT-meanwhile-does-territoriality-drive-human-aggression.html.
4. Leo Tolstoy, *How Much Land Does a Man Need?* (Penguin UK, 2015; originally published in 1886).

supplies are limited, and he tires as the day progresses. Eventually he realizes that sundown is fast approaching. He is nearly exhausted and still quite a distance from the starting point. Pahom runs as quickly as he can back to the starting point, climbs the small hill, and collapses as he puts his hand on the starting point just as the sun dips below the horizon. The locals cheer, but Pahom is dead. His servant takes the spade and buries him in all the land he will ever need.

The instinct to acquire more land that Ardrey describes is manifest in both Gerald O'Hara's outraged expression and Pahom's persistent greed for more land. Whether or not it is instinctual, Gerald and Pahom share pride, greed, and self-identification in terms of the amount of land that they control. Such self-identification in terms of land and possessions is part of that state of nature described by Alma as "without God in the world" and "contrary to the nature of God." (Alma 41:11; see also Mosiah 3:19).

And yet, land is an essential component in many of God's covenants with His children. Increasingly, scholars and policymakers are recognizing that land and property are essential for the achievement of other human rights. Access to land and security of tenure are regarded as an important "means to achieve human rights, as defined by international conventions."[5] Further, it is common for people to identify with locations and even specific properties.

If this natural inclination to acquire land and define ourselves in relation to our land and possessions is "contrary to the nature of God" (Alma 41:11), why does God include land so often in His covenants with His people? How would He have us think about land? And if land is so vital for survival and development, how will land distribution, "ownership," and use function in Zion? How should we understand our predisposition to identify with the places in our lives? These are the issues considered in this chapter.

---

5. EU Task Force on Land Tenure, *EU Land Policy Guidelines*, European Commission (Brussels, 2004), 4, https://ec.europa.eu/europeaid/sites/devco/files/methodology-eu-land-policy-guidelines-200411_en_2.pdf; Jennifer C. Franco, Sofía Monsalve, and Saturnino M. Borras, "Democratic land control and human rights," *Current Opinion in Environmental Sustainability* 15 (2015).

God presents us with an alternative to the natural territorial imperative Gerald O'Hara and Pahom exhibited. In place of a self-image that relies on pride, greed, and how much we own, God offers the alternative called stewardship. This alternative shifts our focus from what we possess to how we relate to the past, the future, our community today, and to God and Christ. A Zion society based on stewardships is also likely have a different view of property rights as well.

Land Covenants

God's covenants with His people frequently include a land dimension. Land has been described as the cornerstone of the Abrahamic covenant. During the Savior's visit to the Nephites, He reiterated four different times that the Father had commanded Him to confirm to the Nephites that their land was theirs for a perpetual inheritance. Faithful Gentiles were also included in this covenant with the remnant of Israel in the Americas (see 3 Nephi 21:22–23; 2 Nephi 10:10–12, 19). As part of the restoration of the gospel, the Saints were assured a land of promise flowing with milk and honey (see Doctrine and Covenants 38:18–19).

In contrast to Gerald O'Hara and Pahom, 1 Kings 21 recounts the story of Naboth, who inherited a vineyard next to King Ahab's palace. Ahab wanted the land to extend his palace grounds.

> And Ahab spake unto Naboth, saying, Give me thy vineyard, that I may have it for a garden of herbs, because it is near unto my house: and I will give thee for it a better vineyard than it; or, if it seem good to thee, I will give thee the worth of it in money. And Naboth said to Ahab, The Lord forbid it me, that I should give the inheritance of my fathers unto thee. And Ahab came into his house heavy and displeased because of the word which Naboth the Jezreelite had spoken to him: . . . And he laid him down upon his bed, and turned away his face, and would eat no bread. (1 Kings 21:2–4)

Ahab was so upset that, with kingly majesty, he went home and pouted.

Naboth was not looking for a better deal. His relationship to his land was quite different from Pahom's. When God made covenants with Abraham and told him to leave Haran, He said that His purpose was to make Abraham a "minister to bear my name." The covenant had three components:

- "A strange land which I will give unto thy seed after thee for an everlasting possession, when they hearken to my voice" (Abraham 2:6).
- "I will make of thee a great nation" (Abraham 2:9).
- "Thy seed after thee . . . shall bear this ministry and Priesthood unto all nations" (Abraham 2:9).

These three elements of the Abrahamic covenant are reiterated throughout the Old Testament. With particular regard to land, one Old Testament scholar has observed:

> There is little doubt that the promise of the land was one of the three major elements in the Abrahamic promise (Gen. 12:7; 15:7; 18–21; 17:8; the other two being the seed and the gospel). Christopher Wright showed how this concept of the centrality of the land was so in pure statistical terms. Out of forty-six references to the promise-plan of God from Genesis to Judges, only seven of the forty-six references do not mention the land. Moreover, twenty-nine have it as the sole feature of its content (cf. Gen. 28:4).[6]

Another author and translator went so far as to describe land as the cornerstone of the Abrahamic covenant. [7]

When Moses and Joshua led the children of Israel to the promised land, the land was surveyed and then apportioned among the twelve tribes by lot, and within each tribe, land was randomly assigned by family group. Just as "the land" was given to Abraham's posterity for an "everlasting possession," these assignments were also permanent.

---

6. Walter Jr. Kaiser, "Ownership and Property in the Old Testament Economy," 2022 (2012). https://tifwe.org/resource/ownership-and-property-in-the-old-testament-economy/.
7. Harry M. Orlinsky, "The Biblical Concept of the Land of Israel: Cornerstone of the Covenant Between God and Israel," in *The Land of Israel: Jewish Perspectives*, ed. L. A. Huffman (Notre Dame, IN: University of Notre Dame Press, 1986).

In particular, the Lord instructed: "No land may be sold outright, because the land is mine, and you come to it as aliens and tenants of mine. Throughout the whole land you hold, you must allow a right of redemption over land which has been sold."[8]

"Land" in these verses refers to farmland. "Sold," as used in the second sentence, is effectively a lease in which the landholder "sells" the productive capacity of the land for up to forty-nine years.[9] The intent of this commandment and the guidelines for redemption and the related "jubilee year" provisions seem to be to keep land as an inheritance within each extended family group.[10]

Eventually, with the help of a duplicitous wife, Ahab succeeded in having Naboth killed so he could get the land. I find three useful observations from the Naboth story. First, Naboth saw the sale of his inherited land as a violation of his family's covenant with God. Second, at least Ahab felt that the land value could be established, suggesting there was some type of land market in operation. Third, absent the dishonesty of Ahab and Jezebel, law and custom did not permit Ahab to force the sale or otherwise seize the inherited land.

While selling an inheritance may have been abhorrent to Naboth, families sometimes run into economic trials and are forced to liquidate assets. In such circumstances, "investors" are often willing to "help them out." Bruce Wells cites one example:

---

8. Lev. 25:23–24, Oxford Study Bible, *The Oxford Study Bible: Revised English Bible with the Apocrypha*, ed. M. Jack Suggs, Katharine Doob Sakenfeld, and James R. Mueller (New York: Oxford University Press, 1992).

9. In the "jubilee year," all such leases are supposed to terminate and the land return to the original landholder. The landholder also has the right to redeem the land prior to the jubilee year. Houses are treated somewhat differently. Within a walled city, houses may be sold at capital value, but they must be redeemed within one year. Absent that redemption, the house becomes the permanent property of the purchaser. Property owned by Levites is treated somewhat differently. See Leviticus 25 and commentaries for a more complete discussion of redemption and inheritance.

10. While there are few indications in the Bible that the provisions of the jubilee were ever implemented, inherited land apparently had a different legal and social status. See Stephen C. Russell, "The Legal Background of the Theme of Land in the Book of Joshua," *Hebrew Studies* 59, no. 2018 (2018), https://www.jstor.org/stable/26557789.

Families who fell on hard times and had to sell inherited land retained the right to redeem it. But cunning investors found ways around this. Documents from the Late Bronze Age (c. 1550–1200 B.C.E.) site of Nuzi in Iraq, for instance, show that one particular businessman was adopted as a son by dozens of families in the area. The texts actually record discounted sales of land disguised as adoptions. People in dire straits sold their land to this man for a reduced price and adopted him into their family. In the eyes of the law, the land never left the family and thus was not eligible for redemption. Similar schemes may be the target of texts such as Mic[ah] 2:2, which condemn those who defraud others of their inheritance.[11]

Keeping land in the family was not simply a cultural artifact. Covenants are more than two-way promises. A covenant establishes a relationship between the parties, between God and man. In this case, land symbolizes the relationship between the God of Israel and His chosen people. "And I will establish my covenant between me and thee and thy seed after thee in their generations for an everlasting covenant, to be a God unto thee, and to thy seed after thee. And I will give unto thee, and to thy seed after thee, the land wherein thou art a stranger, all the land of Canaan, for an everlasting possession; and I will be their God" (Genesis 17:7–8).

Yet by the time of the Savior's mortal ministry, there was apparently an active real estate market in Judea. The Lord Himself acknowledged such markets in His parable: "Again, the kingdom of heaven is like unto treasure hid in a field; the which when a man hath found, he hideth, and for joy thereof goeth and selleth all that he hath, and buyeth that field" (Matthew 13:44).

The intent of the parable may be to communicate the joy and worth of the gospel, but the communication medium draws upon experiences that His listeners would be familiar with the buying and selling of fields. Despite the Lord's historic objections, the early Christians were both familiar with and actually engaged in the sale of real estate.

---

11. "Inheritance Laws in Ancient Israel," Bible Odyssey, Society of Biblical Literature, 2022, https://www.bibleodyssey.org/passages/related-articles/inheritance-laws-in-ancient-israel/.

Lehi and his family also entered a special covenant with God that involved land. Lehi, Ishmael, and their families (along with Zoram) left Jerusalem in 600 BC. From the outset, Laman and Lemuel were not happy about it, and one of their chief complaints was that they were being taken from the "land of their inheritance" (1 Nephi 2:11; 1 Nephi 17:21). To be sure, they were also leaving their accumulated family wealth. But even Sariah complained about having to leave "the land of [their] inheritance" when she feared that her sons had been killed, and she makes no mention of the abandoned wealth (see 1 Nephi 5:2).

Lehi's response was that he had obtained a land of promise by covenant from the Lord (see 1 Nephi 5:5; 2 Nephi 1:5). It is not clear from Nephi's record exactly when Lehi received this promise, but Nephi received a similar promise just days after the family left Jerusalem (see 1 Nephi 2:20; 1 Nephi 13:30).

After wandering in the wilderness for eight years and spending about three years in the land Bountiful, Lehi's party arrived in the promised land in about 588 BC (see 1 Nephi 18:23). Shortly before he died, Lehi gave instructions to his children regarding the land of promise, explaining that the land was consecrated for them and their posterity and all those who the Lord would lead to the land (see 2 Nephi 1:5, 7; 1 Nephi 13:11–15, 14:1–2).

In reviewing 3 Nephi, it is impossible to overlook all the references to "the land of . . . inheritance." Some relate specifically to the remnant of the seed of Jacob in the Americas. The Savior repeats the promise that had been made to earlier Nephite prophets four times. I think this qualifies as emphatic.

> And behold, this is the land of your inheritance; and the Father hath given it unto you. (3 Nephi 15:13)

> Verily, verily, I say unto you, thus hath the Father commanded me— that I should give unto this people this land for their inheritance. (3 Nephi 16:16)

> And the Father hath commanded me that I should give unto you this land, for your inheritance. (3 Nephi 20:14)

And behold, this people will I establish in this land, unto the fulfilling of the covenant which I made with your father Jacob; and it shall be a New Jerusalem. (3 Nephi 20:22)

There are also passages that relate to Israel more broadly and re-emphasize that the Lord's covenant with Israel had not been fulfilled or nullified, including the land of their inheritance. "And because I said unto you that old things have passed away, I do not destroy that which hath been spoken concerning things which are to come. For behold, the covenant which I have made with my people is not all fulfilled; but the law which was given unto Moses hath an end in me" (3 Nephi 15:7–8; see also 3 Nephi 20:13, 25).

Then the Savior explicitly restates Israel's covenant relationship to the land of their inheritance. "I have covenanted with them that I would gather them together in mine own due time, that I would give unto them again the land of their fathers for their inheritance, which is the land of Jerusalem, which is the promised land unto them forever, saith the Father" (3 Nephi 20:29; see also 3 Nephi 20:33, 46).

Regarding the Gentiles and their inheritance, the Savior teaches in 3 Nephi:

> But if they [Gentiles] will repent and hearken unto my words, and harden not their hearts, I will establish my church among them, and *they shall come in unto the covenant and be numbered among this the remnant of Jacob, unto whom I have given this land for their inheritance*; And they shall assist my people, the remnant of Jacob, and also as many of the house of Israel as shall come, that they may build a city, which shall be called the New Jerusalem. (3 Nephi 21:22–23; emphasis added; see also 3 Nephi 16:13)

From just these passages in 3 Nephi, it seems clear that a land of inheritance is still an important part of the Lord's covenant with His people. The remnant of Jacob in the Americas has been given "this land" for their inheritance, and the Gentiles may join them if they can live up to the covenants. Jerusalem is still the land of inheritance for the rest of the house of Israel, and they will be restored to that land after they accept Jesus Christ as their Savior and Redeemer.

How will this concept of land as a perpetual inheritance fit in our Zion? How will the foundation stones of Zion influence how we think about and treat land as we adjust our social institutions and establish Zion? We have two contrasting perspectives before us: the Gerald O'Hara/Pahom relationship to land on the one hand, and Naboth's on the other. Revisiting the nature of stewardships is a helpful starting point in answering these questions and understanding the Lord's preferred approach to land.

Stewards in Zion

President N. Eldon Tanner of the First Presidency testified in 1978 that we are stewards in the Lord's program and all that we call our own belongs to the Lord. "What a great spirit we would have if we would realize that all that we have to administer, all that we call our own, is the Lord's, and we have the responsibility to do it the way he would have it done. So much has been done and is to be done, and it will be done best when we follow the principles of stewardship."[12]

What does it mean to say that God owns the earth and we are only stewards? For believers in sacred writings, it is not difficult to establish that the earth belongs to God. There are a number of scriptural passages in which the Father or the Son states explicitly that They created the earth and everything on it. They created order out of unordered matter (see 2 Nephi 29:7; 3 Nephi 9:15; Doctrine and Covenants 14:9; Moses 2:1; Moses 3:4; Abraham 4:1).

Since the earth and everything on it belongs to the Lord, what does God expect of us as tenants? One key passage outlining these expectations is found in the instructions given to Joseph Smith in 1834.

> It is wisdom in me; therefore, a commandment I give unto you, that ye shall organize yourselves and appoint every man his stewardship; That every man may give an account unto me of the stewardship which is appointed unto him. For it is expedient that I, the Lord, should make every man accountable, as a steward over earthly blessings, which I have made and prepared for my creatures. (Doctrine and Covenants 104:11–13)

---

12. N. Eldon Tanner, "We Are His Stewards," *Ensign*, May, 1978.

Both the Gospels of Matthew and Luke include a parable that provides insights into the Savior's view of stewards (see Matthew 25:14–30; Luke 19:11–26). The two accounts differ in important details. In Matthew's version, the parable of the talents is given after the triumphal entry into Jerusalem, two days before Passover. The sums of money given to the three servants were large and differed based on some prior assessment of ability. Luke's account takes place on the road to Jerusalem prior to the passion week. There are initially ten servants, and the same modest sum is given to each of the ten. Despite these differences, the principles illustrated are consistent:

- Stewards are given charge of their master's assets.
- Stewards have discretion to act as they see fit.
- Stewards are expected to pursue their master's interests, not their own.
- Stewards will be called to give an account of their choices in managing their master's possessions.

Those who are successful in furthering the master's purposes will be rewarded by having their stewardships enlarged. Those who fail to improve and enlarge what they were assigned will lose their stewardship.

There is no indication in either version that the initial assets assigned as stewardships were subsequently returned to the master, except for those who failed to improve on their stewardship. Such "unprofitable" stewards lost what they were given. In both accounts, what the master expected on his return was the profit from the sums given as stewardships. This principle is explained more fully in a revelation to Joseph Smith in November 1831:

> Nevertheless, inasmuch as they receive more than is needful for their necessities and their wants, it shall be given into my storehouse; And the benefits shall be consecrated unto the inhabitants of Zion, and unto their generations, inasmuch as they become heirs according to the laws of the kingdom. Behold, this is what the Lord requires of every man in his stewardship, even as I, the Lord, have appointed or shall hereafter appoint unto any man. *And behold, none are exempt from this law who belong to the church of the living God.* (Doctrine and Covenants 70:7–10; emphasis added)

This requirement that the surplus or profits from a stewardship be given to the Lord's storehouse is further illustrated by the parable recorded in Luke 12 of the rich man faced with a bumper crop. The parable does not identify the rich man as a steward, but from the perspective that we are all stewards over property that belongs to God, the parable is relevant.

The rich man lacked space in his barns to store the harvest, so he tore down his barns and built bigger ones. He reflected with satisfaction on his success and said to himself, "Thou hast much goods laid up for many years; take thine ease, eat, drink, and be merry" (Luke 12:19). The Savior condemns his covetousness, not because he was saving and providing for his future but because his greed meant that others in need went without (see also Doctrine and Covenants 104:15-18).

A final stewardship parable is also worth noting. In the parable of the unjust steward (see Luke 16:1–13), we have a steward who abused his responsibilities and failed to promote his master's interests. When called to give an account, he attempted to provide for his own future by granting heavy discounts to those with substantial debts to his master.

This parable has proven to be difficult for many to interpret. Was the Savior condoning unethical behavior by the unjust steward? James E. Talmage offers this explanation:

> It was not the steward's dishonesty that was extolled; his prudence and foresight were commended, however; for while he misapplied his master's substance, he gave relief to the debtors; and in so doing he did not exceed his legal powers, for he was still steward though he was morally guilty of malfeasance. The lesson may be summed up in this wise: . . . Be diligent; for the day in which you can use your earthly riches will soon pass. Take a lesson from even the dishonest and the evil; if they are so prudent as to provide for the only future they think of, how much more should you, who believe in an eternal future, provide therefor! If you have not learned wisdom and prudence in the use of "unrighteous mammon," how can you be trusted with the more enduring riches?" [13]

---

13. James E. Talmage, *Jesus the Christ* (Salt Lake City, UT: The Church of Jesus Christ of Latter-day Saints, 1916), 464.

The translation of Luke offered in the *Oxford Study Bible* also suggests some key principles:

> If, then, you have not proved trustworthy with the wealth of this world, who will trust you with the wealth that is real? And if you have proved untrustworthy with what belongs to another, who will give you anything of your own? No slave can serve two masters: for either he will hate the first and love the second, or he will be devoted to the first and despise the second. You cannot serve God and Money. (Luke 16:11–13)

Joseph Spencer notes the connection between accountability and stewardships in Doctrine and Covenants 42 and makes this observation:

> In being made accountable to God for the use of one's property, the Latter-day Saint finds it inappropriate to say that what she legally owns or rightfully earns is actually hers. Even as it is owned, whatever is in the hands of a consecrated Latter-day Saint is still to be regarded as a stewardship. Stewardship thus ceases in this revelation [Doctrine and Covenants 42] to be a matter of use without ownership, becoming instead a matter of using things as though not owning them.[14]

The Nature of Land Stewardships

Land as a stewardship is a key element in the covenant that God makes with His people. Land in this view is both a private good (personal possession) and a common pool resource in that the possessor is part of a community of Saints. The implication is that receiving and holding land as a stewardship in Zion has three dimensions.

- Land is a personal inheritance to be used, improved, and enjoyed in the support of the immediate family.
- Land is part of an extended family stewardship to be conserved

---

14. Joseph M. Spencer, *For Zion: A Mormon theology of hope* (Salt Lake City, UT: Greg Kofford Books, 2014), 128.

and retained within the extended family, while managed with an eye to the benefit of the entire community.

- Land is a symbol of a holy stewardship and covenant relationship with God and should be beautified and nurtured.

If stewards in Zion place Christ at the center of their lives and rely on the five foundation stones of Zion, land will be managed as a common pool resource. This means that stewards will cooperate with other Saints for both personal support and community benefit through voluntary donation of the excess productivity.

Excess productivity includes both the actual product coming off the land and the allocation of time and other means of the steward in shared responsibilities. In 1998, Elder D. Todd Christofferson retold a story originally shared by Bishop Vaughn J. Featherstone in 1973. During the influenza epidemic of 1918, George Goates, a farmer in Lehi, Utah, lost a son and three grandchildren to the flu within just six days. At the same time, an early winter had frozen the ground and made it extremely difficult to harvest their beet crop. Every day of delay made it more difficult. After burying his family members, George and his son Francis started for the field to work on bringing in what harvest they could. As they drove their wagon along the road, they passed wagon after wagon, full of beets, going the other way.

> As they passed by, each driver would wave a greeting: "Hi ya, Uncle George," "Sure sorry, George," "Tough break, George," "You've got a lot of friends, George."
>
> On the last wagon was . . . freckled-faced Jasper Rolfe. He waved a cheery greeting and called out: "That's all of 'em, Uncle George."
>
> [Brother Goates] turned to Francis and said: "I wish it was all of ours." [15]

When they arrived at their field, there was not a beet to be found. All those wagons going the other way had been full of George's beets, harvested by his neighbors who were responding to a brother's need. Those brethren who rallied to the support of a neighbor in need understood that stewardship involves shared commitment to the community.

---

15. D. Todd Christofferson, "The Priesthood Quorum," *Ensign*, November 1998.

How does this principle apply in an urban setting and for suburbanites? It involves shared time and equipment (tool "libraries," lawn mowers, snow blowers, chain saws, and so on), shared response to crisis, shared support for community projects.

Consecration means that the steward's possessions, including home and land, are part of the bishop's storehouse and can be called on by Church leaders as needed. When Saints acquire land as a stewardship and an inheritance to pass on to future generations, it may seem that they "own" the land and can do whatever they wish with it, including the right to sell it. But the earth is the Lord's, and the Saints are always only stewards. Land must be managed as the Lord would have it managed if the steward is to be judged a faithful steward.

The Lord's priority is the development of all His children, so all resources under our control should be managed and improved upon so that we can provide for our families *and* lift others (see the parable of the talents in Matthew 25:14–30). To do otherwise runs the risk of putting us in the position of Lazarus, who lived well but failed to help the poor man at his gate (see Luke 16:19–31).

We see this principle in practice as the Nephites were willing to give land to the people of Ammon (see Alma 27:22–26), and the people of Ammon were willing to give part of that land to the converted Zoramites (see Alma 35:14) and other Lamanites (see Alma 62:16–17).

Land stewardships are often acquired by purchase or settlement. When Israel first entered the promised land under the leadership of Moses and Joshua, the Lord "dispossessed" the Canaanites and gave the land to Israel. But taking possession of the land was often by assimilation rather than conquest. According to John Goldingay:

> Contrary to the impression conveyed by some passages taken in isolation, the Joshua narrative as a whole does not describe Israel gaining control of Canaan by blitzkrieg or annihilating the Indigenous peoples, as the wider [Old] Testament narrative

confirms, and it indicates that some local people accepted the Israelites and joined them.[16]

Similarly, in the Restoration, the Saints were instructed to buy their land of promise, even though it belonged to the Lord.

> Behold, the land of Zion—I, the Lord, hold it in mine own hands; Nevertheless, I, the Lord, render unto Cæsar the things which are Cæsar's. Wherefore, I the Lord will that you should purchase the lands, that you may have advantage of the world, that you may have claim on the world, that they may not be stirred up unto anger. (Doctrine and Covenants 63:25–27)

Land given by the Lord as an inheritance helps cement the covenant between man and God, even if the "giving" involves the purchase of the land. But the nature of a stewardship is that the assets under management do not "belong" to the steward, even if purchased, and are always held "lightly" and at the disposal of the Master.

Land and Identity

The book of Joshua recounts Israel's entry into Canaan, as promised to Abraham, and is therefore focused on land. As John Goldingay explains: "Land is integral to peoplehood. Land suggests habitat, home, and security, a place for settling down ([Joshua]1:13,15). Joshua is thus about 'the ideology of homeland.' . . . Land is 'the definitive theme of the book of Joshua.'"[17] Earlier in his book, Goldingay suggests: "Joshua is more a mirror for identity than a model for morality. It tells the Israelites who they are, by telling them what God did and what their ancestors did to make them who they are."[18]

This connection between land and personal and collective identity is an important reason land plays the role it does in God's covenants

---

16. John Goldingay, *Joshua*, ed. David G. Firth and Lissa M. Wray Beal, Baker Commentary on the Old Testament: Historical Books, (Grand Rapids, MI: Baker Academic, 2023), 6.
17. Goldingay, *Joshua*, 264.
18. Goldingay, *Joshua*, 14.

with His people. If you ask my wife where she is from, she will say Springville, Utah, where she lived for only the first five years of her life. Then her family moved fifty miles away, and years later she attended Brigham Young University, where we met. Since we have been married, we have lived in other cities in Utah, California, Virginia, Massachusetts, and Pennsylvania. Up until just a couple of years ago, we lived in Springville for only a few months, spread over many years.

But my wife is "from Springville." Her father was born in Springville. Her grandparents were also born there and spent their lives there. When my wife was a child, her family went home for the holidays to Springville. Her connection to Springville is a connection to family and heritage. It is an important component in her self-identity. Connections to place, whether a particular piece of land or a community, often help establish who we are and how we relate to others.

We can gain further insights into our relationship to land by reflecting again on the story of Ahab and Naboth cited earlier (see 1 Kings 21). Naboth viewed his land as an essential element in the inheritance he had received from his fathers. They had received the land as part of their covenant with God. As such, that parcel of land was critical as an element in Naboth's personal identity and as a symbol of his covenant with God. Ahab offered Naboth compensation for the land in the form of an even better vineyard or "fair market value." Neither could replace Naboth's connection to that particular location.

Was Naboth's response to Ahab simply an instinctive defense of his territory against an intruder as Ardrey might suggest? Was his response fundamentally different from Pahom's? Is my wife's connection to Springville based on instinct or covenants? I suggest that for both Naboth and my wife the connection to place is based on relationships rather than possessiveness. Pahom defined himself in terms of his possessions. For Naboth, his vineyard was a tangible representation of his heritage, his connection to God, and the legacy of both for his descendants. For my wife, Springville represents a tangible connection to prior generations who gave their all in building their families and community. It is a heritage she cherishes and strives to pass on to her descendants.

An ownership view of land tends to foster pride, greed, and individual focus on possessions: a self-image as a self-conscious and protective landowner. Gerald O'Hara and Pahom are the archetypes. A stewardship view of land tends to foster a focus on determining how the Master would have the land managed, and on how the excess returns can best be used to help those in need and the community at large.

Property Rights in Zion

As previously noted, the Lord's land covenants with Abraham, the remnant of Jacob in the Americas, and the Saints in the Restoration have yet to be fulfilled. When they are, there will likely be a permanent or semi-permanent connection between the covenant people and the land the Lord gives them. Land ownership in Zion will likely have a different meaning than it does today even if the land is purchased. Land stewardships will be given as permanent inheritances with inherent social obligations rather than fee simple ownership as we understand the concept. This implies that we may need to rethink property rights.

From the founding of the Republic, the right to privately controlled land and property has been central to our quest for "life, liberty and the pursuit of happiness." But even the Founding Fathers were not unanimous in their understanding of property rights. From the outset, there was a debate over the relative primacy of private rights versus public needs. James Madison, Alexander Hamilton, and John Adams all argued that a principal function of government was the protection of private property.[19] Benjamin Franklin and others took a different view, arguing that "private property is a creature of society, and is subject to the calls of the society whenever its necessities require it, even to the last farthing."[20]

In a completely different context, James Scott asks the right central question: What kind of people will a given activity or institution

---

19. See *Federalist* No. 54 by James Madison.
20. As quoted in Harvey M. Jacobs, "U.S. Private Property Rights in International Perspective," in *Property Rights and Land Policies*, ed. Gregory K. Ingram and Yu-Hung Hong (Cambridge, MA: Lincoln Institute of Land Policy, 2009), 55.

foster?[21] In this case, the question is, What kind of people will the legal regime for property rights tend to foster? Do we want more Pahoms or more Naboths? We know that God's purpose is to foster and enable the development of His children. Land stewardships are an integral part of the covenants that God makes with His children and therefore should contribute to spiritual and temporal human prospering.

In a Zion society, we need a concept of property and property rights that does the following:

1. Acknowledges God as the creator and ultimate owner of all land and property.
2. Sustains the agency of stewards in their right to control how land is used while holding them accountable for their choices.
3. Encourages stewards to consider and value the needs of others.
4. Links land stewardships to the broader and coordinated needs of a Zion society, now and in the future.

The current concepts of property rights in the Western world do not meet this standard. But identifying and developing an approach to property rights that is more consistent with the needs of a Zion society is a fairly technical legal discussion. The issues and my initial thoughts on the question are laid out in the appendix on property rights in Zion.

Land in Zion

There is a significant connection between people and land. Our connections to place and land are an important part of establishing and maintaining our personal identity. Those connections can either lead us to turn inward to our pride and greed, or they can help us to turn outward to consider Divine guidance and the needs of others around us. The connection to land does not require individual ownership in the western sense, with land titling and the right to sell the land. In fact, the connection to self-image is probably stronger if people know that the piece of land will be theirs and their families forever.

---

21. James C Scott, *Two Cheers for Anarchism* (Princeton, NJ: Princeton University Press, 2012), 67.

It appears God would prefer that land be considered a perpetual inheritance and that it not be sold (see Leviticus 25:23–24). The connection to land runs deeper if it is heritable but not saleable. Possessing a land parcel that belonged to our ancestors and will be passed on to our descendants establishes a connection in both directions, further defining who we are. Knowing further that the land was awarded by God as part of a covenant with Him establishes an enduring relationship to God and provides guidance on how land should be managed.

The promise is repeated multiple times in the Book of Mormon: If you keep the commandments, you will prosper in the land, but if you don't you will be cut off from his presence. This is an interesting dichotomy: prosperity "in the land" versus spiritual isolation. Helaman 12:2 seems to define prosperity in terms of material wealth, collective safety, improved relations with "enemies," and "all things [necessary] for the welfare and happiness of [God's] people." Nothing with the Lord is temporal (see Doctrine and Covenants 29:34–35). The prosperity thus promised has spiritual roots and will be perpetuated as long as we keep the covenants that yield that prosperity.

Rather than view land as a personal possession, God offers the Saints in Zion a stewardship view of land. As such, the Saints in Zion will manage land to fulfill the Lord's purposes, both short and long-term. The five foundation stones of Zion will ensure that all have access to land as part of their Zion covenant. I think it unlikely that land will be sold since doing so would violate the covenant status of land, though land leases will likely be used. Importantly, land will always be central to individual and family identity as members of the covenant community.

CHAPTER 10

Organizations and Institutions in Zion

We Believe in Gathering

*I*n the 1890s, Rudyard Kipling published "The Miracle of Purun Bhagat," the story of a highly educated, politically powerful, high-caste Brahmin man who abandoned all and became a wandering beggar. After successfully navigating both Indian and British society, Purun pursued spiritual progression by abandoning the worldly and following the path of the wandering holy man. Purun Bhagat eventually settled in an abandoned mountain shrine as he sought solitary enlightenment. While the story is fictional, it represents what many world religions see as a powerful path to God.

I am not aware of any celebrated "wandering souls" or hermits in the Latter-day Saint culture. We are committed to gathering with other saints and progressing spiritually through relationships, connections, and social interaction. Joseph Smith taught that both temporal and spiritual blessings flow from gathering and efforts in concert with others:

> The great profusion of temporal and spiritual blessings, which always flow from faithfulness and concerted effort, *never attend individual exertion or enterprise*. The history of all past ages

abundantly attests this fact. *In addition to all temporal blessings,* there is no other way for the Saints to be saved in these last days, as the concurrent testimony of all the holy prophets clearly proves, for it is written "They shall come from the east and be gathered from the west, the north shall give up, and the South shall keep not back."— "the Sons of God shall be gathered from far, and his daughters from the ends of the earth."[1]

The gathering to Zion doesn't just result in congregations of people. It results in the businesses, social clubs, service organizations, and other groups that people living together inevitably create. The question considered here is how the foundation stones of Zion should influence those various organizations and institutions and what we can do today to nudge organizations in the direction of Zion.

The Lord's pronouncement to Moses clearly states His priorities: "This is my work and my glory, to bring to pass the immortality and eternal life of man" (Moses 1:39). In suggesting guiding principles for organizations, my starting point is the proposition that the purpose of mortality is to maximize human development and the achievement of human potential. If God's work and glory is to bring to pass the eternal life and happiness of His children, then a central purpose in Zion is to assist in achieving that goal. The way our organizations and institutions function can either help or hinder the achievement of that potential. Organizations will contribute more positively and effectively if they are grounded on the five-fold foundation of Zion.

The Why of Organizations

Men and women are fundamentally social beings. Elder Alexander Morrison reiterated this point in a 1998 address: "People are by nature social beings whose lives and feelings are eternally connected and

---

1. Joseph Smith Papers, *History 1838–1856*, vol. C-1, *The Joseph Smith Papers* (Salt Lake City, UT: Church Historian Press, The Church of Jesus Christ of Latter-day Saints, 1842), 1147; emphasis added.

intertwined with those of others. Almost invariably, individuals reach their full potential only in association and in community with others."[2]

Human capacities and possibilities are enhanced and greatly extended by cooperation and collaboration through organizations. Even the option of a Purun Bhagat living in isolation on the side of a mountain was only feasible because of the support provided by villagers in the valley below. All of us benefit from living in social organizations. The Lord has consistently commanded His people to gather together. We see the value of collaboration demonstrated in the success of cooperative efforts among the Latter-day Saints in the nineteenth and early twentieth centuries.

Collaboration and cooperation in and through organizations both support and enhance individual agency and self-reliance, and therefore human learning and development, by expanding the range of choices and possible actions available to the individual and the family. The various types of organizations enhance agency in different ways.

Enterprises in Zion will exist (1) to provide employment, skill development, capacity development, and creative outlets for those within the firm, both managers and staff; and (2) to meet meaningful needs of community members. In Zion, however, every enterprise will be in the human development business at least as much as anything else.

Other associations such as humanitarian aid organizations will be created as a means for joint action on the part of the organizers and members.

Still other organizations will exist to serve their members by expanding their awareness, alternative choices, and opportunities for social interaction. Consider, as an example, the hypothetical case of Belinda who wants to read more widely and have more social interaction. She opts to join a local book club. What is she gaining by doing so? Belinda will likely be exposed to books she otherwise may not have seen or chosen to read. She may connect strongly with some of the books and may object to others.

Belinda will also be able to discuss the books with new friends. Those friends may read the same books as Belinda, but because of

---

2. Alexander B. Morrison, "A Caring Community: Goodness in Action," *Ensign*, February 1999.

their differing life experiences, they may differ markedly in their reaction to the books. Over time, the experience may help Belinda understand her own priorities and preferences more fully. Some of the goals Belinda embraces may differ greatly from those she pursued before joining the club.

In other instances, organizations can make options available that would not be obtainable by the individual without cooperation and group resources. When I was a boy, I enjoyed playing Little League baseball, although I was never very good at it. This option was only available to me because an organization made it possible. Local markets or a well-functioning market economy also make options available that would otherwise be out of reach of most consumers. Most people cannot raise both bananas and pine nuts in their home garden. Broadening the range of choices also implies that the individual's ability and capacity to act on their choices is enhanced.

While organizations can provide many advantages, in our current society, we have, to a great extent, become dependent on large, hierarchical organizations for our comfort and livelihood. Such dependence may not help our progression. We move at an early age into schools modeled after regimented factories. The attitudes of subservience fostered in schools are further reinforced "by an adult working life lived largely in authoritarian settings that further abridge the workers' autonomy and independence."[3] Even participation in large voluntary associations can include heavy conformity expectations. The consequences for human development consistent with the goals of Zion are bleak. The challenge is to create organizations and institutions that help rather than hinder the achievement of human potential.

The Challenges of Organizations

History is replete with examples of collective human efforts that undermined and thwarted human development. Not all participation in organizations and institutions is voluntary, and involuntary organizations are particularly prone to infringe on the agency and freedom

---

3.   Scott, *Two Cheers for Anarchism*, 78.

that are essential for development. As nurturing and vital as families can be, even families can hinder the light and truth of development if the family is following incorrect traditions. In the Doctrine and Covenants we learn:

> Every spirit of man was innocent in the beginning; and God having redeemed man from the fall, men became again, in their infant state, innocent before God. And that wicked one cometh and taketh away light and truth, through disobedience, from the children of men, and *because of the tradition of their fathers.* (93:38–39; emphasis added)

Organizations and institutions also have "traditions" through behaviors, policies, and practices that persist over time. Even when the purpose of the organization is not explicitly focused on subjugating or constraining its members, human nature and organizational structure all too often tend to combine in traditions that elevate some members by suppressing or exploiting others. As Joseph Smith wrote, "We have learned by sad experience that it is the nature and disposition of almost all men, as soon as they get a little authority, as they suppose, they will immediately begin to exercise unrighteous dominion" (Doctrine and Covenants 121:39).

Since almost all people have this nature and disposition, it should be no surprise that nearly all organizations are hierarchical and authoritarian. And the organizations we belong to exert a profound influence on us. As James Scott said, "We live most of our lives in institutions: from the family to the school, to the army, to the business enterprise. These institutions to some considerable degree shape our expectations, our personalities, and our routines."[4]

Organizations can constrain individual choices in a variety of ways, some of which may be necessary or trivial. Some workplace rules associated with our employment may fall into this category. As a missionary, I wore a white shirt and tie, which was definitely not my first choice of attire but was an expectation and behavior that went with my choice to accept a call to serve as a missionary. In a more significant example, constraints are placed on members of society "to

---

4. Scott, *Two Cheers for Anarchism*, 76.

secure the public interest" (Doctrine and Covenants 134:5). Thus, limits may be placed on free speech or other actions that are thought to undermine public safety.

Organizational constraints become problematic when they limit individual agency or influence choices in ways that are inconsistent with the eternal goal of human development. One relevant example is illustrated by a letter from the Church's First Presidency. The letter addresses the practice of voting a "straight ticket" in U.S. elections, rather than voting for each candidate separately. Some political parties encourage this practice. It is intended to make it easier for party loyalists to vote only for their party's candidates, but it cedes to a political party the need for voters to individually study candidates and make choices. The First Presidency does not think highly of this practice: "Merely voting a straight ticket or voting based on 'tradition' without careful study of the candidates and their positions on important issues is a threat to democracy and inconsistent with revealed standards."[5]

In another example, a large national bank set aggressive sales targets for their employees and then put heavy pressure on them to meet those targets. A number of employees responded by creating millions of false accounts for customers and enrolling customers in financial products and services without their knowledge or consent. When knowledge of the practice became public, the bank faced severe consequences. The actions of the employees involved were reprehensible and inconsistent with a righteous use of agency, but the employees were responding to the policies, practices, and constraints of the organization. The bank implemented a number of internal reforms intended to redirect employee efforts and restore its reputation, but its mission is still focused on financial products and services, not the development of managers and other employees.

As noted in the previous quotation from Joseph Smith, rich spiritual and temporal blessings flow from our connectedness to others. But organizational life can also constrain individual agency. Organizations often serve the purpose of simplifying and focusing

---

5. Quoted in Scott Taylor, "First Presidency Letter Emphasizes Latter-day Saints' Participation in Elections and Civic Affairs, Reaffirms Political Neutrality," *Church News*, June 6, 2023.

the range of choices for individuals. Choosing to join a group with a particular agenda or perspective, such as a major political party, or volunteering for a service organization may begin as an expression of the individual's perspective. However, the choice to affiliate with a group represents at least an initial acceptance of the organization's perspective on many issues not carefully considered by the individual previously, and the organization is likely to influence the perceptions and choices members adopt.

When we join an organization, we assume some degree of responsibility and accountability for its success, and therefore for the results of the organization's actions, positive and negative. This includes the way the organization both enhances and constrains the agency of individuals, including ourselves.

Expanding on the previous hypothetical illustration, Belinda sacrificed a certain amount of her freedom of choice in joining her book club. If the club follows the recommended book list of the National Book Foundation, Belinda is allowing someone else to choose the books she reads. Belinda probably has only the vaguest of ideas of why the books on the list were chosen. She may be unwittingly accepting someone else's social agenda or their efforts to make a profit. Belinda's priorities may be changed by the choices she freely and willingly makes as her experience and understanding changes, but it is also likely that the choices presented to Belinda will be framed in part by those choosing the books and by the reactions of other club members. In this sense, organizations and institutions can broaden the range of choices presented to individuals both through education and socialization. But the framing of the choices also has a constraining effect on agency. A comparable example in a family happens when Mom asks little Bethany if she wants to wear the red dress or the blue dress. The option of wearing shorts or nothing at all is not presented. But in Belinda's case, if she finds that she does not like the books, she can leave the book club.

Given both the enhancing and constraining effects of organizations, what principles and goals should guide organizations? That consideration begins with how organizations frame their purpose and goals.

Organization Mission and Vision

Every organization makes at least one attempt to clarify and specify its purpose. This visioning exercise may be initiated at the creation of the organization to attract members and supporters in response to a crisis or a change in leadership, or simply to sharpen the focus of activity and resources. Whatever the rationale, the intent is to guide the organization as it sets goals and moves forward.

Some families also craft a mission statement.[6] My family's mission statement still hangs on the wall in our family room even after multiple moves. To be honest, like many mission statements, it is rarely explicitly referenced, but it was meaningful when we created it. It is still valued because the vision it articulates is still relevant.

These clarifying mission and vision statements are intended to state in simple terms the purpose of the organization. From a simple statement of purpose, goals and objectives are crafted to set a course direction. Below is a selection of fairly famous corporate mission statements:

- Tesla: To accelerate the advent of sustainable transport by bringing compelling mass market electric cars to market as soon as possible.[7]
- TED: To discover and spread ideas that spark imagination, embrace possibility and catalyze impact.[8]
- LinkedIn: To connect the world's professionals to make them more productive and successful.[9]
- Google: To organize the world's information and make it universally accessible and useful.[10]

---

6. Stephen R. Covey, *The 7 Habits of Highly Effective Families: Creating a Nurturing Family in a Turbulent World* (St. Martin's Griffin, 1997).
7. "Tesla mission," 2023, accessed August 2023, https://www.tesla.com/blog/mission-tesla.
8. "TED mission statement," 2023, accessed August 2023, https://www.ted.com/about/our-organization.
9. "LinkedIn Mission," 2023, accessed August 2023, About.linkedin.com.
10. "Google Mission," 2023, accessed August, 2023, https://www.google.com/search/howsearchworks/our-approach/#:~:text=Google's%20mission%20is%20to%20organize,it%20universally%20accessible%20and%20useful.

Effective mission and vision statements are simple and memorable, and they drive planning and decision-making. Activities, both new and old, are evaluated for their contribution to achieving the stated mission and vision. As the examples illustrate, mission and vision statements attempt to focus on what the organization produces and why. Organizational leaders then focus their efforts on achieving the articulated goals as efficiently and effectively as possible. At least, that is what organizational stakeholders expect from managers and leaders.

The Lord's pronouncement to Moses can be viewed as a mission statement: "This is my work and my glory, to bring to pass the immortality and eternal life of man" (Moses 1:39). By comparison, what is missing from most mission statements is any reference to the growth and development of the people inside the organization or, in many cases, even the customers, clients, or society in general. What would an organization's mission look like if it were grounded on the five-fold foundation of Zion?

Although not in the least concerned about building Zion, anthropologist James C. Scott posed a question about human development in organizations, which is exactly the question for Zion: "What if we were to ask a different question of institutions and activities than the narrow neoclassical question of how efficient they are in terms of costs (e.g., resources, labor, capital) per unit of a given, specified product? What if we were to ask what kind of people a given activity or institution fostered?"[11]

In a Zion society, erected on the five foundation stones, organizations will pay at least as much attention to human development and "the kind of people" an activity will "foster" as to the quality and efficiency of their goods and services. Development in this sense includes encouraging the exercise of personal agency, encouraging the love of others, requiring accountability, and building and supporting unity in the organization and the community. If we learn the principles of Zion at home and at church, organizations become the training ground where we practice and internalize those principles.

---

11. Scott, *Two Cheers for Anarchism*, 67.

Organizations in Zion will focus on the development and support of people, including:

- Those who provide the resources used by the organization
- Those who provide leadership and management within the organization
- Those who provide the labor within the organization
- Those who directly benefit from the output of the organization
- Those who are affected indirectly by the organization's activities, either positively or negatively

Organizations can contribute to human development by providing an environment in which people interact, learn from each other and together, have shared experiences, give and receive feedback, see the examples provided by others, and have the opportunity to experiment and improve their understanding and skills. The opportunities for development differ somewhat based on the role or roles played in the organization.

Development for those who provide capital and other resources to organizations involves coming to a greater understanding of consecration and greater love for all God's children. Flowing from that development will be greater demonstrations of love for others, while pride and class distinctions will be shunned. Higher levels of development will manifest in consecration to help others by providing work opportunities, joining cooperatives, and entering into partnerships. Likewise, as "those who have" grow in their development, they will show greater sensitivity to the needs of the community and to the indirect effects of organizational activities. They will also be mindful of our stewardship of the earth. While providers of capital may expect a return on their investment, their expectations will be modest, and earnings in self-reliant enterprises will be distributed largely to those working in the organization.

The personal development of those leading the organization will foster the development of others within the organization. Personal development will always include a deeper understanding and commitment to the five foundation stones and the doctrine of Jesus Christ. That understanding and commitment encourages leaders to focus on the one, on the development of the individuals within the organization and those served by the organization, as well as the accomplishment of the organization's level of productivity and success.

Fostering the development of others within the organization will include effective communication of the mission of the organization and the meaning of quality work. The commitment to individual growth will require implementation of policies that promote that growth. Such policies embrace the oft-cited "workplace empowerment" policies: promote individual initiative, assure that members have the resources they need, allow members to manage their own time and pursue their own goals, provide development opportunities, and encourage feedback and open communication. All of these assume that mutual trust is nurtured within the organization. A leader who loves his neighbor as himself would not expect to be remunerated at a level hundreds of times higher than his "neighbors" in the organization.

For those who labor in the organization, personal development will include improving their task-related skills, their ability to cooperate effectively with others, their love and support for others, and their stewardship for the success of the organization.

Organizations will also acknowledge a responsibility for the needs and development of their customers and clients and the broader community. The exercise of agency requires that those making a choice have adequate information and an understanding of the implications of their choice. Assuring that "men are instructed sufficiently" requires that organizations are honest, forthright, and complete in the product information they provide, and the potential consequences associated with using their product or service. Organizations may provide some of this information themselves, but they will likely also cooperate with other organizations for broader development and dissemination of important information.

With this general perspective in mind, the next section considers the implications of the foundation stones in greater detail.

How the Foundation Stones Influence Organizations

Individuals in Zion will strive to emulate the Savior and lead as He would lead. In particular, they will follow the counsel of President

Thomas S. Monson, who taught, "Never let a problem to be solved become more important than a person to be loved."[12] Building an organizational culture that promotes and supports Zion represents a commitment to the foundation stones of love for God and others, respect for the agency of all while still requiring accountability, and unity in collaborative actions.

A concept taught in tax policy circles seems relevant. The notion is that businesses do not pay taxes. Only people pay taxes through a combination of lower profits to owners, lower wages paid to employees, or price increases to customers. A similar concept applies when we consider how the foundation stones apply to organizations. Organizations do not love—only people love. At the direction of the people involved, organizations may adopt policies and practices to either bless or unduly constrain the lives of those inside or outside the organization. But it is the people directing and acting through the organization who are demonstrating their love or lack of it.

Two other foundation stones for organizations follow from our understanding of the purpose of social interaction. If freedom to choose and to act on the choices we make is essential for eternal development, then it seems clear that respecting and protecting individual agency is an organizational foundation stone.

In an address delivered at BYU in 1987, then-Elder Dallin H. Oaks explained that "free agency, the power to choose, is a gift of God, conferred on his children and exercised by them in the premortal existence. It is an essential precondition of the further progression we seek in mortality."[13] As Elder Oaks notes, freedom to act on our choices can be constrained, but freedom is also required to realize our full potential.

Protecting the agency of all to the greatest degree possible is a foundational principle for all organizations and institutions. As used here, agency is also accompanied by the self-reliance corollary. It is both the ability and the responsibility to act to contribute to the extent possible and improve life both for the individual and for society.

---

12. Thomas S. Monson, "Finding Joy in the Journey," *Ensign,* November, 2008.
13. Dallin H. Oaks, "Free Agency and Freedom" (Brigham Young University devotional, October 11, 1987), 5, speeches.byu.edu.

Eternally significant development is based on the responsible use of agency. But agency is based on law, not unbridled liberty. The challenge facing all organizations is to recognize when constraints on individual agency help realize development in a broad sense, and when limiting autonomy also limits development.

Drawing on his work in various developing countries, including Malaysia, James Scott notes a widespread desire for personal autonomy:

> I suspect that the tremendous desire one can find in many societies for a piece of land, one's own house, one's own shop owes a great deal not only to the real margin of independent action, autonomy, and security it confers but also to the dignity, standing and honor associated with small property in the eyes of the state and of one's neighbors.[14]

Thomas Jefferson felt that small farmers were the bedrock of democracy. The equivalent view today would have to include the self-employed and the "gig" workers in the world, the individuals and families who value their autonomy enough to sacrifice other dimensions.

Often the self-employed face expenses and risks not borne by those who work for large organizations. Matthias Benz and Bruno S. Frey asked why self-employed people are willing to work for lower wages and lower returns on their investments compared to those who work in organizations. Their review of data from twenty-three countries concludes:

> Both autonomy and the chance to pursue interesting activities should be seen as important elements of a broader human need for self-determination. . . . In a broader context, it also suggests that people do not value only outcomes such as income or leisure, but derive independent utility from processes allowing for self-determination.[15]

---

14. Scott, *Two Cheers for Anarchism*, 89.
15. Matthias Benz and Bruno S. Frey, "The Value of Doing What You Like: Evidence from the Self-employed in 23 Countries," *Journal of Economic Behavior & Organization*, 68, no. 3–4, 2008.

These findings are consistent with Scott's observation of trends among industrial workers in the United States.

> An astonishingly higher percentage pines to open a shop or a restaurant or to farm. The unifying theme of these dreams is the freedom from close supervision and autonomy of the working day that, in their mind, more than compensates for the long hours and risks of such small businesses.[16]

We also see the desire for autonomy and independence in the current debate over at-home work versus return-to-the-office requirements following the widespread shutdowns during the COVID outbreak. Gleb Tsipursky describes three recent reports examining the controversy. Collectively, the reports find that requirements to return to the office result in higher levels of employee attrition and increased difficulty in recruiting. In addition, "a staggering 76% of employees stand ready to jump ship if their companies decide to pull the plug on flexible work schedules." One of the studies found that shifting from a flexible work schedule to a more traditional in-office schedule was comparable to a 2% to 3% pay cut.[17]

Despite institutional efforts to restrain agency, workers still yearn for it and are increasingly willing to actively seek it in the workplace.

The second pertinent foundation stone is accountability. Individual choices and actions are inextricably connected to responsibility for the consequences of those actions. If human development comes through the exercise of individual agency, understood as a cycle of instruction, alternatives, choice, action, and consequences, then the second organizational cornerstone must be individual accountability. In an organizational or institutional setting, this individual accountability extends to responsibility for both the actions and the success of the organization. Peter Block's definition of a citizen resonates with this concept of accountability.

---

16. Scott, *Two Cheers for Anarchism*, 91–92.
17. Gleb Tsipursky, "We're Now Finding Out the Damaging Results of the Mandated Return to the Office—and It's Worse than We Thought," *Fortune*, August 1, 2023.

A citizen is one who is willing to be accountable for and committed to the well-being of the whole. That whole can be a city block, a community, a nation, the earth. A citizen is one who produces the future, someone who does not wait, beg, or dream for the future. The antithesis of being a citizen is the choice to be a consumer or a client.[18]

Accountability (citizenship) in a mortal organization will involve regular reporting of activities and outcomes to others with the capacity and responsibility to evaluate performance and provide coaching on potential improvements. But it also includes a commitment to the success of the organization and concerted effort to promote and enhance that success.

Transparency is another component of accountability, including clarity about motivations and actions. Individuals are held accountable when they report to peers and leaders in this way. Organizations are held accountable when they report regularly and fully to their stakeholders.

Accountability does not imply punishment for mistakes, either for individuals or organizations. The objective is human development. Accountability is linked to recognition and learning, rather than rewards and punishment.

Organization members will support and strive to further the mission and objectives of the organization. They will build coalitions with other members to seek improvements and creative ways to further both their personal and organizational development.

In designing, creating, and managing organizations in Zion, the people involved will be motivated by love for those in the organization and those affected by the organization. Human development will be as important as any product or service provided. Thus, respect for the agency of all involved will be a prime consideration. The accountability of organization members will include accepting responsibility for the success of the organization in achieving all its goals and the effect of organizational activities on society. Unity will follow from this shared

---

18. Peter Block, *Community: The Structure of Belonging* (San Francisco, CA: Berrett-Koehler Publishers, Inc., 2009), 63.

sense of responsibility and from the mutual trust that is cultivated at all levels. If this summarizes how the foundation stones will influence organizations, then the foundations of Zion will also influence the actions of members when they disagree with their organization.

Changing an Organization

I have given a good deal of thought to the propensity we have as people to give up our agency to organizations and institutions. There seems to be a fine line between extending our capacity to act through collaborative efforts and simply ceding decisions to other entities or people. When we collaborate with others or join an existing organization, it seems unlikely that the joint and multiple purposes of the organization will exactly match our own. This is the essence of compromise. The question is, How far should we be willing to compromise our own goals, standards, and objectives to obtain the benefits from cooperation and membership?

The answer lies in the work of Albert O. Hirschman in his influential book, *Exit, Voice and Loyalty: Responses to Decline in Firms, Organizations, and States.*[19] As the title suggests, when our collaborative efforts fail to meet all our expectations, our first response will likely be loyalty to the organization. When the personal differences reach a certain point, we, as active, caring citizens in Zion, will speak up and voice our concerns in an attempt to convince others to make needed adjustments. If that fails, the ultimate response is to exit the organization and seek other opportunities. Just as Zion is a choice, so is our association with most organizations.

Of course, things are rarely as simple as that sounds. The loyalty given to organizations should be carefully considered. Sometimes inertia keeps us in organizational relationships when reflection suggests we should speak up or look for other opportunities. Just as we might change our dining habits if we learn that our favorite restaurant has multiple health code violations, should we not also consider

---

19. Albert O. Hirschman, *Exit, Voice, and Loyalty* (Cambridge, MA: Harvard University Press, 1970).

changing our membership if we learn that an organization we favor routinely cheats their employees or engages in deceptive practices?

And then there are organizations intimately tied to our understanding of our personal identity. Being a member of The Church of Jesus Christ of Latter-day Saints is an essential aspect of my identity. For me, that means being committed to building the kingdom of God on the earth. I am a former university professor who taught aspiring public servants how to improve government, not quite as central to my sense of self, but close to it. The combination meant that the ideal professional venue for me was Brigham Young University.

I put my whole heart and soul into my work at BYU for fifteen years. Then a crisis arose. My colleagues soundly rejected my professional vision and voice. The only reasonable course was to leave BYU, but leaving forced me to reevaluate my identity as a professional committed both to public service and to building the kingdom.

My four-year stint at another institution was a vital period in my personal growth and expanding international vision for building the kingdom. I eventually returned to BYU but with a broader understanding of how my efforts could help bless the lives of God's children around the world.

My point in sharing this personal story is to acknowledge that the "exit, voice, and loyalty" paradigm can be very painful. Our sense of self may be expressed in deeply held connections to organizations. If those organizations are large, they are also likely to be hierarchical and difficult to change through the exercise of our voice. Loyalty to our self-image may make loyalty to the organization difficult or impossible, but exiting the organization may be soul-wrenching.

In such a personal crisis, we spend sleepless nights humbly pondering such questions as:

- Why am I in the organization?
- Can I achieve my purposes without the organization?
- Can I change the organization?
- How certain am I that I am right?
- Do I even know enough about what is going on to understand what needs to change?
- Do I care enough about the organization to try and change it?

- Is trying to change the organization worth the personal cost?
- How easy is it to exit the organization?
- How will exiting affect me?

Association with some organizations may be so central to our understanding of who we are that exiting is simply out of the question. In such cases, our loyalty requires that we work for meaningful change and improvement within the organization with a focus on the foundation stones of Zion. And we must be humble enough to hold open the possibility that we are the ones who may be wrong and who must change.

Most of us probably belong to at least one organization that does not adhere to the vision for organizations I have described in this chapter. On reflection, we may choose to leave some of those organizations. In other organizations we may choose to encourage changes that will bring the organization closer to Zion.

A productive strategy for such change efforts can be summarized as "one by one." Whether striving to build relationships and coalitions to support change, or seeking to change a single policy, change agents will focus not only on what needs to change but also on who needs to change.

As I learned at BYU, simply articulating a vision for the future is not sufficient. It is essential that others within the organization understand and support the new narrative and vision as well. At least initially, that support is likely to come "one by one."

Wholesale change in large organizations is very difficult. Patience and a narrower focus may prove a better long-term strategy. Identifying particular small changes, one by one, will yield significant cumulative results over time.

We must remember that the scope and scale of the Church's activities as an institution are insufficient to produce the changes in organizations needed in the establishment of Zion. Its focus is on individuals and families rather than private organizations or the operations of government. The scope of the Church of Jesus Christ does not cover the full range of human interactions and cooperative efforts.

Zion will include a broad range of organizations, all grounded in the five-fold foundation of Zion. Never doubt that the world's organizations need to change if we are to establish Zion. Those changes will happen only as all stakeholders connected to organizations are persuaded, with gentleness, meekness, and love unfeigned, as the Savior would, that the five-fold foundation for Zion applies to all organizations.

A Word about Government

My personal focus is on the principles that should guide organizations in Zion, with a particular emphasis on governments. It is necessary to distinguish between private organizations and government institutions because of government's inherent power to compel behavior. There is no question that numerous governments throughout history have exercised "unrighteous dominion" to the detriment and death of millions. It is also clear that this pattern continues today, and many efforts to "reform" government are intended to limit government's capacity to harm.

Even with a largely benign government, one challenge we face as a society is to assess the degree to which outside intervention in someone's life is appropriate to minimize "natural" consequences. Children are physically prevented from touching hot stoves because they lack the information and understanding we feel is necessary to make an informed decision. If they are burned, we tend to hold caregivers accountable rather than the child.

As a society, we have deemed it necessary to abridge freedoms, and therefore the natural accountability for individual actions, in a number of ways. In the name of public safety, we put up traffic lights, stop signs, and crosswalks, and we occasionally punish people for violating traffic laws. We design public playgrounds with play apparatus deemed safe. To protect neighborhood property values, we impose building codes, land use restrictions, and nuisance laws.

We require personal automobiles to have multiple safety restraints. I met a professional driver in China who felt that a government requirement that his passengers wear seat belts was an insult to his professionalism. It suggested that he was not capable of avoiding serious accidents. I sympathized, commended his skill, and wore my seat belt.

Some of these restrictions may be needed because even responsible adults may lack access to all the information needed to make an informed decision, especially about the actions of others. As in the last example, a person may be a good driver and still experience the consequences of another driver's poor decision. Once a house has been constructed, the prospective buyer has no inexpensive way to determine the adequacy of building systems employed but no longer visible. Because the builder's choices have such long-term consequences, we have come to rely on building codes and inspectors to monitor the construction process.

The question I attempt to answer in part 4 takes a more positive approach: On what guiding principles should governments in general be founded and structured to maximize the realization of human potential for all the governed and support a Zion society?

Some may be under the impression that when Zion is established, there will be no need for a civil government distinct from the Church of Jesus Christ. Joseph Smith did not share that view. In March 1844, he began to assemble a confidential council that eventually included about fifty men, both Church members and nonmembers, with the stated aim "to look to some place where we can go and establish a Theocracy either in Texas or Oregon or somewhere in California."[20] In their second meeting, they appointed a committee to draft a new constitution. While the council came to be known as the Council of Fifty, the minutes of their early meetings indicate they were directed by revelation to refer to themselves as the kingdom of God.[21]

With particular regard to civil government, Joseph Smith offered this instruction to the Council of Fifty after an extended debate on whether there was a meaningful difference between church and state in Zion:

> There is a distinction between the Church of God and the [civil] kingdom of God. The laws of the [civil] kingdom are not designed

---

20. Joseph Smith Papers, *Council of Fifty, Minutes, March 1844–January 1846*, 1, 25.
21. Joseph Smith Papers, *Council of Fifty, Minutes, March 1844–January 1846*, 1, 30–31.

to effect our salvation hereafter. It is an entire, distinct and separate government. The church is a spiritual matter and a spiritual kingdom. . . . The literal [civil] kingdom of God, and the church of God are two distinct things. The gifts of prophets, evangelists &c never were designed to govern men in civil matters. The [civil] kingdom of God has nothing to do with giving commandments to damn a man spiritually. It only has power to make a man amenable to his fellow man.[22]

The design and operation of governance in Zion is the subject of part 4.

---

22. Joseph Smith Papers, *Council of Fifty, Minutes, March 1844–January 1846*, 1, 201–03.

PART 4
Governance

Governance has become a bit of a buzzword over the past several decades. It has been applied to both for-profit firms and not-for-profit organizations, including churches, in addition to governments. By "governance" I do not mean the structure of government (legislatures, presidents, administrators, and so on). Multiple definitions have been offered in many contexts, but all the definitions relate to rules for using power. There are both formal and informal rules. When the rules are formal and the entity applying the rules can compel obedience in others, we call that entity government. Other types of organizations can expel members for noncompliance, but they cannot compel conformity. When freedoms and human rights are valued, stewarding the formal rules which inevitably and necessarily limit freedoms for some groups are among the most difficult decisions we make as a society.

Informal rules are no less important. Because they are tacit, they may go largely unnoticed. Such rules both derive from and influence what lies in the hearts of people in a community. Informal and diffuse forms of power and authority can prompt social action even in the absence of immediate state action. When the informal rules for using power based on righteousness wither in a people, the consequences for righteous government are dire.

Achieving righteous governance, both formal and informal, is challenging and requires committed citizens acting on the five-fold foundation of Zion. The next two chapters consider governance in Zion, both the design principles for government and the requirements for effective informal governance in Zion.

CHAPTER 11

The Need for Good Government

Resident Dallin H. Oaks observed:

> The science of government is a consideration of the procedures by which and the extent to which the official representatives of one group of citizens can impose restrictions on the freedom of another group. Decisions on the extent to which government power should restrict the *freedom* of individuals are among the most difficult decisions we face in an organized society. . . .
>
> We have to accept some government limitations on freedom if we who live in communities are to have life, liberty, and the pursuit of happiness. A condition of uninhibited individual freedom would allow the strong to oppress the weak. It would allow the eccentric desires of one person to restrict the freedom of many.[1]

Because of their experience in Missouri and Kirtland, the Saints recognized the need for a government structure that would protect their rights and afford them the freedom to establish Zion as they understood it. As we seek to build up the kingdom of God in our pre-millennial world in preparation for the coming of the Savior, we

---

1. Oaks, *The Lord's Way*, 6–7; emphasis in original.

continue to have that need. Whether civil government will persist in Zion is a good question.

On the one hand we have these pronouncements:

> But, verily I say unto you that in time ye shall have no king nor ruler, for I will be your king and watch over you. Wherefore, hear my voice and follow me, and you shall be a free people, and ye shall have no laws but my laws when I come, for I am your lawgiver, and what can stay my hand? (Doctrine and Covenants 38:21–22)

> For the Lord shall be in their midst, and his glory shall be upon them, and he will be their king and their lawgiver. (Doctrine and Covenants 45:59)

On the other hand, as previously noted, Joseph did not foresee a time when a civil government could be eliminated. In Mosiah 26, King Mosiah was unwilling to judge Church members who had sinned but had not violated the law of the land. Alma did judge the sinner, but the extent of the punishment available to the Church was expulsion and "blotting out" their names. Joseph drew a similar distinction between Church and state in Zion.

The Council of Fifty debated whether there is a difference between civil and Church government. The point was made that at least in the beginning, there will be good people in the community who are not members of The Church of Jesus Christ of Latter-day Saints. Joseph went so far as to invite three persons who were not members of the Church to join the council, stressing that one central purpose of their joint effort was to guarantee religious freedom for all.[2] To ensure that religious liberty would be protected, some argued there had to be a difference between the Church and a civil government designed to protect the rights of all.

The minutes of the Council of Fifty record that Joseph taught the Council:

---

2.   Joseph Smith Papers, *Council of Fifty, Minutes*, March 1844–January 1846, 1, 140

The literal kingdom of God, and the church of God are two distinct things. The gifts of prophets, evangelists etc. never were designed to govern men in civil matters. The kingdom of God has nothing to do with giving commandments to damn a man spiritually.[3]

As was the case during the days of Alma and Mosiah, there were limits on the sanctions that could be imposed by the Church in 1844. Any action that merited imprisonment, the seizure of property, or worse required an action by the civil government, not the Church.

The plan of happiness is developmental. When the Savior returns, He will indeed be our King and Lawgiver, but His laws will always be designed for our eternal development and exaltation. There will forever be a range of activities and social interactions, including in public governance, where we can use our agency and practice the principles of Zion.

Even though God is the Creator and therefore Owner of the entire world, He directed the Saints to purchase land in Missouri, stating: "Behold, the land of Zion—I, the Lord, hold it in mine own hands; Nevertheless, I, the Lord, render unto Cæsar the things which are Cæsar's" (Doctrine and Covenants 63:25–26). The land purchases in Missouri were nearly all from the United States government.

Joseph believed there will be an ongoing need for civil government even as we usher in the Millennium. God has made us agents, and we have seen repeatedly in the scriptures that the Savior expects us to do what we can do for ourselves, and He does for us what we cannot do. Based on that principle, and in sympathy with Joseph Smith's viewpoint, this chapter discusses the design and organization of government in Zion.

Design of Government

One attempt to design a government took place when the Saints settled Nauvoo, Illinois. To protect their liberty, the Saints in Nauvoo obtained a charter that was intended as a bulwark against persecution

---

3. Joseph Smith Papers, *Council of Fifty, Minutes*, March 1844–January 1846, 1, 128–29.

and legal abuse. While few of its provisions were unique to Nauvoo, in combination the provisions created problems for the Church in the end:

> The broad provisions of the Nauvoo Charter were intended to enable the Mormons to establish a peaceful sanctuary, free from the kinds of violence and harassments they had experienced at the hands of Missouri officials. Nonetheless, it is a twist of historical irony, that while the Saints relied on their charter to be an unbreachable wall defending the rights of Zion, many of their non-Mormon neighbors came to view it as an offensive barrier. The implementation of the constitutional provisions of the charter exacerbated the Mormons' problems by isolating and thereby alienating the affairs of the city from the rest of the county and state.[4]

From one perspective, it could be argued that the design of a civil government in Zion may not matter. If the people qualify to live in Zion, they can make any type of government work. If they are not a Zion people, no form of government will be adequate. Judge Learned Hand, often considered to be the greatest American judge to never sit on the Supreme Court, expressed a similar view in his "Spirit of Liberty" speech on July 4, 1944:

> I often wonder whether we do not rest our hopes too much upon constitutions, upon laws and upon courts. These are false hopes; believe me, these are false hopes. Liberty lies in the hearts of men and women; when it dies there, no constitution, no law, no court can even do much to help it. While it lies there it needs no constitution, no law, no court to save it.[5]

After rejecting the notion that liberty means the right to do whatever you please, Judge Hand goes on to provide a stirring and insightful view on the spirit of liberty:

---

4. Kimball, "Protecting Nauvoo by Illinois Charter in 1840," 302.
5. Learned Hand, *The Spirit of Liberty: Papers and Addresses of Learned Hand*, 1952 ed., ed. Irving Dilliard (New York: Knopf, 1944).

What then is the spirit of liberty? I cannot define it; I can only tell you my own faith. The spirit of liberty is the spirit which is not too sure that it is right; the spirit of liberty is the spirit which seeks to understand the mind of other men and women; the spirit of liberty is the spirit which weighs their interests alongside its own without bias; the spirit of liberty remembers that not even a sparrow falls to earth unheeded; the spirit of liberty is the spirit of Him who, near two thousand years ago, taught mankind that lesson it has never learned but never quite forgotten; that there may be a kingdom where the least shall be heard and considered side by side with the greatest.[6]

Zion is precisely the kingdom that Judge Hand envisioned. I share Judge Hand's faith that such a kingdom grounded in Christlike charity and the other foundation stones of Zion is possible.

While I recognize that righteousness must lie in the hearts of the people or no government can succeed, I am convinced that there is a place for civil government in Zion. As Joseph indicated, there is a difference between the Church of God and the kingdom of God on the earth. The Nauvoo Charter was intended to shield the Saints while they established Zion. What I am seeking are the principles that underlie and guide the design and operation of the civil side of Zion—principles which can be promoted and implemented today, as well as supported in a Zion of the future. Good and righteous people still need to be guided by sound principles, and the design of government and governance matter a great deal. Government must protect against wrongdoing, but it is also an important vehicle for collective action.

I am impressed that J. Reuben Clark Jr. and Dallin H. Oaks, two of the best minds the Church has ever produced, have devoted decades to the study of this question. Both have concluded that the Constitution of the United States is inspired and went so far as to say that the fundamental principles embodied in that document are integral to their religion.

---

6. Hand, *The Spirit of Liberty: Papers and addresses of Learned Hand.*

Much of the faith that President Clark and President Oaks place in the Constitution stems from the revelation given to Joseph Smith in 1833 regarding the Lord's hand in establishing the Constitution. President Clark stated: "I declare that the divine sanction thus repeatedly given by the Lord himself to the Constitution of the United States as it came from the hands of the Framers with its coterminous Bill of Rights, makes of the principles of that document an integral part of my religious faith."[7]

Another important source for guiding principles regarding government is Doctrine and Covenants 134, which is a declaration of belief about governments and laws. This declaration was approved by a conference of the Church for inclusion in the 1835 edition of the Doctrine and Covenants. While the section has been included in every edition since and is often quoted by Church authorities (including Presidents Clark and Oaks), the minutes of the conference in which the declaration was read and approved for publication are clear that it was accepted as the "belief, or 'opinion' of the officers of the Church" and not as a revelation.[8]

At the October 1928 general conference of the Church, President Heber J. Grant affirmed that section 134 is "a declaration of the belief of our Church regarding the governments and laws."[9] Because of its long history as the most formal and officially accepted statement of the Church's beliefs about government and law, it is worth careful examination and comparison with the foundational principles articulated here.

The principles gleaned from these sources can be divided into two categories: the divinely inspired structural components of government and the equally divine rights to be protected by government.

---

7. J. Reuben Clark, "The Constitution," *Improvement Era*, June 1957, 399.

8. Hyrum M. Smith and Janne M. Sjodahl, *Introduction to and Commentary on the Doctrine and Covenants, Rev. Ed.* (Salt Lake City, UT: Deseret Book, 1972), 852.

9. Heber J. Grant, in Conference Report, October 1928, 9, 11.

Divinely Inspired Structural Components

President Dallin H. Oaks has spoken repeatedly about the Constitution over the years. As he notes in several of his talks, he spent decades as a law professor, three and one-half years as a Utah State Supreme Court justice, and many years as an Apostle. In the course of his studies, he also reviewed and reflected on the constitutional views of President J. Reuben Clark. I begin by drawing from then-Elder Oaks's 1992 *Ensign* article in which he identifies the components of the Constitution that he feels are divinely inspired. He makes it clear that he does not consider either the wording or all elements of the Constitution to be inspired. But there are five "great fundamentals" in which he sees the hand of God guiding the Founders. He said:

> To summarize, I see divine inspiration in these four great fundamentals of the U.S. Constitution:
>
> - The separation of powers in the three branches of government
> - The Bill of Rights
> - The division of powers between the states and the federal government
> - The application of popular sovereignty[10]

President Oaks adds one more divinely inspired fundamental: "The rule of law and not of men. . . . There is divine inspiration in the fundamental underlying premise of this whole constitutional order. . . . The rule of law is the basis of liberty."[11]

Regarding the separation of powers, President Clark wrote: "It is this union of independence and dependence of these branches—legislative, executive and judicial—and of the governmental functions possessed by each of them, that constitutes the marvelous genius of this unrivalled document. . . . As I see it, it was here that the divine inspiration came. It was truly a miracle."[12]

Concerning the division of powers between states and the federal government, President Oaks states: "This principle of limited national

---

10. Dallin H. Oaks, "The Divinely Inspired Constitution," *Ensign*, February 1992.
11. Oaks, "The Divinely Inspired Constitution."
12. Quoted in Oaks, "The Divinely Inspired Constitution."

powers, with all residuary powers reserved to the people or to the state and local governments, which are most responsive to the people, is one of the great fundamentals of the U.S. Constitution."[13]

My own experience is that one of the best checks on the abuse of government authority is to divide related tasks between offices and agencies as well. It may seem less efficient, but it has often proven more reliable in producing good outcomes.

On the subject of popular sovereignty, President Oaks writes:

Perhaps the most important of the great fundamentals of the inspired Constitution is the principle of popular sovereignty: The people are the source of government power. . . .

The sovereign power is in the people. I believe this is one of the great meanings in the revelation which tells us that God established the Constitution of the United States,

"That every man may act . . . according to the moral agency which I have given unto him, that every man may be accountable for his own sins in the day of judgment.

"Therefore, it is not right that any man should be in bondage one to another.

"And for this purpose have I established the Constitution of this land." (Doctrine and Covenants 101:78–80.) . . .

Popular sovereignty necessarily implies popular responsibility. Instead of blaming their troubles on a king or other sovereign, all citizens must share the burdens and responsibilities of governing. As the Book of Mormon teaches, "The burden should come upon all the people, that every man might bear his part." (Mosiah 29:34.) . . .

A government based on popular sovereignty must be responsive to the people, but it must also be stable or it cannot govern. A constitution must therefore give government the power to withstand the cries of a majority of the people in the short run, though it must obviously be subject to their direction in the long run.[14]

---

13. Oaks, "The Divinely Inspired Constitution."
14. Oaks, "The Divinely Inspired Constitution."

President Oaks reiterated his views on popular sovereignty in 2009 at a Brigham Young University–Idaho devotional:

> This principle of sovereignty in the people explains the meaning of God's revelation that He established the Constitution of the United States "that every man may act . . . according to the moral agency which I have given unto him, that every man may be accountable for his own sins in the day of judgment" (Doctrine and Covenants 101:78). In other words, the most desirable condition for the effective exercise of God-given moral agency is a condition of maximum freedom and responsibility—the opposite of slavery or political oppression. With freedom we can be accountable for our own actions and cannot blame our conditions on our bondage to another. This is the condition the Lord praised in the Book of Mormon, where the people—not a king—established the laws and were governed by them (see Mosiah 29:23–26). This popular sovereignty necessarily implies popular responsibility. Instead of blaming their troubles on a king or tyrant, all citizens are responsible to share the burdens of governing, "that every man might bear his part" (Mosiah 29:34).[15]

The subject of popular sovereignty is discussed more fully in the next chapter.

As noted, President Oaks added one more item to his list of fundamentals: the importance of the rule of law. The whole idea of the rule of law, in which no person is above the law and all are to be governed by law, is fundamental to the very idea of a constitution. "As the Lord declared in modern revelation, constitutional laws are justifiable before him, 'and the law also maketh you free.' (Doctrine and Covenants 98:5–8.) The self-control by which citizens subject themselves to law strengthens the freedom of all citizens and honors the divinely inspired Constitution."[16]

Doctrine and Covenants 134 begins by simply stating the belief that "governments were instituted of God for the benefit of man; and

---

15. Oaks, "Religious Freedom" (Brigham Young University–Idaho devotional, October 13, 2009), byui.edu/speeches/devotionals.
16. Oaks, "The Divinely Inspired Constitution."

that he holds men accountable for their acts in relation to them, both in making laws and administering them, for the good and safety of society" (Doctrine and Covenants 134:1). Latter-day Saints believe there is individual accountability for the collective actions taken by their government[17] as well as specific benefits that flow from well-run governments. This accountability is inescapable and extends both to "making laws and administering them." Thus, active engagement in the functioning of government is inherent in citizenship.

In order to promote the "good and safety of society," the declaration states that policies and laws should be adopted and implemented that promote the public interest and protect the individual's free exercise of conscience. "All governments have a right to enact such laws as in their own judgments are best calculated to secure the public interest; at the same time, however, holding sacred the freedom of conscience" (Doctrine and Covenants 134:5).

The declaration also makes clear a commitment to the rule of law and to quality administration in government.

> We believe that all governments necessarily require civil officers and magistrates to enforce the laws of the same; and that such as will administer the law in equity and justice should be sought for and upheld by the voice of the people if a republic, or the will of the sovereign.
>
> We believe that all men are bound to sustain and uphold the respective governments in which they reside, while protected in their inherent and inalienable rights by the laws of such governments; . . . that to the laws all men owe respect and deference, as without them peace and harmony would be supplanted by anarchy and terror; human laws being instituted for the express purpose of regulating our interests as individuals and nations, between man and man. (Doctrine and Covenants 134:3, 5–6)

---

17. Which "men" are held accountable may seem somewhat ambiguous. By one possible reading, the passage applies only to the government officials who make and administer laws. However, this does not seem compatible with popular sovereignty as explained by President Oaks or "government of the people, by the people, and for the people" which has been the most common view at least since Lincoln used the phrase.

The declaration further states that "for the public peace and tranquility all men should step forward and use their ability in bringing offenders against good laws to punishment" (Doctrine and Covenants 134:8), a view that is quite consistent with the principle of accountability as citizens. President Oaks also made this point in his discussions of the role of citizens.[18]

Divinely Inspired Rights

Regarding the Bill of Rights, President Oaks wrote:

I have always felt that the United States Constitution's closest approach to scriptural stature is in the phrasing of our Bill of Rights. Without the free exercise of religion, America could not have served as the host nation for the restoration of the gospel. . . . I also see scriptural stature in the concept and wording of the freedoms of speech and press, the right to be secure against unreasonable searches and seizures, the requirements that there must be probable cause for an arrest and that accused persons must have a speedy and public trial by an impartial jury, and the guarantee that a person will not be deprived of life, liberty, or property without due process of law. President Ezra Taft Benson has said, "Reason, necessity, tradition, and religious conviction all lead me to accept the divine origin of these rights."[19]

Doctrine and Covenants 134 identifies three "inherent and inalienable" rights which governments should secure to each individual through the legal system: "We believe that no government can exist in peace, except such laws are framed and held inviolate as will secure to each individual the free exercise of conscience, the right and control of property, and the protection of life" (Doctrine and Covenants 134:2).

Thus, while the need for governments to curtail individual freedoms is acknowledged in the need to pass and enforce laws "for the good and safety of society," there is a minimum set of rights necessary

---

18. Oaks, "The Divinely Inspired Constitution."
19. Oaks, "The Divinely Inspired Constitution."

for individuals to be able to exercise their individual agency. That set of rights is summarized in the declaration and in other non-Church documents both before[20] and after the 1835 declaration as the protection of life, liberty (free exercise of conscience), and property.

The Bill of Rights expands on this list somewhat and is augmented by the thirteenth (abolition of slavery), fourteenth (equal protection), fifteenth (right to vote not denied by race), and nineteenth (women's voting rights) amendments. The exploration, explication, and defense of these rights have occupied volumes, and it is not my objective to review this vast literature here. But it is worthwhile to consider each in light of the foundational principles identified in section 134.

Free Exercise of Conscience

The declaration of belief contained in section 134 is clear that men and women are amenable only to God for the exercise of their religion unless their actions infringe on the rights and liberties of others. The law and those who administer it should "never control conscience" nor "suppress the freedom of the soul." The Constitution also affirms the free exercise of religion, and President Oaks has spoken out vigorously in defense of freedom of religion.[21]

But both section 134 and the Constitution go beyond the individualized practice of personal religion. Section 134 affirms that it is "just to preach the gospel to the nations of the earth, and warn the righteous to save themselves from the corruption of the world" (Doctrine and Covenants 134:12). Consistent with the right to attempt to influence others in religious matters, and with accountability for the quality of governance overall, the Constitution affirms positive rights of free speech, free press, freedom of assembly, and suffrage.

---

20. See the Declaration of Independence and the natural law writers, especially John Locke. Of course, Jefferson replaced the word "property" with "pursuit of happiness" in the Declaration of Independence.
21. See, for example, "President Oaks Tells Students in Rome Why Religious Freedom Matters," *Church News*, December 14, 2021, https://newsroom.churchofjesus-christ.org/article/president-oaks-rome-religious-freedom-summary.

Thus, the minimum standard established in these two documents includes both the right to freely exercise one's personal religion (subject to a similar right for others) and the right to meet, discuss, and attempt to influence other members of the community. While section 134 is particularly concerned with religion, clearly the Constitution encompasses a similar right for all efforts to influence other members of society and the government itself. Freedom of conscience then includes both individual and collective agency at least to the extent of free expression and dialogue, and personal practices that do not compel others or infringe on the rights of others.

A commitment to similar constitutional rights in other countries has facilitated the spread of the gospel and planted the seeds of Zion in those lands.[22]

Right and Control of Property

It is possible to conceive of a society in which all social needs are met by voluntary contributions. However, as President Oaks has observed:

> The science of government is a consideration of the procedures by which and the extent to which the official representatives of one group of citizens can impose restrictions on the freedom of another group. Decisions on the extent to which government power should restrict the freedom of individuals are among the most difficult decisions we face in an organized society.[23]

Is it permissible to curtail the freedom of one group (through taxes or restrictions on property rights) in order to expand the freedoms of another group (e.g., better education, health care or access to land)? The answer is yes, within limits, if approved by the voice of the people. Access to land offers one case study.

It may appear that in an industrial society people do not require access to land to support themselves. But families need a minimal

---

22. James Goldberg et al., "Our Inspired Constitutions," *Liahona*, October 2023.
23. Oaks, *The Lord's Way*, 6.

amount of space for healthy living (even if the land area is shared with others by stacking the dwelling units) and work. People also need access to roads and walkways to enable moving about and carrying out life's activities. As argued in the chapter on land in Zion, land often has an important connection to self-identity. And ultimately land is required to grow crops and the food necessary to feed people and produce materials that are converted into clothing, shelter, and so on.

In the 1830s, the term *property* was used to describe both material things belonging to a person or group as well as land under one ownership.[24] Thus, in reading section 134 and the Constitution, it cannot be assumed that the term *property* applies only to land. At the same time, the right to property does not necessarily imply the right to total ownership of a piece of land and all properties on it. The key concept may well be a steward's right to access, control, and benefit from the materials and land necessary to provide for living space and familial support.

From one perspective, private ownership of tangible property is inconsistent with scriptures that declare that the "earth is the Lord's, and the fulness thereof" (1 Corinthians 10:26; Psalm 24:1; Deuteronomy 10:14). If the earth belongs to God as its Creator, then our possession of it is as stewards.

> For it is expedient that I, the Lord, should make every man accountable, as a steward over earthly blessings, which I have made and prepared for my creatures. I, the Lord, stretched out the heavens, and built the earth, my very handiwork; and all things therein are mine. (Doctrine and Covenants 104:13–14)

> For it is required of the Lord, at the hand of every steward, to render an account of his stewardship, both in time and in eternity. For he who is faithful and wise in time is accounted worthy to inherit the mansions prepared for him of my Father. (Doctrine and Covenants 72:3–4)

---

24. Oxford English Dictionary.

Similarly, scriptures in which God grants possession of certain lands to particular groups as a land of inheritance do not appear to contemplate the sale of that land to others. Under the regulations contained in the Torah, for example, in the jubilee year the Israelite nation was to return all property to its original owner, except the houses of laymen within walled cities (see Leviticus 25).

The Constitution seems to make clear that a family's possessions should be safe from unwarranted or unlawful seizure by the government. It seems reasonable to presume that society would protect an individual's security of possession from similar seizure by private individuals or entities. Beyond this level of security, a minimal standard in this domain would require that all persons have access to adequate living space for themselves and their family, and security in that possession. This requirement does not necessarily imply private ownership but simply security of tenure.

Families also require access to the tangible property necessary for personal and family support in order to be self-reliant, and they should have free access to public rights-of-way. These minimal rights related to property ensure to each individual the capacity to act on the choices they make and receipt of the product or result of those choices.

In this domain, as well as in the free exercise of conscience, societies may choose to articulate property rights beyond the minimum level just described. Property rights in Zion will likely be articulated differently than current Western views. (See the chapter on land in Zion and the appendix on property rights in Zion.)

Protection of Life

At one level, the protection of life may seem the most straightforward of the three rights. It seems clear that individuals and families should be safe from violence either from the government or from others in the community. Murder, assault, all forms of abuse, and other acts of violence should be prohibited and physical safety should be vigorously protected.

But it could well be argued that ignoring the nutritional needs of a starving individual is hardly protecting that individual's life. Here again, though, the voice of the people may respond differently in different settings. It would certainly be conceivable that a society could choose to act collectively through government to establish safety nets to assure such things as adequate food, shelter, and/or healthcare. Other societies may elect to meet these basic needs through the voluntary sector and the generosity of private individuals, depending on the will of the people. In most societies today, voluntary associations of private individuals provide a valuable expression of and extension to individual agency.

No matter how communities, states, and nations elect to assure the protection of the rights discussed here, "no government can exist in peace" unless these rights are protected (Doctrine and Covenants 134:2).

Limitations

If in the Zion society "the most desirable condition for the effective exercise of God-given moral agency is a condition of maximum freedom and responsibility," as President Oaks argues, government actions will of necessity be limited. Cooperative action through government will be undertaken only when other forms of voluntary cooperative action cannot accomplish the same goal or cannot accomplish it as completely. Any other course undermines voluntary cooperation and therefore the moral agency of families.

For example, the Saints today are charged with caring for the poor and eliminating poverty in Zion. Could this be done through the government's tax system? Yes, by taxing wealthier households at a higher rate and redistributing the revenue to the poor in some form. Many public finance experts argue that redistribution at the national level is an appropriate and needed function of government.

But attempting to solve the problem of poverty through the tax system has several negative effects on society. First, by using compulsion to raise taxes the agency of taxpayers is restricted, the opposite of what we would like to see in society. Compulsion replaces the grace of giving with the grumbling of the gouged.

Second, citizen taxpayers may become disconnected from the problem being solved. Many may adopt the attitude of Scrooge in Charles Dickens's *A Christmas Carol.* They paid their taxes and thereby did their part in solving the problem. If poverty remains, it is someone else's problem, or the government is corrupt and inefficient and should be reformed, ignoring the fact that poverty is not eliminated by money alone. It also requires donations of time for mentoring and the provision of opportunities.

The third negative effect is more subtle but perhaps the most serious. By replacing voluntary cooperative action with government compulsion, we undermine the strength of families acting in unison with other families.

When the Martin and Willy handcart companies were stranded in Wyoming, there was no government program to rescue them. Families cooperated to send men and supplies voluntarily. When Herbert Hoover led the effort to feed the people of Belgium during World War I, families acted cooperatively to gather supplies and charter ships, often over the objection of governments. Such actions today are hard to imagine because we have international organizations—extensions of governments—to address hunger, refugees, emergency shelter, and the like.[25] Families' recognition of the need to act, understanding of their personal responsibility to act, and even their awareness of how to act effectively have been diminished because of the growth of government.

I am not suggesting that these programs never should have come about. Much suffering has been relieved because of them. I am arguing that there is a price in addition to the monetary cost. Some call it social capital, but whatever the label, the ability of individuals and families to voluntarily join with other families to resolve a problem is reduced when government acts. As a result, government action should be a last resort if a condition of maximum freedom and responsibility is to exist in Zion. The Lord expects us to see a need and do our best to fulfill it:

> For behold, it is not meet that I should command in all things; for he that is compelled in all things, the same is a slothful and not a wise servant; wherefore he receiveth no reward. Verily I say, men

---

25. There are also large and often effective voluntary organizations collecting resources and distributing them to meet very real needs.

should be anxiously engaged in a good cause, and do many things of their own free will, and bring to pass much righteousness; For the power is in them, wherein they are agents unto themselves. And inasmuch as men do good they shall in nowise lose their reward. (Doctrine and Covenants 58:26–28)

It is true that the Lord intends that "the poor shall be exalted, in that the rich are made low" (Doctrine and Covenants 104:16), but the principles of agency and accountability imply that this sharing will be voluntary and based on the laws of the celestial kingdom.

At the same time, I am not suggesting that all government programs to assist those in need should be immediately dismantled. There will need to be a transition period, which will likely be painful. The Saints in Zion and the remaining good people of the earth will need to relearn the lessons of charity, unity, initiative, and voluntary cooperative action. While the transition is underway, some duplication of effort may be needed to minimize the suffering of those in need.

Even in Zion a civil government will be needed. The focus of that government will most likely be limited, as many of the current social functions of government will be assumed by individuals and families acting cooperatively through other channels.

The central structural features of government will include the four fundamentals that Presidents Clark and Oaks identified: the separation of powers in the three branches of government, the division of powers between sub-national and national government, the application of popular sovereignty, and the preeminence of the rule of law.

Another central function of government will be the protection of rights, particularly minority rights. The national track record on protecting minority rights is poor, including the treatment of African Americans, Native Americans, Japanese Americans, Latter-day Saints, and others. These fundamental rights are currently enumerated in amendments to the Constitution and are summarized in Doctrine and Covenants 134 as the free exercise of conscience, the right and control of property, and the protection of life. How these rights are articulated may change and evolve and must certainly improve. But in Zion the objective will remain the same: the achievement of the maximum degree of freedom and responsibility so that individuals can exercise their agency in a spirit of liberty. Given that objective, it is reasonable to ask what the role of government will be in Zion.

The Role of Government in Zion

As noted, civil governments have a role in Zion. Joseph Smith spoke of religious rights to be protected. President Oaks and President Clark spoke of other rights enumerated in the Constitution and protections for minority interests. Thus, one accepted role for civil government in Zion is the protection of human rights and the prevention of discrimination.

The need for protection is readily extended to the enforcement of private contracts. Suppose, for example, two couples—Bob and Susan and Jeremy and Ethel—are responsible individuals in possession of all relevant information, and they choose to enter into a contract with each other. Let's say they make a real estate transaction in which Bob and Susan agree to sell their home and land to Jeremy and Ethel. The couples agree on a price, other terms, and a date to finalize the transaction, all of which are specified in the contract. Jeremy and Ethel do all that is required under the contract, but at the last minute, Bob and Susan have a change of heart and refuse to finalize the sale. What can Jeremy and Ethel do? It depends on several factors, but in the end, Jeremy and Ethel can turn to the government for help in enforcing the contract or recovering any financial damages they may have incurred.

Beyond protections of this sort and the prosecution of wrongdoers, is there any role for government? Government is one mode for collective action, and how widely it is used will depend on the community and the will of the people. Many governments provide a range of basic services, including clean water, sanitary sewage disposal, garbage collection, roads, fire protection, emergency medical services, public parks, and others. Could these be provided by families themselves or by private self-reliant associations in Zion? Nearly all could be.

In addition to the millions of homes on private wells, hundreds of privately owned and operated companies have a strong track record of reliably providing clean water to thousands of homes. Many of these are regulated by government agencies to ensure quality service and fair prices. Many sewage treatment facilities are also privately owned, and about 60 million homes in the United States are served by private septic systems.[26]

Garbage collection has been privatized in many communities. Private highways are probably more common in Asia and Europe, but they do exist in the United States as well. Even if the highway was originally built with public money, it may be operated by a private company.

Several states have privately owned fire departments, and privately owned emergency medical services are not uncommon. Even national parks can be privately owned. The Tallgrass Prairie National Preserve is 99.7 percent private land but is managed by the National Park Service in exchange for public access and education.

Who decides which services will be owned and operated privately and which will be by the government? Ultimately, it's the people in each community, state, or nation, but the answer may change over time. What has been traditionally a publicly owned and operated service may be wholly privatized, or the public may retain ownership but turn management over to a private entity.

Many communities retain certain services, such as the provision of electricity, believing that the public entity can provide the service at a lower cost to the consumer. In other instances, the challenges of upgrading and maintaining a system may prove more costly than the community is willing to bear, so they privatize all or part of the operation. Or the choice may go in the opposite direction and a service that was privately operated may be taken over by a government agency. Such decisions depend on the perceptions of the decision-makers and the priorities of the community.

An interesting variation on the public versus private provision is the homeowner's association (HOA). In the United States, HOAs are private entities that often provide public-type services. Membership is established when a family buys property within the boundaries of the HOA. The decision to buy the property is also a decision to join

---

26. "Septic Systems Overview," United States Environmental Protection Agency, 2018, accessed September 3, 2023, https://19january2021snapshot.epa.gov/septic/septic-systems-overview_.html#:~:text=More%20than%2060%20million%20people,or%20other%20decentralized%20treatment%20systems.

the HOA, and there is a contractual agreement to abide by the rules of the HOA and pay any required fees. HOA rules typically relate to how yards and buildings will be maintained and used, and can be much more restrictive than municipal ordinances. HOA services vary widely from simply providing group insurance on commonly owned property to a full range of what are typically municipal services. Normal HOA fees act very much like property taxes.

For other types of services, public and private provision may be mixed. A community may have a public law enforcement agency, but a large enterprise may elect to supplement public protection with their own security personnel. National defense may seem the purview of national governments, but mercenary armies have existed for centuries and continue to supplement government forces today, especially in the Middle East.

In all cases, public services must be paid for, and higher levels of reliable service will generally be more costly. There are principally two methods used to pay for government services: fees and taxes. Some services can be divided into units, such as gallons of water, kilowatts of electricity, admissions to a recreation center, or marriage licenses issued. Such services are generally paid for through fees based on the number of service units provided.

With other services, it is difficult to isolate a unit of service. For example, how much fire protection does a typical home receive in a year? Such services are frequently paid for through the tax system. At times, the public benefit of a service may be large enough that even if a fee is charged, the cost of the service may be partially borne by taxpayers. An example might be the registration of births, marriages, and deaths.

In some instances, requiring participation in a service may be in the public interest. When I was in a smaller community in Brazil, not all streets were paved. Those that were typically had cobblestones. In residential areas, if a homeowner wanted the street in front of their house paved with cobblestones, they were required to pay a fee. If all the neighbors paid but a particular homeowner did not, the street was paved, except for the half street directly in front of the non-paying property. Drivers and missionaries on bicycles had to remain alert.

It is not uncommon in some localities to require families to participate in a service. For example, a family may be on their own septic system, but if the community decides to move to a central sewage system and installs a sewer line in the road, the community may require the family to connect to the sewer line in order to spread the cost of the new system across a broader base. This may especially be the case if the development density on private septic systems is causing groundwater contamination. Public health and safety considerations may push communities to require new construction projects to participate in such services as sanitary sewage disposal, solid waste collection and disposal, water services, and electricity.

In other instances, citizens may choose to act through government to restrict or prohibit some private actions and require others. In the appendix on property rights, the discussion of trespass laws by Simon Winchester points out that while trespassing on private property without permission is generally prohibited in the United States, several European countries have no such restrictions.

In the past sixty years, the world in general has become more aware of the potential environmental harm from some manufacturing processes. Many countries now require firms to adopt technologies and practices to limit their adverse impact on water and air quality. Some of these policies remain controversial because of the financial burden placed on those firms. But when the value of a market transaction such as the sale of electricity does not reflect the full cost to the community in terms of degraded air quality or other effects, communities and nations can act through regulation to minimize any impacts not reflected in the market price.

In other cases, there are what economists call "public goods." These are services that if provided at all are automatically provided to everyone, and no person's consumption of the service diminishes anyone else's use or consumption. National defense is often cited as a case in point, but I like the example of clean air. If we can ensure the air is clean for me, then it is also clean for everyone else in the community. My consumption of clean air does not diminish the amount of clean air for others. These "public goods" are generally paid for through the tax system. For example, clean air is often paid for through tax credits and tax exemptions for air pollution control technologies installed by polluting firms.

Government is not all about restricted freedom and required taxes. Some services can be provided at a higher level and a lower cost if the service is provided at a more aggregated level. When my mother was a child, she lived on a farm in a rural county. The cost of the sole schoolteacher was shared among families by providing room and board for the teacher, two weeks at a time per family. It was definitely hard on the teacher and was likely not the best learning environment for the children. Now we have specialized educational opportunities provided to rural areas via video connections over dedicated computer networks. It still is not ideal for many people, but it is a vast improvement and the service cost can be justified since it is provided to a larger population.

Some services simply could not be provided adequately at the state or local level. Most people feel that the U.S. federal government does a reasonable job of responding to natural disasters, protecting the public from terrorists, and ensuring that the foods we eat and our medicines are safe. The internet is an outgrowth of federal defense spending, as is the national highway system. Even long-term fully amortized home mortgages required federal guarantees when they were first developed. Could these services have been developed by private entities? Yes, but it is highly unlikely that the private sector would have taken the risks and made the investments without federal support and guarantees, paid for and supported by federal tax dollars.

In a Zion society committed to supporting individual agency and personal accountability to the extent possible, how should decisions be made regarding restrictions on personal freedom through laws and regulations, and through required taxes and fees? It depends on what the communities, states, and nation want and are willing to pay for. Here again, I would argue that some of the costs of acting through government are non-monetary. The ability of individuals and families to voluntarily join with other families to resolve a problem is reduced when government acts. This is not an argument against government as a tool for public action. It is a caution to consider all the implications of such collective choices.

I am not arguing that everything government does is done well. On the contrary, there is much room for improvement at all levels of government. However, some things can be done through government more economically, more effectively, or more completely than through other forms of private associations. Identifying what those things are in a given setting and reaching a reasonable consensus on how much to do and how to pay for it is a key function and challenge for popular sovereignty.

Judge Hand argued that these formal governance rules and roles of government are insufficient to ensure a free society, that the spirit of liberty must reside in the hearts of men. He offered his vision for what that spirit is when he said:

> The spirit of liberty is the spirit which seeks to understand the mind of other men and women; the spirit of liberty is the spirit which weighs their interests alongside its own without bias; the spirit of liberty remembers that not even a sparrow falls to earth unheeded; the spirit of liberty is the spirit of Him who, near two thousand years ago, taught mankind that lesson it has never learned but never quite forgotten; that there may be a kingdom where the least shall be heard and considered side by side with the greatest.[27]

Zion will be that kingdom. The next chapter discusses how such a spirit can be fostered, nurtured, and sustained.

---

27. Hand, *The Spirit of Liberty: Papers and addresses of Learned Hand.*

CHAPTER 12

Governance in Zion

The preceding chapter outlined the inspired principles for structuring the government of Zion, many of which are already embedded in the constitutional framework of the United States. Scripture proclaims that God Himself "established the Constitution of this land, by the hands of wise men whom I raised up unto this very purpose" (Doctrine and Covenants 101:80) and the Saints should befriend "that law which is the constitutional law of the land" (Doctrine and Covenants 98:6). Does that mean that we have a righteous civil government and that it will remain so as long as we sustain and defend the Constitution? Are the current Constitution and laws enough to protect religious freedom now and to govern Zion in the future?

The question requires an answer on at least two levels. What more do we need to govern Zion in the long run? And what steps do we need to take today to move our society closer to Zion?

Is Our Democracy in Trouble?

Joseph Smith said that his only complaint about the U.S. Constitution was that it did not give the federal government enough power to protect the rights of individuals as expressed in the

Constitution.[1] That concern has been largely addressed with the adoption of "equal protection" under the Fourteenth Amendment in 1866 and subsequent expansion of federal authority.

However, the U.S. population has become increasingly skeptical about the country's ability to solve the problems it faces. According to a report from the Pew Research Center, the percentage of people in the United States who trust "the government to do what is right just about always" or "most of the time" has fallen from about 75 percent in the early 1960s and has hovered in the 15-to-25-percent range since 2020.[2] National polls also regularly show that the large majority of Americans feel the country is "on the wrong track."[3]

The challenges are not just in America and are not just a matter of public opinion. The publishers of *The Economist* in the United Kingdom have developed a Democracy Index evaluating conditions in 167 countries. Their data includes information on electoral processes, civil liberties, political participation rates, government functioning, and political culture. At this writing, the data only goes back about fifteen years, but during that time, countries have become less democratic in virtually every region of the world. Since 2006, the condition of democracy in the United States has declined noticeably on this scale, and the United States now ranks below Canada, Austria, Denmark, Finland, Germany, and several other European countries.[4]

In a recent survey of twenty-two countries (all members of the Organization for Economic Cooperation and Development [OECD]), the overall finding was that about 60 percent of those residents surveyed do not trust their national governments. It is noteworthy that

1. Joseph Smith Papers, *Council of Fifty, Minutes, March 1844–January 1846*, 1, 201–03.
2. "Public Trust in Government: 1958–2022," Pew Research Center, 2022, accessed July 1, 2023, https://www.pewresearch.org/politics/2022/06/06/public-trust-in-government-1958–2022/.
3. For example, Chuck Todd et al., "Poll finds 71% of Americans believe country is on wrong track," *NBC News First Read* (2023). https://www.nbcnews.com/meet-the-press/first-read/poll-finds-71–americans-believe-country-wrong-track-rcna68138.
4. EIU, *Frontline Democracy and the Battle for Ukraine: Democracy Index 2022*, Economist Intelligence Unit Limited (London, UK, 2022), https://www.eiu.com/n/campaigns/democracy-index-2022/.

while the United States is a member of the OECD, it did not choose to participate in this survey.

> Results from multiple questions in the Trust Survey consistently illustrate that governments are seen as unresponsive to people's demands both in policy making and in more obviously democratic processes. Only one third of people (32.9%) think their government would adopt opinions expressed in a public consultation, for example. . . . And only about four in ten respondents, on average across countries, say that their government would improve a poorly performing service, implement an innovative idea, or change a national policy in response to public demands. . . . When considering more overtly democratic political processes, only three in ten say the political system in their country lets them have a say.[5]

These trends have led multiple observers and authors to wonder about the future of democracy.[6] All this suggests that while essential formal principles for the design of government are present in the Constitution, they are not sufficient to assure the permanence of democracy today or that Zion, once achieved, will remain a free society governed by the will of the people. If the polls and pundits are correct, our democracy is moving in the opposite direction.

We have the principles needed to govern Zion. We need the values that Judge Learned Hand said must lie "in the hearts of men and women" if liberty is to thrive[7] and a citizenry committed to both the

---

5. OECD, *Building Trust to Reinforce Democracy: Main Findings from the 2021 OECD Survey on Drivers of Trust in Public Institutions*, (Paris: OECD Publishing, 2022), Section 1.2.

6. See for example, Robert Kuttner, "Can Democracy Survive?" *The American Prospect* (October 25, 2022); Richard Haass, "Can Democracy Survive?" *Nine Questions for the World* (2021); Anne Applebaum and Peter Pomerantsev, "How to Put Out Democracy's Dumpster Fire," *The Atlantic*, April 2021; Tom Ginsburg and Aziz Z. Huq, *How to Save a Constitutional Democracy* (Chicago, IL: The University of Chicago Press, 2018); George Soros, "Can Democracy Survive the Polycrisis?," *Project Syndicate: The World's Opinion Page* (2023); William A. Galston and Elaine Kamarck, *Is Democracy Failing and Putting Our Economic System at Risk? The Brookings Institution and States United Democracy Center* (Washington, DC, 2022).

7. Hand, *The Spirit of Liberty: Papers and Addresses of Learned Hand.*

formal and informal governance system that is grounded in and operates based on those principles.

The Need for Committed Participation

What are the values that must lie in the hearts of men and women in a Zion society? Judge Hand was focused on the spirit of liberty. President John Taylor spoke of the need to get the law of consecration in the hearts of the people. Both are encompassed in the foundation stones discussed in part 2: devotion to the Father and the Son, charity as Christlike love for all, individual agency, personal accountability, and the unity required by celestial law. Unanimity of understanding and agreement on how the foundation stones should influence social action often takes time and public deliberations, and the answers are never fixed and unchangeable.

When the Council of Fifty debated whether there was a difference between church and state, Joseph did not give his views until after a protracted debate among council members.[8] Could he have spoken up sooner and rechanneled the discussion? Possibly, but it is equally likely that his views and inspiration were informed by the debate. That is one reason the Church is governed by councils with decisions made after careful deliberation. Councils are intended to provide a forum for deliberations that both clarify our personal thinking and bring out a shared perspective that is richer than any one individual's views. We hear with some frequency the phrase attributed to Elder Boyd K. Packer: "Revelation is scattered among us."[9]

Governance in Zion will occur through popular sovereignty, as stated by President Oaks. Effective and sustainable democratic sovereignty requires public discussion and the exchange of ideas. It requires active and engaged citizens who participate in the process. The need for charity and unity in Zion requires that the citizens in Zion listen to each other and share their perspectives, regardless of apparent differences. That can be difficult to do.

---

8. Joseph Smith Papers, *Council of Fifty, Minutes, March 1844–January 1846*, 1, 201–03.
9. Neil L. Andersen, "Align with the Brethren" (Leadership Enrichment Series, August 15, 2012). See also https://ca.churchofjesuschrist.org/a-special-code.

Society and the challenges we face are constantly changing, and our governance system must be able to accommodate and adapt as those changes emerge. The key is a commitment to the foundations of Zion, a solid grounding in popular sovereignty, and broadly based public engagement with the process.

Unfortunately, the level of public engagement in the United States and elsewhere has declined over the decades. Rather than engaging in meaningful discussions, we all too frequently think that if you don't agree with me, you are either ignorant, stupid, or evil.

It has probably always been hard to talk to people who are different, and there seems to be an initial bias against those who aren't like us. But over time those biases can change. For example, between 1820 and 1860, the Irish constituted more than one-third of all immigrants to the United States. In the 1840s, they comprised nearly half of all immigrants to the United States. The influx of immigrants who were perceived to be different in religion and habits prompted resentment and fear.

> Ill will toward Irish immigrants because of their poor living conditions, and their willingness to work for low wages was often exacerbated by religious conflict. Centuries of tension between Protestants and Catholics found their way into United States cities and verbal attacks often led to mob violence. For example, Protestants burned down St. Mary's Catholic Church in New York City in 1831, while in 1844, riots in Philadelphia left thirteen dead.[10]

The story of how the view of the Irish changed is both important and fascinating, involving cooperation, corruption, perseverance, and champions such as Mary Harris ("Mother") Jones. Somehow, we are now quite willing to claim an Irish connection every St. Patrick's Day.

It has always been hard to talk to those outside our circle, but when we do, our views and our understanding of our core values

---

10. "Irish-Catholic Immigration to America," Classroom Materials: Immigration and Relocation in U.S. History, The Library of Congress, 2023, accessed June 25, 2023, https://www.loc.gov/classroom-materials/immigration/irish/irish-catholic-immigration-to-america/.

change. And so do those of the "others." The foundation stones of Zion do not change, but our understanding of them and our resulting actions become more consistent with those foundations.

Examples of Active Citizenship

Often, breaching the barrier has required champions to lead the way. Some "barriers" may simply be social inertia: we keep doing what we have been doing because that is what we have done before. Active citizens emerge to raise our sights and elevate our actions. Aurelia Spencer Rogers was one such active citizen. At the age of thirteen, she and her sister assumed the care for four younger siblings when their mother died. Just a few months later, their father was called on a three-year mission, leaving the two sisters to care for the other children, move the family to Salt Lake, and settle in the Salt Lake Valley.

Brigham Young established programs for teenage youth in the mid-1870s, but more than 40 percent of Utah's population was under the age of fourteen. Now an adult, Aurelia had been concerned for some time about the need for better discipline, especially among young boys. Her bishop shared her concern and called a meeting of the mothers in the area. Aurelia later wrote to Eliza R. Snow reflecting on her experience:

> The subject of training children was thoroughly discussed and the responsibility of guiding their young minds was thrown almost entirely upon the mothers. I had children of my own, and was just as anxious as a mother could be to have them brought up properly. But what was to be done? It needed the united effort of the parents, and, as is often the case in a community, some of them were careless. A fire seemed to burn within me, and I had a desire at one time to go to the Young Men's Mutual Improvement Association meeting and talk to them; but I did not yield to the impulse, thinking too much, perhaps, of what people might say. The query then arose in my mind could there not be an organization for little boys wherein they could be taught everything good, and how to behave.[11]

---

11. Jill Mulvay Derr et al., eds., *The First Fifty Years of Relief Society: Key Documents in Latter-day Saint Women's History* (Salt Lake City, UT: Church Historian's

Aurelia presented the idea to General Relief Society President Eliza R. Snow and her companions. Not long after, Aurelia's bishop asked if she would be willing to start such an organization. She said:

> I felt willing, but very incompetent. From that time my mind was busy thinking how it was to be managed.
>
> Up to this period the girls had not been mentioned; but my mind was that the meeting would not be complete without them; for as singing was necessary, it needed the voices of little girls as well as boys to make it sound as well as it should. After some consideration, a letter was sent to Sister Eliza asking her opinion in regard to the little girls taking part.[12]

Eliza responded:

> My dear sister Rogers: The spirit and contents of your letter pleased me much. I feel assured that the inspiration of heaven is directing you, and that a great and very important movement is being inaugurated for the future of Zion.[13]

Aurelia Rogers saw the need for an instructional program focused on younger children and started a Primary organization for the children in Farmington, Utah, on August 11, 1878. Two weeks later, more than two hundred children gathered for the first meeting. Eliza R. Snow soon launched a Primary in Salt Lake City, and the Primary organization became an officially sponsored Church organization in 1880 under the leadership of Louie B. Felt.

In the early years, the Primary was not a resounding success. Attendance averaged about half of those enrolled. Eliza R. Snow traveled widely working with local Relief Societies and promoting the new Primary. Emmeline B. Wells published supporting editorials in

---

Press, 2016), 206.

12. Derr et al., *The First Fifty Years of Relief Society*, 209.

13. Derr et al., *The First Fifty Years of Relief Society*, 209.

the *Woman's Exponent*, and President John Taylor added his support for the fledgling organization.[14]

Louie B. Felt's decades of leadership also had a powerful impact on the Primary's success. She was the first General Primary President and served in that calling for forty-five years. It took years for the Primary organization to mature and for specialized materials and songbooks to be developed.

I share this long example because it illustrates some key points:

- One person who understood and was committed to the foundations of the gospel saw a need and took action. She did not wait for the institutional structure to present a response to the need.

- She did not work alone but sought both counsel and cooperation from others. She found the support of a champion in Eliza R. Snow.

- The success of the effort was the result of concerted, cooperative effort over many years.

This example demonstrates the power of individual active citizens responding to community needs and the potential of that action to result in rich blessings flowing from very humble beginnings.

A commitment to the foundations of Zion often leads to individual action in response to observed needs in the community. The following contemporary example illustrates many key principles for initiating and sustaining local "informal governance" as the power to affect change in a community.

The My Hometown Initiative

Mark Rupp was a bishop and later a stake president in West Valley City, Utah, the second largest city in the state by population. Through his service he developed a detailed knowledge of the needs of

---

14. RoseAnn Benson, "Primary Association Pioneers: An Early History," *A Firm Foundation: Church Organization and Administration*, ed. David J. Whittaker and Arnold K. Garr (Provo, UT: Religious Studies Center, Brigham Young University, 2011).

his neighbors. Those needs were great, both in the Church and among all his neighbors.

President Rupp's stake, the Salt Lake Granger North Stake, included about four thousand homes, or about ten percent of the city's housing, and was a microcosm of West Valley City on several dimensions. More than 40 percent of West Valley's housing stock was built in the post-war baby-boom years prior to the official incorporation of the city in 1980. At the same time, only 8 percent of the homes in West Valley have been constructed since 2010, compared to nearly 21 percent statewide.

Residing in this modest and aging housing is a very diverse population. The U.S. Census Bureau reports that about 45 percent of the West Valley population considers itself "white, non-Hispanic." More than one in five residents were born outside the United States, and more than 40 percent of the families speak a language other than English at home.[15] At one point Mark Rupp asked his congregations to identify the countries where household members were born. The stake then built an award-winning parade float featuring the forty-five national flags of those countries.[16]

Low incomes and poverty are also challenges in many areas in West Valley City. Overall, per capita income levels are about one-third lower than the state average, while the poverty rate is about 24 percent higher.

Faced with aging housing and neighborhoods, as well as a large immigrant population struggling to survive economically, Mark Rupp described his stake as having "ten times the needs and one-tenth the resources" of most stakes.[17]

For years, President Rupp worked to fulfill the needs of his congregants and the community. He met with city officials and drove through the area with them. He also sought guidance from his ecclesiastical leaders. Then in 2019, years of previous impressions and conversations began to bear fruit.

15. U.S. Census Bureau, "QuickFacts: West Valley CIty City, UT," 2023.
16. Mark Rupp, "Operation MyHometown Origins and Development," interview by Lawrence Walters, October 5, 2023.
17. Rupp, interview.

In late 2017, Mark Rupp's brother, Jeffrey, was called to serve as the stake president in the Draper Utah Stake. A little over a year later, on July 17, 2019, President Mark invited President Jeffrey and his counselors to tour the Salt Lake Granger North Stake. On the drive to West Valley, the discussion centered on how the Draper stake might help the West Valley community. On the drive back to Draper, the discussion centered on how a collaborative effort would be mutually beneficial.[18]

Having met with city administrators several times previously with few results, President Mark Rupp decided to schedule another meeting with administrators and invite two other local stake presidents, a couple of bishops, and a stake Relief Society president to go with him. On August 13, 2019, a meeting took place with Assistant City Manager Nicole Cottle, Community Development Director Steve Pastorik, and other city staff to discuss needs and begin to establish a plan. President Rupp clearly remembers an engaging discussion, but as the meeting was nearing conclusion, he felt that no action plan had been agreed upon and "that could not be the result of this meeting." He stated to the others present, "We need to pick a street, and start now to make a difference." Nicole Cottle responded that she would meet with her team and get back to President Rupp in two weeks.

The problems Mark identified were not new for city leaders. West Valley city managers had divided the city into seventy-five neighborhoods and had ten years of statistics documenting trends. Through their "neighborhood help audits," they knew about declining neighborhoods and poverty. They knew where the police calls were coming from and where the housing code violations were. For years, the city and county had invested millions of dollars in various projects to improve neighborhoods, with little, if any, results.[19] They had learned that reversing these trends could not be achieved by the city alone. As City Manager Wayne Pyle described, there was no way the city could

---

18. Rupp, interview.
19. Nicole Cottle, "Operation MyHometown Origins," interview by Lawrence Walters, October, 6 2023.

overcome these challenges since residents saw the city as government and believed government was not to be trusted.[20]

Assistant City Manager Nicole Cottle had been with the city for more than twenty years as an attorney. In that capacity, she worked with and gained the respect of all the key city department heads. As the assistant city manager, one of her assignments was problem solving and constituent services. When she went into the meeting with Mark Rupp and others from the Church, she knew they had been in before and expected them to ask the city to solve a problem.[21]

But Nicole had a unique experience. Mark Rupp and the other local leaders did not ask the city to solve their problems. They asked the city to help them solve their problems. Nicole was not certain how to respond to this novel request and asked for two weeks to think about it.

The meeting with Mark Rupp was different because these local leaders were asking for cooperation and collaboration, not for someone else to solve the problems. Shortly thereafter, Nicole felt she had a clear vision of who needed to do what in city government, where to start, and even what to call the initiative.

Discussions continued with the assigned Area Seventy, Mark Durham. Subsequently, a meeting was held on October 8, 2019, with Elder Durham, two other stake presidents, and Elder Craig C. Christensen, the Area President over Utah. Nicole Cottle was also invited.

They began to exchange ideas and plans, and in a subsequent meeting between Mark Rupp, Elder Mark Durham, Nicole Cottle, and one of the bishops in the Granger North Stake, plans were considered and a proposal finalized.

Nicole proposed a location for the initial pilot effort that was in the "middle of the bottom" grouping of neighborhoods. The area was known as the Hillsdale neighborhood on city records but was referred to as the Stansbury area by residents. Nicole felt there was a base to draw on in terms of people committed to their families. This

---

20. Wayne Pyle, "Interview Regarding Operation MyHometown," interview by Lawrence Walters, October 4, 2023.
21. Cottle, interview.

neighborhood of 1,060 houses, apartments, and mobile homes[22] also featured an elementary school, a chapel of The Church of Jesus Christ of Latter-day Saints, and thirty other churches.[23]

The proposed plan was submitted to the Area Presidency and eventually the Quorum of the Twelve Apostles. With their approval and that of the West Valley City leadership, Operation Hometown was born, which eventually came to be known as the My Hometown Initiative.

The fundamental challenge in the Stansbury area was the lack of trust and cohesion. One year prior to launching the My Hometown Initiative, the city had allocated one million dollars for homes in the Stansbury area for improvements, weatherization, and the like. Whether through a lack of understanding or a reluctance to fill out a form and self-identify, not one application was received.[24]

The My Hometown Initiative first had to organize and reach out to residents. Mark Rupp and ward leaders began by selecting approximately thirty-five block captains, each assigned to approach residents at ten to fifteen homes and identify the needs and capacities of each household. These block captains were selected from people Mark and ward leaders knew, whether or not they were members of The Church of Jesus Christ of Latter-day Saints. The criterion was simple: who do we know who cares about the neighborhood?

The block captains were the heart of the My Hometown Initiative. They were on the front line, breaking down barriers between neighbors. Nicole Cottle explained that many in the neighborhood didn't trust anyone because they didn't know each other even if they had lived next to each other for years. The language barriers and concerns about immigration status encouraged isolation. But neighbors just a few houses away could reach out and begin to listen.

Another key was the service and mentoring provided by volunteers from other parts of the Salt Lake Valley. These "sister stakes" as well as other churches provided volunteer labor, but at least as important was

22. Tad Walch, "Church, city reshape neighborhood with Operation My Hometown," *Deseret News*, February 24, 2021.
23. Cottle, interview.
24. Cottle, interview.

the encouragement and mentoring offered. The ultimate objective was to make the improvement process self-sustaining by using residents' own resources where possible and local resources as needed. The My Hometown Initiative provided the required infusion of vision and a demonstration of the power of cooperation.

The initial intent was to start with both a community resource center (CRC) housed in the LDS chapel and a "Days of Service" program. Then COVID forced a change in the initial focus. In February 2020, My Hometown launched with the "Days of Service" program and an explanation of the future CRC at a neighborhood dinner attended by about 150 participants. Over eight different days, the coalition of neighbors, volunteers, and the city completed 110 projects and made significant improvements to 55 homes in Hillsdale.[25] As of this writing, more than 100,000 hours of service have been rendered during these service days.[26]

As it became feasible again, the local Latter-day Saint chapel became a multi-use building, serving as a community resource center while still fulfilling its regular function as a chapel. People took their neighbors to the resource center. As Mark Rupp described, the intent was to break down barriers and help people improve their lives. To achieve this goal, volunteers were available to support a variety of services, including helping others to understand the process of getting a driver's license, learn English, and access immigration services. Block captains and My Hometown volunteers learned that parents in the neighborhood wanted their children to have music lessons, so the resource center identified volunteers to teach piano lessons.[27]

A key to the success of the mentoring offered was the relationships that were established. Whatever hesitations volunteers may have experienced about entering "someone else's neighborhood,"[28] those sentiments changed as relationships developed. Volunteers recognized that it takes more than simply telling someone what they need to do. It takes demonstration and going with them to get that driver's license

---

25. Walch, "Operation MyHometown."
26. Rupp, interview.
27. Rupp, interview.
28. Cottle, interview.

or access to well-baby immunizations.[29] It takes mentoring and ministering one by one.[30]

The initiative has proven successful in building a sense of community where little existed. As just one indicator, more than 1,300 people attended a My Hometown interfaith Christmas celebration.[31]

Of course, home and neighborhood improvements, as well as resource centers, often require more than labor. The Church continues to provide the chapel for the resource center and limited humanitarian assistance for some projects. West Valley City provides dumpsters, hosts block parties, and prints materials for events and venues. Additional resources are obtained through corporate and private donations.[32]

My Hometown has become self-sustaining as local residents step up and become local leaders. Block captains meet regularly to compare notes and assess needs. The interfaith council of churches meets monthly to cooperate and collaborate. Former Assistant City Manager Nicole Cottle said, "This is the way to save communities and bolster neighborhoods. This is the only thing I have seen in 25 years that is as impactful. It is the way. Period."[33] Mark Rupp quotes Elder Craig C. Christensen as saying, "This is the most meaningful thing I've participated in while serving as Utah Area President."[34]

Neither Aurelia Rogers nor Mark Rupp launched national or even regional campaigns, though their efforts grew beyond their initial vision. Both started at a local level, where effective collective action begins—in neighborhoods and communities, in both formal and informal counseling and deliberation together.

It may be difficult to conceive of a national deliberative process involving millions of people spread over thousands of miles. We have national elections for political office, but there is little, if any, counseling together or deliberation on specific needs such as immigration

---

29. Rupp, interview.
30. Cottle, interview.
31. Rupp, interview.
32. Cottle interview; Rupp, interview.
33. Cottle, interview.
34. Rupp, interview.

reform, climate change, welfare reform, or health policy. On the other hand, it is quite possible to design a process that starts at the local level and undergoes a systematic aggregation and validation procedure to obtain public input on selected structured issues. There are fairly well-defined processes for engaging the public in policy discussions and deliberations. Specific suggestions and strategies are presented in the appendix on deliberative processes.

As successful as the My Hometown Initiative is proving, the type of neighborhood interaction it illustrates could be facilitated more effectively by careful urban design such as that contemplated for the city of Zion. In this regard, it is insightful to revisit the design of the city of Zion as envisioned by Joseph Smith and his counselors.

The City of Zion: Neighborhood Engagement and City Form

Two versions of the plat for the city of Zion were sent from Kirtland to Bishop Partridge in Missouri. Both versions included a city with square blocks of ten acres each, 660 feet on each side. Each block was to be divided into 20 half-acre lots, each 66 feet by 330 feet. The revised plat for the city shows 2,640 lots organized into a city described as 1.5–miles on a side (actual dimensions as drawn are 1.72 miles by 1.58 miles). All lots were laid out on a north-south, east-west grid of streets that were mostly 82.5 feet wide.[35]

One of the unusual features of the plat was the intended population density, which the First Presidency stated was 15,000 to 20,000 people. That puts the population density between 5,500 and 7,345 people per square mile. Of the 326 cities and towns currently in Utah, only two have densities in that range: Kearns (7,930/mile) and Midvale (6,092/mile). Thus, the city of Zion was to be more densely developed than other frontier cities, even though the lot sizes would be considered quite large today.

---

35. Joseph Smith Papers, *Revised Plat of the city of Zion, circa Early August 1833, The Joseph Smith Papers* (Salt Lake City, UT: Church Historian Press, The Church of Jesus Christ of Latter-day Saints, 1833).

The combination of layout, density, and community design led the American Planning Association to designate the plat for the city of Zion as a National Planning Landmark.[36] Beyond the physical aspects of the city plan, historian Steven L. Olsen has written about the spiritual symbolism and implications of the plat for Zion. In 1993 Olsen wrote: "The three most popular academic explanations of Zion's uniform cardinal and orthogonal layout have been (1) the democratic land distribution practices on the American frontier, (2) a lack of aesthetic creativity on the part of Joseph Smith and (3) the historical experience of the Prophet in urban centers of America."[37]

Olsen, however, finds symbolic ties to core spiritual concepts in the plan for Zion: the gathering "from the four quarters of the earth" (Doctrine and Covenants 33:6) and "an earthly model of a spiritual ideal and a territorial symbol of the order of human relationships approximating the order that was found in the City of God."[38]

Olsen argues that Zion's social order was to be based on priesthood organization of temporal affairs, with the inhabitants living in an equal and self-sufficient society, and interpersonal interaction governed by the highest moral principles. "Zion's social order complemented its territorial order—both were centrally focused on and mutually ordered by religious principles."[39]

If Olsen is correct, then the territorial design of the city of Zion should have implications for local governance and neighborhood deliberations. Unfortunately, while the dynamics of neighborhood growth and decline have received a good deal of attention from researchers, the topic of neighborhood governance has not been their focus.[40] But

---

36. "National Planning Landmarks," American Planning Association, 1996, https://www.planning.org/awards/landmarks/#Utah.

37. Steven L. Olsen, "Joseph Smith's Concept of the city of Zion," in *Joseph Smith: The Prophet, The Man*, ed. Susan Easton Black and Charles D. Tate, Jr. (Provo, UT: Religious Studies Center, Brigham Young University, 1993), 207.

38. Olsen, "Joseph Smith's Concept of the city of Zion," 208.

39. Olsen, "Joseph Smith's Concept of the city of Zion," 209–10.

40. Peter Somerville, Ellen Van Beckhoven, and Ronald Van Kempen, "The Decline and rise of Neighbourhoods: The Importance of Neighbourhood Governance," *European Journal of Housing Policy* 9, no. 1 (2009).

there is at least one living example of how the basic plan for Zion will affect public engagement in practice: the city of Barcelona, Spain.

Barcelona is similar in many ways to the plan for Zion. The 1855 plan for Barcelona's expansion includes square blocks, with about twenty dwellings per block, large interior spaces for gardens and parks, wide streets, and similar block arrangements. The central figure in Barcelona's modern design was Ildefons Cerdà (1815–1876). Cerdà's plan for the city expansion was laid out on a northwest-southeast orientation to maximize the amount of natural light available to all buildings, whereas the plat for Zion has a north-south, east-west orientation for reasons explained by Steve Olsen.[41]

As in the Zion plat, Cerdà's blocks are square though somewhat smaller than planned for Zion (372 feet on a side as opposed to 660 feet), since Cerdà's design viewed Barcelona as densely urban rather than largely agricultural. Cerdà also planned wide streets (115 feet), similar to Zion (82.5 to 132 feet). Even though the blocks were somewhat smaller and the intended density higher, each block also included substantial household garden areas and communal green space (more than 6 percent of each block).

The Barcelona example is relevant to the discussion of governance in Zion because of the impact Cerdà's design has had on social interaction in Barcelona. First, while the plan has been criticized as boringly uniform (as has the plat for Zion), that uniformity has proven "endlessly adaptable." "The goal was to combine the advantages of rural living (green space, fresh air and food, community) with the advantages of urban living (commerce, culture, free flow of goods and ideas)."[42]

The wide streets, ample open space, and greenery promote pedestrian traffic and socializing. Vehicles are permitted but are not the dominant use. The result is a greater sense of community and engagement, what is currently termed "mixed use public spaces." And Barcelona plans to expand such areas in the future.

---

41. "Barcelona's Remarkable History of Rebirth and Transformation," Vox Media LLC, 2019, https://www.vox.com/energy-and-environment/2019/4/8/18266760/barcelona-spain-urban-planning-history.
42. Roberts, "Barcelona's Remarkable History of Rebirth and Transformation."

The plan for Zion would encourage a similar outcome if the community could support a similar vision. For example, Salt Lake City streets are typically 130 feet wide, as suggested by the initial plat for Zion. However, the city has missed an opportunity by focusing on vehicular traffic and paving most of the rights of way. The city now struggles to make space for non-motorized transit and to become more pedestrian friendly. Wide public rights of way are a good idea if an emphasis is placed on using those spaces to facilitate socializing and interaction over vehicles. Vibrant neighborhoods lend themselves to effective neighborhood deliberation and governance.

Unfortunately, as previously noted, few attempts have been made to systematically study the potential for neighborhood governance. Several findings from the limited research are, however, relevant and at least suggestive for the current discussion. First, neighborhood attachment matters, echoing the discussion of land in Zion. According to Somerville, et al., "Research . . . suggests that residents' attachment to their neighbourhood (irrespective of how satisfied or dissatisfied they may be with it) is the most important factor associated with their participation in neighbourhood life generally, and in neighbourhood governance in particular."[43]

Second, participation in neighborhood governance increases when participation is valued and even invited, and if participants are "confident of the collective as well as individual benefits that their participation will bring."[44]

Third, the evidence suggests that "a strong association structure or a high level of neighborhood social cohesion can lead residents to develop their own participation instruments."[45]

Unfortunately, few efforts have been made in this country or elsewhere to develop methods for aggregating the product of neighborhood deliberations. Somerville, et al. wrote:

---

43. Somerville, Van Beckhoven, and Van Kempen, "The Decline and Rise of Neighbourhoods: The Importance of Neighbourhood Governance."
44. Roberts, "Barcelona's Remarkable History of Rebirth and Transformation."
45. As cited in Somerville, Van Beckhoven, and Van Kempen, "The Decline and Rise of Neighbourhoods: The Importance of Neighbourhood Governance."

Relatively little has been done to put mechanisms in place to ensure that all neighborhoods in a city have the opportunity to develop and articulate collective neighborhood views and to ensure these can be brought together at a city-wide level other than through traditional local electoral mechanisms, which are increasingly viewed as inadequate.[46]

A better understanding of the different modes of neighborhood governance still needs to be developed. Olsen sees Zion as "centripetal," with the temple as the central focus and expansion beyond the central place still focused on a central and largely hierarchical governance structure. But the dispersed geographic development of the Church, with wards, stakes, areas, and multiple temples, each functioning largely independently while still receiving centralized coordination (and some services), suggests another model for neighborhood governance.

Somerville and colleagues identify what they refer to as "co-governance" of neighborhoods, a term that suggests cooperation and partnerships between neighborhoods, and between neighborhoods and higher levels of government. Such cooperation might amount to coalition building around particular concerns, or it might involve partnerships with other neighborhoods or entities to accomplish particular functions. The whole concept of largely independent but cooperating neighborhoods suggests more of a polycentric system of governance, which "may exist if the decision-making centers [neighborhoods] take each other into account in competitive and cooperative relationships and are capable of resolving conflicts."[47]

In the United States, we have extensive experience with polycentric local governments. A given home site may fall within the boundaries of an independent school district, one or more special public service districts, a city or town, a county, a multi-county water conservation district, and a state. Each government entity is reasonably

---

46. Somerville, Van Beckhoven, and Van Kempen, "The Decline and Rise of Neighbourhoods: The Importance of Neighbourhood Governance."
47. Keith Carlisle and Rebecca L. Gruby, "Polycentric Systems of Governance: A Theoretical Model for the Commons," *Policy Studies Journal* 47, no. 4 (2019): 928.

autonomous and has a defined service provision role. These overlapping jurisdictions may go largely unnoticed until the annual property tax notice arrives and lists the taxes charged by each entity. But the system allows for inter-local and cooperative agreements and dispute resolution between entities and works reasonably well in most cases.

What is lacking is a neighborhood counterpart that invites and promotes neighborhood deliberation, collaboration, and cooperation to encourage neighborhood governance, and then a mechanism for systematically aggregating neighborhood views and actions to a higher level.

The plan for Zion was used as the basic approach in laying out hundreds of new communities in the Utah Territory. While many of the larger communities have Church-defined wards and stakes, and more organic neighborhoods, few if any demonstrate effective neighborhood governance. Some have city sponsored "neighborhoods," but these do not match the functional governance need described here.

Where to Start in Building Governance for Zion

Initiating and realizing community changes to bring society closer to Zion can be a daunting task. We all have our own lives and demands to meet. We may believe in Zion as a concept, we may be working to qualify personally to live there, and we may be encouraging others to qualify for Zion. We would like our neighborhood, city, state, and nation to draw closer to Zion. But when it comes to promoting changes in the way things work in our communities, we may instead decide it is a good time to clean out the garage. Therefore, a key question is, Where do we start in transforming our governance systems?

What can we learn from the My Hometown Initiative? Over several years, Mark Rupp and his stake leaders developed a detailed inventory of needed changes. They realized that addressing the needs was beyond their resources, so they looked for partners and identified champions who could support and expand their efforts to bring change. In the Church, these champions included Area Seventy Mark Durham and Area President Craig Christensen. Their support was critical in forming partnerships with sister stakes around the valley and in obtaining permission to repurpose the church building as a community resource center. In the city, their champion became Assistant City Manager Nicole Cottle, who had the ear of city leaders and a solid relationship with all city departments.

Overcoming public resistance and fears required building public support through the system of block captains. Starting with who they knew, they were able to nurture relationships within clusters of neighbors and build on those relationships through the Days of Service and the community resource center.

Just as the My Hometown Initiative was about to launch, COVID forced them to postpone the community resource center and shift their focus to the Days of Service efforts. They had to be adaptable and adjust as the initiative developed, even adding piano lessons in the community resource center in response to neighborhood requests.

Most fundamentally, My Hometown changed the narrative of what it means to live in the Stansbury area. That change in narrative is touching hundreds of lives, even for those whose homes have not received upgrades and for those just learning about My Hometown.

Clearly, My Hometown is not a short-term solution. It is not a single service project. It is an extended effort to build leaders and help people and neighborhoods become self-reliant. It may seem frustrating when those emerging leaders move on, but when they do, they take their skills with them to bless others.

The My Hometown Initiative, which the Church is now expanding into other areas, is an example of embracing the foundation stones of Zion. The initiative is expanding in Salt Lake City, Ogden, Provo, and other areas outside of Utah. Regarding My Hometown, Area President Elder Craig Christensen said, "Service without condition—unconditional service, without motive, ulterior motive—cuts through everything. I think this is an example of how the Church really can do best."[48]

My Hometown in West Valley City has now been extended from the original 1,060-home neighborhood to an area of 40,000 homes. The principles learned from the Stansbury area are being shared with

48. "Church, city reshape neighborhood with Operation MyHometown," *Deseret News*, February 24, 2021.

other neighborhoods. If all goes well, a coalition of neighborhoods will emerge that can confront broader issues within the city.

Zion is a complete package. Establishing Zion will require a covenant people who dwell together in righteousness and peace, without contention. As previously mentioned, I do not believe those conditions will be delivered from on high. We need to build Zion-eligible lives, and we need to build a Zion society. How do we get from here to there?

My recommendations are drawn from work I did originally for the United Nations Human Settlements Programme (UN-Habitat) and the Global Land Tool Network (GLTN).[49] That work looks at how local communities can begin the process of change in their financial structure. While the specific focus in that book is on generating more revenue, most of the principles apply to initiating change more broadly.

Building Zion communities begins with an initial inventory. The inventory can be taken by a single individual, but gathering a small group of like-minded friends for a frank discussion may work best. The questions that will guide the discussion include: What do we need to change? Why do we need to change? Where does the change need to happen? What is preventing the change from happening? Helpful inventories are as concrete and specific as possible.

The next phase is to search for opportunities and carry out a more detailed assessment by considering the following:

- The legal environment. Are there legal reasons that would prevent or facilitate the changes sought?
- The administrative capacity of any government or other agencies that must be dealt with or that will need to implement or approve the changes sought. Do they have sufficient trained staff to implement the changes? Is there someone in the agency that could be recruited as an ally?

---

49. Lawrence C. Walters, *Where to Start? A Guide to Land-based Finance in Local Governance* (Nairobi, Kenya: United Nations Human Settlements Programme, 2020).

- The historical and cultural context within which the changes will need to function. Is there a history that would make the kind of changes sought more difficult or easier? Do cultural norms need to be considered in working for change?
- Potential colleagues, allies, and champions who may be recruited. Could individuals with specific skills, knowledge, or contacts help with the change effort?
- Any other context-specific factors. Could anything else help or hinder efforts to bring about the desired changes?

It is important to recognize the challenges and common impediments that will likely be encountered. The conditions the group wants to change came about for a reason, even if no one remembers why. Organizations and communities have their own inertia. We keep doing things a certain way out of habit. Some people who benefit from the current arrangements will oppose change. It is also common that in adopting changes, decision-makers may compromise principles and policies the group sees as vital.

The best way to overcome these challenges is to build public support for the proposed changes. Here is where the group might initiate both a public information campaign and a public engagement process, as was done in the Stansbury area. Transparency and accountability contribute to public trust, but they require systematic reporting and listening. Effective communication creates a narrative explaining the need for change and the benefits to be achieved.

Change advocates should be prepared to adjust or modify expectations and adapt to changing conditions and new knowledge throughout the process. Again, the My Hometown response to COVID is a good example.

Forging the political will and creating sustainable support for change requires the creation of a new narrative, a change in the perception of officials and the public. This is exactly what local leaders of the My Hometown Initiative did. They changed what it meant to live in Stansbury. Such changes in the prevailing narrative may result from changes in circumstances or occurrences that may challenge current attitudes and create new opportunities to promote the changes sought.

At the heart of any coalition for change there is nearly always a champion or group of champions, individuals of stature who are willing to take risks to advance the agenda for change. Identifying and recruiting the support of such individuals is an important step in successful change efforts. In the case of My Hometown, the champions included Nicole Cottle, Elder Mark Durham, and President Craig Christensen.

Many successful efforts to bring about change follow a process of trial and error, with short feedback loops, where certain small interventions are tried, tested, and then adjusted. Advocates will often celebrate small wins and avoid being discouraged by setbacks.

Ultimately, the goal is to build Zion. That can only happen if we embrace the foundations of the gospel of Jesus Christ and the methods and attitudes that Christ instilled in His disciples, ancient and modern.

In 1996 Professor Jean Elshtain from the University of Chicago spoke at BYU about the state of democracy in America. She argued that we now live in a political age of resentment of and withdrawal from civic life. She described at some length the weakening of democratic civil society. I believe she is correct. Conditions have not improved in the past quarter century. The ability of democratic societies to bring together diverse views, critically examine arguments, and take action continues to erode.[50]

This erosion seriously impedes our ability to establish Zion. In this chapter and in the appendix on deliberative processes, I have provided a framework for how the foundation stones of Zion can inform our actions as citizens in Zion. Agency requires freedom and is coupled with accountability. Both will be exercised most effectively in a Zion society with active citizens engaged in small-scale deliberative processes in their neighborhoods and communities. I have attempted to describe a framework for how such processes should be designed and evaluated. And I have suggested one path for moving our communities closer to the Zion standard.

---

50. Lawrence C. Walters, "Citizenship" (Brigham Young University devotional, April 1, 2014), speeches.byu.edu.

CHAPTER 13

Organizing a Zion Society

*I*n this final chapter I strive to pull together the essential insights outlined in the preceding chapters into a framework for the establishment of Zion. I believe the observations here follow from those earlier discussions. As with any writer, there is inevitably some degree of personal bias. Just the choice of my initial questions reflects a bias on my part. Other conclusions reached here may also include my own point of view, and readers are, of course, free to reach different conclusions. I look forward to ongoing discussions.

Again, I stress that I am not trying to articulate a far-distant view of a future Zion. Rather, I seek to outline the principles, values, and goals that should motivate and guide the efforts of those who actively seek to establish Zion today. Personal righteousness is required of all, but that alone will not establish Zion. Zion is the name the Lord applies to His people, those who live together in the unity required by the celestial law. Those who seek to live in Zion will recognize that building the kingdom and establishing Zion requires that we create, adjust, support, and actively lead the institutions and organizations in this current world to a higher and holier plane. The five foundation stones of Zion should affect every relationship and organization we are associated with.

Zion Tomorrow

A Zion society exists because the people choose to live together in righteousness and unity. The choice to live in righteousness is grounded in the two great commandments: devotion to the Father and the Son and Christlike love for all God's children. The Savior will always be the central focus of such service and love. The foundation of Zion also rests firmly on the heavenly gifts of individual agency and personal accountability.

Achieving Zion is a choice to fully enter into the covenants with God the Father and His Son Jesus Christ. And it is a choice to internalize and live the second great commandment, to place the interests of others on a par with our own, "without bias," as Judge Hand put it. This Christlike love of others, charity, is a heavenly gift bestowed on all the true followers of Jesus Christ and is the foundation of social relationships in Zion.

The guiding principles in Zion will be the principles inherent in the gospel of Jesus Christ, which I have summarized as devotion to God and Christ, charity, agency, accountability, and unity. These foundation stones have not and will not change, but our understanding of them undoubtedly will as we elaborate them in subsidiary values. For example, what we mean by and how we apply justice and mercy will likely evolve as we more fully grasp the eternal nature of the interaction among charity, agency, and accountability.

The law of consecration has never been revoked and will be more fully lived in Zion. We enter into the law of consecration in the temple. It is not necessary to deed anything to the Church, the bishop, or anyone else. Such deeds are a mere legal artifact of our culture. We have already consecrated all that we have or will have to the Church for building the kingdom and for Zion. We must embrace the covenant, act in charity for others, and limit our consumption to levels that allow us to assist others until all have sufficient. Based on the Nephite experience, it will take time to achieve this condition as a people, even with strong personal commitment.

As we do so, we will join with other consecrated disciples in unity and cooperation. That unity and cooperation will be foundational for effective collective action and success. The central operating concept in a Zion society is cooperative action by families to achieve joint purposes. This cooperation must extend to all spheres of activity: raising and educating children; providing for basic needs of food, shelter, and health; and creating public and civic infrastructure.

The disciples of Christ are commanded to gather with other disciples and establish a unified community of Saints. Historically, that gathering was to a designated land or city. In Enoch's day, the city was separated from the surrounding society. In Melchizedek's day, the city of Salem perhaps did not have the same degree of separation. The city the Saints planned to build in Missouri would have been surrounded by non-believers, at least initially. The Saints today will gather to Zion in designated locations (stakes) in their individual homelands, and our Zion communities will be in the midst of skeptics and critics, at least initially.

Poverty can be eliminated. For this to happen, the inhabitants of Zion must:

- Inspire hope among the poor and a brighter vision for the future grounded in real opportunity
- Provide a context-appropriate model for living and prospering
- Encourage and support cooperative action by the poor themselves, in concert with non-poor families
- Enable full integration and participation of the poor as equals in the broader society
- Facilitate cooperative arrangements to mitigate the impacts of both community and personal disasters
- Support and actively pursue stable and effective governance in society.

I think the scriptural record is clear that the covenants made regarding land will be fulfilled. Stewardship will replace ownership. Consistent with the Lord's covenants regarding land, the Saints in Zion will steward land to fulfill the Lord's purposes, both short and long term. Keeping the second great commandment will ensure that all have access to land as part of their Zion covenant. As mentioned previously, one implication is that there will likely be a very limited market for land sales, though leases may be more common.

A commitment to the foundations of Zion will lead individuals to act in response to observed needs in the community. Effective action will often involve collaboration and cooperation with neighbors. This engagement will take place within neighborhoods and clusters of neighborhoods. The physical layout of cities and towns in Zion can facilitate this interaction and engagement if communities have that vision.

The emphasis on the family in this framework again stresses the connection between agency and self-reliance. In Zion, self-reliant families will do far more than provide for life's necessities. They will actively take responsibility for the success of Zion as a society. They will look to the Church for those things that only the Church can provide (ordinances, temples, and so on). They will look to government for those protections and enabling functions that only government can provide. For other opportunities and actions beyond the capacity of a single family, self-reliant families will join with other families to organize new ventures, or they will join already functioning organizations that help them fulfill their goals.

All organizations, including families, exist to benefit their members. Organizations serve their members by expanding the range of opportunities, providing the information and teaching needed to understand the implications of the available choices, and enhancing the capacity to act on those choices.

Families will act jointly and cooperatively to accomplish their purposes through several types of organizations. The family is the basic unit of a Zion society. The nucleus consists of parents and children (either natural or adopted) but will likely extend to other generations and more distant connections. Families bear the responsibility to act to provide for themselves, maximize the opportunities and development of their family members, and engage with other families in cooperation and collaboration for their mutual benefit and that of the larger community.

The Church of Jesus Christ will continue with a defined purpose and scope of action that include providing priesthood authority and keys, covenants and ordinances, prophetic direction, scriptures, support to families for gospel learning and teaching, and service and leadership opportunities. The Church will continue to be funded through tithing and other voluntary contributions. It will probably engage in commercial activities only to the extent that those activities directly contribute to the Church's core purpose and scope of action (e.g., publishing and perhaps food production and distribution).

Voluntary associations will be a principal organizational mechanism for families to pursue their joint actions. The purpose and scope of action for both self-reliant and community-supported organizations will vary depending on the objectives of those families who come together to form and support the association (e.g., commercial, church, music, theater, sports, additional support for the poor, education, and insurance). Leadership will be provided by either election or appointment from within the association members. Associations will be accountable to their membership, within the legal framework. Members will be accountable for the success and effect of their associations. They will be funded through commercial activity and voluntary contributions.

Joseph Smith stated that there is a difference between the Church and the political kingdom of God. Civil governments will exist in Zion. Their purpose and scope of action will be to provide protection, enforce laws, and provide public infrastructure, broadly understood. Governments provide the framework within which church, voluntary, and commercial activities take place, and they protect families. The scope of the protection includes protection of human rights, contract enforcement, protection from and prosecution of lawbreakers, and national defense. The provision of public infrastructure includes any system that benefits the entire community, region, or nation and which voluntary associations cannot provide or cannot provide as completely (e.g., the governance system, roads, national defense, police protection, courts, information gathering and dissemination, basic research, other public goods). Leadership will be chosen by elections using majority vote, and elected officials will likely appoint professionals to administer and carry out public purposes and projects.

The U.S. Constitution contains inspired principles for structuring civil governments, including (1) the separation of powers, (2) the division of powers between national and sub-national governments, (3) the application of popular sovereignty, and (4) the rule of law.

The U.S. Constitution and Doctrine and Covenants 134 also identify divinely inspired human rights, including the Bill of Rights and other constitutional amendments, especially the free exercise of conscience, the right and control of property, and the protection of life.

This is the vision and the ultimate goal. It is consistent with the description of the cornerstone of Zion provided in Doctrine and Covenants 124. What must we do today to improve our communities and move our organizations closer to Zion?

What We Must Do

Establishing Zion begins with our own heart, attitudes, and commitment. President Russell M. Nelson expressed it this way:

> As I have stated before, the gathering of Israel is the most important work taking place on earth today. One crucial element of this gathering is preparing a people who are able, ready, and worthy to receive the Lord when He comes again, a people who have already chosen Jesus Christ over this fallen world, a people who rejoice in their agency to live the higher, holier laws of Jesus Christ.
>
> I call upon you, my dear brothers and sisters, to become this righteous people. Cherish and honor your covenants above all other commitments. As you let God prevail in your life, I promise you greater peace, confidence, joy, and yes, rest.[1]

This prophetic admonition and encouragement has not changed in the past fifty years. President Spencer Kimball was quite clear and succinct in 1978 that there are three fundamental actions we must take if we are to establish a Zion society.

- We must eliminate the individual tendency to selfishness.
- We must cooperate completely and work in harmony with others.
- We must lay on the altar and sacrifice whatever is required by the Lord.

---

1. Nelson, "Overcome the World and Find Rest."

President Kimball promised:

My brothers and sisters, *if we can do this, then we will find ourselves clothed in the mantle of charity* "which is the greatest of all, for all things must fail—

"But charity is the pure love of Christ, and it endureth forever; and whoso is found possessed of it at the last day, it shall be well with him." (Moro. 7:46–47.)

Let us unite and pray with all the energy of heart, that we may be sealed by this bond of charity; that we may build up this latter-day Zion.[2]

For me, the place to start is with the question, What lack I yet?

As we strive to establish Zion and prepare for the Second Coming, I see the need for both individual and social actions. First, as President Kimball urges, it is imperative that we all strive earnestly for the gift of charity as the fundamental guiding principle in our relations with others. And then we must allow that gift to guide us in our service.

The personal development needed to qualify to live in Zion is a lifelong process. Part of that personal development is the increased ability and willingness to turn outward, as the Savior did so consistently, and consider the needs of others. That will begin with a focus on those closest to us, both physically and emotionally, in an effort to inspire in them the vision and passion for Zion. But it won't stop there.

As we seek to extend our own capabilities and energies, we will unite with others and co-create opportunities to cooperate and collaborate in establishing Zion. Relationships define Zion. Relationships grounded in love and devotion to Christ and in the celestial unity at the heart of the cause of Zion.

We begin the collaboration to establish Zion with like-minded Saints who agree on a goal, assess the opportunities and impediments they face, actively seek to teach and expound on their vision, and build coalitions for change. At the same time, we must avoid the "circumcision trap" and stay close to the prophet, always confirming that

---

2. Kimball, "Becoming the Pure in Heart"; emphasis added.

our goals are aligned with the goals of Zion as those goals continue to be revealed and elaborated.

We should consider and evaluate our organizational commitments carefully and work to build support for the principles of Zion in the organizations we choose to affiliate with.

Second, we need to elevate and strengthen families by embracing the changes made in the Church by scaling back the size and role of government at all levels, and by encouraging the cooperative efforts of families. This is not likely to be easy or quick. The status of the family as "fundamental" has eroded and been displaced over decades, and it will take years to redevelop the family capacities required in Zion.

Here again, the path forward will be pursued one family at a time, as individual families seek to develop greater self-reliance through their own capacities and their engagement with other families. In the meantime, we will need patience and caution in any attempts to dismantle or otherwise restrict the many government programs that have supplanted the family. To do otherwise runs the risks of inflicting even more harms in our communities.

We must work for change in our governments at all levels to both create a vision of governance consistent with the foundations of Zion and to implement policies that will promote the vision and practices of Zion. It is also worth considering what it will take to maintain Zion for a millennium once it is established. The Nephites were able to convert everyone but were able to sustain their society for only about two hundred years. Eventually nearly everyone will be converted in the latter-day Zion as well. From my perspective, two family attributes will be required in order to sustain a Zion society in the long term: engagement and vigilance. Families will need to remain committed to the foundations of Zion. They will need to remain engaged and take responsibility for the success of Zion. And they will need to remain vigilant in assuring that all aspects of Zion continue to conform to the five-fold foundation of Zion.

When the Savior returns, He will indeed be our King and Lawgiver, but His laws will be designed for our eternal development and exaltation. There will always be a range of activities and social interactions where we can use our agency and practice the principles of Zion. I have attempted to identify some of those activities where those who seek to establish Zion can take action to further the cause of Zion. One domain of practice will be how we organize and conduct our social interactions through organizations and institutions, including government.

We must remember and strive to follow the counsel of Presidents Nelson and Kimball. May we all choose Jesus Christ and His covenants and come together in righteousness and unity. I am convinced the results will be well beyond our expectations.

APPENDIX A

Property Rights in Zion

As discussed in chapter 9, Zion needs a concept of property and property rights that:

1. Acknowledges God as the creator and ultimate owner of all land and property;
2. Sustains the agency of stewards in their right to control how land is used;
3. Encourages stewards to consider and value the needs of others; and
4. Links land stewardships to the broader and coordinated needs of a Zion society, now and in the future.

The current concepts of property rights in the Western world do not meet this standard. For many years, property ownership was conceived as a coherent combination of rights that constituted what Blackstone defined as "that sole and despotic dominion which one man claims and exercises over the external things of the world in total exclusion of the right of any other individual in the universe."[1]

However, over the last century, the most common approach to property rights has come to view land ownership as a bundle of rights. For example, Elinor Ostrom has summarized property ownership as typically including the following rights.

1. Access—a right to enter a defined physical property.
2. Withdrawal—a right to harvest the products of a resource such as timber, water, and food for pastoral animals.

---

1. Anna Di Robilant, "Property: A Bundle of Sticks or a Tree," *Vanderbilt Law Review* 66 (2013): 877.

3. Management—a right to regulate the use patterns of other harvesters and to transform a resource system by building improvements.
4. Exclusion—a right to determine who will have the right of access to a resource and whether the right can be transferred.
5. Alienation—a right to sell or lease any of the above rights. [2]

Similarly, Simon Winchester describes the bundle as the right to possession; the right of control; the right of exclusion; the right of enjoyment; and the right of disposition. Winchester then appropriately notes: "All of these are legal terms that extend in law far beyond their common-sense dictionary definitions, and which, to the enduring pleasure of the legal community, are still open to all manner of shades of interpretation."[3]

Most scholars and jurists who accept this "bundle of sticks" approach see the precise set of sticks in the bundle as both flexible and malleable, and subject to change by the political authority. Particular rights can be added or subtracted. For example, the right to manage and improve land may be restricted or prohibited by local land use regulations or because that right was previously split off and sold separately to preserve open space.

On the other hand, some cities add sticks to the bundle in an effort to increase the supply of housing. Those cities sell private landowners "density bonus" permits which allow for greater than normal building densities, subject to other legal provisions.

Even the right to exclude others is not universally accepted. Simon Winchester provides a fascinating discussion of how the concept of trespass has been modified and even rejected in a number of countries. Scotland has essentially eliminated trespass laws. Anyone now has an absolute statutory right to wander anywhere in the country at any time no matter who the land belongs to. The right to wander in

2. Elinor Ostrom, "Design Principles of Robust Property Rights Institutions: What Have We Learned?," in *Property Rights and Land Policies*, ed. Gregory K. Ingram and Yu-Hung Hong (Cambridge, MA: Lincoln Institute of Land Policy, 2009).
3. Simon Winchester, *Land: How the Hunger for Ownership Shaped the Modern World* (New York, NY: HarperCollins Publishers, 2021), 35.

Nordic countries is so universally accepted it does not require legislation to enforce it. In Bavaria, the "mushroom clause" gives all the right to forage for and harvest wild plants in regional forests. "In all of these decidedly non-American places there is an unspoken abhorrence of the very notion of trespass, because—though not to belabor the point—it is so strongly felt that access to land is every bit as much a right as the right to air or water."[4]

The bundle of sticks approach to property rights is especially appealing to public officials and land use regulators who see government as active managers of private property rights, constantly balancing and adjusting private rights and public needs to meet the changing conditions of society.[5]

The view is also attractive to those who wish to avoid the claim that they are "taking" property through some public action. In the United States, taking private land for public purposes requires compensation to the landowner. If it can be argued that only one or two "sticks" are being removed from the bundle of rights but the majority remain, compensation may not be required. Of course, landowners tend to argue that the harms are broader and more permanent.

Anna di Robilant provides a nice summary of the arguments for the bundle of sticks approach. She observes that the most important intuitions of the approach can be summarized in four points.

1. Property is a set of analytically distinct entitlements rather than a full and monolithic aggregate of rights;
2. Property entails delicate relations among individuals concerning a given resource (i.e., each owner's entitlements correspond to other owners' vulnerabilities);
3. An owner's entitlements are "bundled" and backed by the state, rather than derived from the law of nature; and
4. The property bundle is malleable (i.e., the owner's entitlements may be recombined into different bundles to achieve a variety of policy purposes).[6]

---

4. Winchester, *Land: How the Hunger for Ownership Shaped the Modern World*, 223.
5. Jacobs, "U.S. Private Property Rights in International Perspective."
6. Di Robilant, "Property: A bundle of Sticks or a Tree," 878.

Until recently, this was the dominant view among legal scholars. and it is still a view taught by law schools in every first-year property law class.

This "bundle of sticks" approach is not without its legal critics, however. Advocates of what di Robilant terms the "ownership" theory are much closer to Blackstone's definition. They argue that the bundle of sticks approach to property rights fails to define precisely what property is and focuses exclusively on the relationships between people without specific reference to land itself. They argue that the fundamental property right is exclusion, the right to exclude everyone else from access to or use of a particular parcel of land. James Penner, a noted proponent of this view, argues property rights reveal "a coherent tripartite structure of title—the right to immediate exclusive possession, the power to license what would otherwise be a trespass, and the power to transfer."[7]

The strength of the "ownership" approach lies in its simplicity and efficiency. Landowners have the right not to be interfered with in their use of the land. This non-interference is the path most likely to result in economically efficient land use. The right to exclude others is not a value or an end in itself, nor is it absolute. Spillovers and scale issues may require government intervention. But exclusion is at the heart of property rights, in this view, and efficient land use is the value pursued.[8]

Neither of these approaches to property rights are consistent with Zion's stewardship approach to land. The bundle of sticks approach identifies a malleable and fungible set of rights without any ethical grounding, let alone an acknowledgment of a commitment to a larger social order. The ownership school does have an ethical grounding, but it is narrowly defined and focused on efficiency. Despite their widespread acceptance, neither provides an adequate foundation for property rights in a Zion society.

Another way to conceive of property rights holds much greater promise for guiding how we think about and design land policies in

7.   James E. Penner, *Property Rights: A Re-Examination* (Oxford University Press, 2020).
8.   Di Robilant, "Property: A Bundle of Sticks or a Tree," 892.

Zion. It was developed in the mid-twentieth century largely by Italian legal scholars[9] but has been largely neglected since. The theory was developed at a time when the shortcomings of the codified views of land and property ownership were recognized to be insufficient to deal with the changing nature of property in the twentieth century. At the same time, the rise of fascism in Italy in the 1920s and 1930s meant that private property rights were under threat as the national policy focus attempted to subordinate private interests to national economic production.[10] It was against this backdrop that a group of property scholars sought to develop a new view of property.

The key insight of this new approach was to conceive of property rights as a tree. The trunk of the tree is the essence of property and includes two components.

1. The "owner's right to have the exclusive ultimate control over how and by whom the thing will be used". And "the owner's core entitlements are the entitlements the state can limit or reshape only for extremely weighty social goals."

2. And the recognition that "owners should exercise their use-control entitlements, while remaining mindful of property's social function. The social function of property is part of the trunk of the tree."[11]

In classical-liberal ownership, Barassi wrote, the interest of the individual owner trumped the interest of the collectivity. In Fascist property, the interest of the Fascist state trumped the interest of the individual owner. By contrast, the new tree [concept of] property envisions the individual owner immersed in society. The owner's dominion is a civic dominion qualified by social obligations.[12]

---

9. The scholars involved included Francesco Ferrara (1877–1941), Salvatore Pugliatti (1903–1976), Lodovico Barassi (1873–1961), Widar Cesarini-Sforza (1886–1965), Filippo Vassalli (1855–1955), and others.
10. Di Robilant, "Property: A Bundle of Sticks or a Tree," 899.
11. Di Robilant, "Property: A Bundle of Sticks or a Tree, " 905–07.
12. Di Robilant, "Property: A Bundle of Sticks or a Tree," 908.

The tree-concept theorists argued that social function alludes to the multiple values and interests implied by different resources.[13] Thus, the branches of the tree represent how the owner's control and the interests of society interact and reflect the specific development and application of law to different types of property. Agricultural land will be treated differently than residential land. Industrial complexes will have different guiding regulations than other types of land. But all will be tied to the same trunk: autonomous decisions about use within the context of broader social obligations.

I don't purport to be an expert on this legal viewpoint. First, most of the resources that develop the concept appear to be in Italian and beyond my current skill level. I found di Robilant's article to be a very useful starting point, but it is only a start, especially as the ideas apply to a Zion society. But the basic concept of land stewardships as the steward's ultimate control over use embedded in a network of connections to family and society seems to me to be much more consistent with what the Lord has revealed about how his stewards should think and act.

---

13. Di Robilant, "Property: A Bundle of Sticks or a Tree," 909.

APPENDIX B

Governance and Deliberative Processes for Zion

*P*opular sovereignty places the ultimate power and responsibility for public action with the people. If such a system is to be effective in reaching decisions satisfactory to participants and enduring, it must include effective public deliberative processes. The public must be able to speak and be heard. They must be able to confer with other members of the public. Governance systems based on popular sovereignty will either develop and rely on meaningful deliberative processes, or they will degrade over time into rule by ever smaller elites.

By "governance system" I do not mean the structure of government (legislatures, presidents, administrators, and so on). Many writers have offered definitions of governance, but the one I like is the definition attributed to Goran Hyden: "Governance is the stewardship of formal and informal political rules of the game. Governance refers to those measures that involve setting the rules for the exercise of power and settling conflicts over such rules."[1]

The exercise of power involves one person (A) getting another person (B) to do something B would not otherwise do, or preventing B from doing something B would otherwise have chosen to do. Power is also exercised when A prevents issues important to B from being considered in the public forum. We know that "it is the nature and disposition

---

1. Avijit Biswas, "Governance: Meaning, Definition, 4 Dimensions, and Types," https://schoolofpoliticalscience.com/definitions-and-types-of-governance/, accessed March 9, 2024.

of almost all men, as soon as they get a little authority, as they suppose, they will immediately begin to exercise unrighteous dominion" (Doctrine and Covenants 121:39). The "political rules of the game" are intended to keep such tendencies in check and minimized. Indeed, in Zion we may hope to see such tendencies largely eliminated. As noted, there are formal rules in this regard, but there are also informal ones, and the informal rules must derive from the foundation stones of Zion, from what lies in the hearts of men and women.

Criteria for a Deliberative Process

Governance, the formal and informal rules determining how power is used, refers to how a society organizes and directs its resources to accomplish public purposes. In a democratic society, these collective decisions are made through deliberative processes at various levels. The deliberative processes we employ determine how popular sovereignty is expressed and how the rules of society are determined. The quality of governance can be assessed by asking three questions.

Are those affected by a policy able to influence its formation and interpretation? Governance should be responsive to stakeholders. It should be transparent, meaning that how the system functions and reaches decisions should be clear to all. All concerned parties should have a voice and should be able to engage in the process in a meaningful way and at a personal cost that is manageable.

Do governments have the capacity to act and to effectively formulate and implement appropriate policies? I include under this question an assessment of whether there is an independent judiciary, whether management is efficient and effective, and so on. The separation of governmental powers into different branches slows the processes of government, but as President Oaks has observed it is one of the great fundamentals in the Constitution. The advantages outweigh the cost in most cases.

Does the governance system support and embody respect for all people? Are the rights of citizens referred to by President Clark and President Oaks respected and protected both by other citizens and by the institutions and organizations? Our governance system should place a high value on the dignity and worth of all people, on the lack of corruption, political stability, respect for the rule of law, freedoms from hinderance, and freedoms to pursue objectives.

Deliberative Process Design

I don't see that there is any essential distinction between what we call sectors (public, private, voluntary), except for two factors:

- A governance system must be evaluated based on the questions above, especially the level of respect for persons. Some arrangements are more likely to exhibit that respect than others.
- Governments most fundamentally embody a socially accepted capacity for coercion not allowed to the same degree in other social arrangements. As such they merit special attention and a different set of guiding principles.

Governments are social institutions entrusted with the power to compel compliance with officially adopted rules of behavior. In granting such power, society expects government to act in the public interest. Thus, any law, regulation, or exercise of compulsion that is not in the public interest undermines the legitimacy of that government. There exists, therefore, a fundamental stewardship relationship between any government and the people being governed. The people agree to give up certain freedoms and grant to government the right to compel obedience. In exchange, the government is expected to protect remaining freedoms and to promote the public interest and well-being of the governed.

Since all humans live within social structures, this stewardship relationship called government is fundamental to human existence, at least in contemporary society, if not throughout human history. In their highest and best form, governments are created and sustained under the influence and guidance of God (see Doctrine and Covenants 134:1). This is not to say that such influence and guidance exists or persists in all governments. The stewardship relationship can be and often has been violated, and the Divine influence is withdrawn.

To discharge its stewardship responsibilities, governments should consult regularly with the governed. The criteria for such deliberative processes are described above. We turn next to the design of the deliberative process. A number of scholars join Presidents Clark and Oaks to advocate in favor of deliberative democracy and broadly based participatory processes. Such a deliberative process requires the following elements if it is to be effective:

1. The participants should possess the necessary deliberative skills.
2. Good information should be widely available and accessible to all.
3. There must be public "space" for the process and dialog.
4. There needs to be a referee who can keep the space open to all, enforce agreed upon ground rules, and supervise preference aggregation.

All four are necessary, and only in combination are they sufficient to yield an effective deliberative process. That does not mean that a consensus decision will always emerge, but the result will be better informed and more nuanced than decisions reached through some other process. Effectiveness in this case means that people trust the process. They feel they have been heard, their views and preferences carefully considered, and the eventual decision is fairly based on the best available information.

There are training programs intended to develop deliberative skills in people. It seems clear that in recent years the internet has greatly expanded the second and third characteristics from the above list. It can be argued whether the deliberative skills are more important than items 2 and 3 on the list above. With good skills, good information can be sought out and public space can be demanded. Without the skills, information and space may generate bandwidth and YouTube videos, but there is no reason to think that shared understanding and trust in the decision process will emerge. People tend to seek out communities and information sources they agree with.

The question in my mind is, What about number 4? Skills, good information, and available space are not sufficient. Good governance involves filling this role as referee in a society in which people are allowed to influence the policies that affect their daily lives. In the Arab Spring movements of 2010, we saw people demanding the space for dialog and change. These demands were facilitated by access to social media. But lacking any honest broker to serve as referee, the movements in Egypt and elsewhere struggled with implementing change. On the other hand, we witnessed local governments struggling to fill this role regarding the Occupy movements in 2011. Governments strove to keep the space for dialog open, while still enforcing accepted ground rules. The difficulty was that the Occupy participants lacked or at least failed to exhibit the deliberative skills necessary to engage in a meaningful deliberative process.

In the U.S. elections of 2016, we saw an uptick in efforts to undermine the quality of available information on social media. Following the election of 2020, we find many more people willing to challenge the legitimacy of the referee and the accuracy of the vote gathering process.

Hence good governance in Zion must address all four elements: the development of deliberative skills in the populace, the availability and access to sound information, the creation and protection of public spaces in which deliberation can occur, and the guidelines for filling the role of impartial referee. Within such a dance hall, a free and independent people will maximize their dancing skills.[2]

Deliberation and Decision-Making

It is also critical in designing the deliberation to understand the objectives for participation. People come to participatory processes with expectations. If there is a mismatch between the expectations of participants and those of the sponsors, the result can further undermine trust and engagement. In a paper I wrote with James Aydelotte and Jessica Miller, we identified five purposes for reaching out and convening a public deliberation setting:[3]

- Discovery—Group deliberation can aid in the search for problem definitions, alternative solutions, or even the criteria that should be used to choose between options. Discovery may also involve gaining greater understanding of what people value and what their priorities are.

---

2. I borrow the reference to government providing the dance hall and the music from Charles Lindblom.
3. Lawrence C. Walters, James Aydelotte, and Jessica Miller, "Putting more public in policy analysis," *Public administration review* 60, no. 4 (2000).

- Education—Sometimes deliberation can help to educate participants about an issue and proposed alternatives.
- Measurement—Some forms for deliberation provide a means to assess public opinion and priorities regarding a set of issues or options.
- Persuasion—Some forums for deliberation are intended to provide an opportunity to persuade the group about a recommended course of action.
- Legitimization—Sometimes there are public norms or legal requirements that must be complied with before finalizing a decision.

The purpose or combination of purposes that should be pursued depends on the type of issue to be addressed and the stage of the decision-making process. Problems and issues can generally be divided into two categories: those which can be solved and those which cannot be solved. You may have seen some version of this distinction cross-stitched or embroidered on a wall at some point, but I want to go beyond "try to find it" and "never mind it."

There is a fairly well-defined process for finding at least approximate solutions to problems that can be solved. My co-authors and I reviewed the best thinking on this process and summarized it as (1) define the problem; (2) define the criteria that will be used to choose between alternative solutions (how will you know when the problem is solved?); (3) identify or generate potential alternative solutions to the problem; (4) evaluate each potential solution using the chosen criteria; and then (5) recommend the alternative that best solves the problem or best solves enough of the problem.[4]

As we demonstrated in our paper, the type of public engagement sponsored should be linked to this decision-making process. If the task is to define the problem or to develop decision criteria, then the engagement tools will focus on discovery: discovering how participants view the problem, what their values are in seeking for a solution, what trade-offs they see in considering alternatives, and so on.

---

4. Walters, Aydelotte, and Miller, "Putting More Public in Policy Analysis."

To accomplish these objectives, focus groups, a task force, open and informal chat sessions, and so forth can be effective.

If, on the other hand, the problem has been defined, criteria have been developed, and research on alternatives has been carried out, the purpose for public deliberation may be to educate participants, to gauge their views on the alternatives given the research, or even to persuade participants regarding a particular alternative. It such cases, more formal presentations, hearings, and polling may be best. The key is to match public expectations for the deliberative process with the organizer's expectations for what is desired from the participation. Further details and examples are provided in our paper.

The process works reasonably well for problems that have a solution. For more complex issues, things get more complicated, as you might expect. As H.L. Mencken put it, "For every complex problem there is an answer that is clear, simple and wrong."[5] The challenge is that there are some decision situations for which (1) there is no agreement on what the problem is; (2) there is no agreement on what criteria should be used to address the problem or on what a solution to the problem would look like; (3) there is no agreed upon approach to identify or generate appropriate potential solutions; and (4) the best available information is incapable of predicting with any precision how well any proposed solution will work. Such problems have a technical name: wicked problems.

On a personal level, "never mind it" may be the best that can be hoped for when faced with a wicked problem. For society, "never mind it" may have disastrous consequences. In a book that Peter Balint, Ron Stewart, Anand Desai and I wrote, we discuss at length one particular type of wicked problem: environmental management.[6] Doing nothing with regard to the environment is not an option. Every course of action is a decision with implications, albeit the exact implications

---

5. Quoted in Avi Nelson, "Candidates Need 'Workable' Theories," *The Boston Herald*, October 24 1976. Mencken's original phrase appears to have been worded slightly differently.
6. Peter J. Balint et al., *Wicked Environmental Problems: Managing Uncertainty and Conflict* (Washington, DC: Island Press, 2011).

are unknown until they happen. But there are other wicked problems as well.

Public education is another example. What should schools teach? How should the subjects be taught? How should teachers be trained? What opportunities should schools make available beyond the basic curriculum? All these questions are controversial. And heaven forbid that the schools should experiment on my child! As just one more example, in my professional career advising governments of all sizes and in many countries, I have never found a more controversial decision than drawing the boundaries for an elementary school.

But with wicked problems, decisions are made, even if the decision is to do nothing. The question is, Can public deliberation improve the decisions? My co-authors and I believe that public participation is essential in making decisions when the problems are wicked. The process is a bit complex but not unreasonable. It involves multiple and different forms of public participation over a period of time. It should also be acknowledged that wicked problems cannot be solved, they can only be managed. Management in the case of wicked problems involves regular monitoring and adjustments in the decision as new learning and knowledge come to light, and as public attitudes and preferences evolve.

About the Author

*L*awrence (Larry) Walters fell in love with public service while living in and working for small towns in Utah. He dug ditches, fought fires, read water meters, fixed power lines, drove snowplows, and loved every minute of it. The satisfaction that came each day from serving the public prompted Larry to go back to school and become more effective in his public service. He earned a bachelor's degree from Brigham Young University and a PhD from the University of Pennsylvania. For the past forty-five years, he has devoted his professional life to training public servants and building more effective governments.

Larry is passionate about good government. He has advised governments and trained government officials on five continents and at all levels, from international organizations and national governments to states and small towns. His career has included time spent as a city manager and a Utah State tax commissioner. He spent thirty years as a professor and graduate program director at Brigham Young University and George Mason University.

Larry has published four books and seventy articles and research reports on tax issues, environmental management, education finance, and productivity analysis. In this book, Larry turns his attention and local government experience to building a Zion society.

Larry and his wife, Carol, have seven children and twelve grandchildren spread across the country and the world.